# BRAVE NEW PEOPLE

## Ethical issues at the commencement of life

D. Gareth Jones

*Professor of Anatomy*
*in the University of Otago, New Zealand*

WILLIAM B. EERDMANS PUBLISHING COMPANY
GRAND RAPIDS, MICHIGAN

*First published 1984 by Inter-Varsity Press, England*
*Revised edition published 1985 through special arrangement with Inter-Varsity by*
**Wm. B. Eerdmans Publishing Company**
*255 Jefferson S.E., Grand Rapids, MI 49503*





**Library of Congress Cataloging in Publication Data**

Jones, D. Gareth (David Gareth), 1940–
Brave new people.

Bibliography: p.
Includes index.
1. Bioethics. 2. Genetic engineering—Moral and ethical aspects. I. Title.
QH332.J66 1985 174′.2 85-4582
ISBN 0-8028-0070-X

Printed in the United States of America by Eerdmans Printing Company, Grand Rapids, Michigan

# Contents

Preface vii
Preface to the Revised Edition ix

**1 Future prospects and present concerns 3**
Tensions and dilemmas
Living through a revolution
Creatures of God
In the image of God
Fractured humanity
Redeemed humanity

**2 Biomedicine and technology 23**
The dilemma of science
Science and values
Technology and human life
Technology and biomedical ethics
Health and disease
Levels of biomedical technology
Limitations and hazards of biomedical technology

**3 Improving the quality of life 48**
Quality-of-life decisions
Genetic diseases
Prenatal diagnosis of genetic diseases
Genetic screening
Improvement in quality

**4 New techniques and the beginning of life** **78**

Fertilization and conception
*In vitro* fertilization (IVF) and embyro transfer (ET)
Artificial insemination
Cloning
Recombinant DNA technology

**5 New beginnings for human life** **99**

IVF as technology
The humanizing possibilities of IVF
Fetal harm and fetal consent
Spare embyros
IVF and research
An assessment of IVF
Legal and social issues in IVF
Artificial insemination

**6 Tampering with heredity** **132**

The mass production of humans
Conformity or creativity?
Drawbacks of human cloning
Why not clowns instead?
Dehumanization
Human engineering

**7 The ethics of therapeutic abortion** **150**

Genetic abortion
Status of the fetus
Perspectives on abortion
Biblical guide-lines
Possible grounds for therapeutic abortion
Abortion for genetic reasons
Living on a knife-edge

**8 Human technology and human values** **187**

Towards an uncertain future
Quality control and foreknowledge
Towards the ideal human
Human responsibility
Suffering
Accountability
Compassion and forgiveness
Individual uniqueness

Bibliography 208

Index of names 215

Index of Scripture references 217

Subject index 219

# Preface

A book such as this one is a journey of personal discovery, as well as an exploration of ideas and principles. In no sense is it a theoretical treatise; the subject-matter is too emotional and intense for that. Nevertheless, a serious attempt has to be made to discover what principles are of importance in making decisions about human life around the time of its inception. For Christians, the aim will be to discover what light the Bible can provide in this area. Even when this has been done, however, an enormous amount of thought is still required to transform the general principles provided by the Bible into the specific guide-lines required for decision-making. There are no slick answers and there are many controversies and dilemmas.

Frequently, it is the controversial aspects of these issues that dominate discussions. While there can be no escape from controversy, my hope is that even those who disagree with my stance on various points will look beyond such disagreement to the underlying principles. To some, my stance on certain issues may appear liberal; to others it may appear conservative. Whatever the reaction, the one thing I ask is that my arguments be taken seriously and that they are used as the basis of urgent and serious debate in this realm.

I have written as a medical biologist, with a deep interest in ethical issues. I have not written as a practising doctor, since this is not my sphere of activity. Nevertheless, I hope that the discussion will prove of value to those who find themselves having to make immediate decisions in these areas, whether as physicians or as parents.

Inevitably, perhaps, this book has had a long gestation. Consequently it is now quite different from my original intention, because of the rapidity of developments in this area. These in turn may quickly render some of the information in the book out of date. In spite of this, the general tenor of the book will, I am sure, remain relevant for some time to come.

This book has not been written in a vacuum. I owe a great debt of gratitude to the writings of many bioethicists, and also to discussions in which I have been involved in many parts of the world. Some of the questions debated in these pages have been confronted in the real world in my own family situation, and I am grateful to Beryl for living out these principles. I am deeply indebted to Barbara Telfer for helping with the checking and re-checking of the manuscript, and for being willing to question ideas she did not understand or agree with. My thanks also go to Paula Williamson who typed the manuscript.

D. GARETH JONES

# Preface to the Revised Edition

My aim in writing *Brave New People* was to try to help people, especially evangelical Christians, find appropriate ways of responding to some of the excruciating problems confronting all of us in the biomedical realm. The issues are contentious ones, and even evangelicals do not generally agree on most of them. My aim was to explore ways in which Christians can attempt to formulate adequate responses to these issues in the light of biblical, biological and medical information. My hope was that I might provide a perspective within which Christians, and the public in general, could approach some of the most pressing issues facing us in the bioethical realm.

In taking on such a project I was well aware that this would prove an immensely controversial area, and also that in crossing the boundaries of biological, theological, ethical and philosophical disciplines I would get into some deep water. I do not claim to have professional expertise in all these areas, and it would be foolhardy for me to pretend that some of my perceptions are not shallow and may even be misleading. To the best of my ability, however, I attempted to avoid such pitfalls. Perhaps, in the end, the only justification for my having taken on this project is that those most affected by the developments in biomedicine are ordinary people—you and me, the general public, our families, our children and our grandchildren. While this is a legitimate area for highly skilled philosophical debate, it is—first and foremost—an intensely practical matter, affecting each one of us in one way or another.

It is unfortunate, then, that in the public arena bioethics appears to be nothing less than a minefield of volatile emotions. The issues are narrowed down to simple black-and-white alternatives, and anyone who dares to venture into this field is labelled in stark, polarized terms: one is in favour of technology or against it, is in favour of *in vitro* fertilization (IVF) or opposed to it, approves of abortion or disapproves of it. According to this scenario there is no 'middle-way'; there are never exceptions to any general principle, and ethical issues are never complex.

In expressing myself in this way I have already revealed something of my own position and I have already condemned myself in the eyes of those who insist on seeing these issues in simple, absolutist terms. This book does not contain a set of dogmatic assertions aimed to appeal either to the political right or to the political left. Neither was it my aim to produce a list of conclusions that might serve as the basis of legislative proposals.

In this book, rather, I am 'thinking aloud', as I look at the pros and cons of each of the issues tackled here. Quite often I debate with myself as I move from one competing argument to another. In this manner I arrive at my conclusions, although where these are tentative or where there is still a considerable element of doubt in my own mind, I say so. My intention is always to make my readers think for themselves and come to *their own conclusions*. It was for this reason that I wrote the following in the original Preface:

> my hope is that even those who disagree with my stance on various points will look beyond such disagreement to the underlying principles. To some, my stance on certain issues may appear liberal; to others it may appear conservative. Whatever the reaction, the one thing I ask is that my arguments be taken seriously and that they are

used as the basis of urgent and serious debate in this realm. (Pp. 7–8)

## Criticisms of Brave New People

I was, therefore, very saddened by the response to *Brave New People* by certain sectors of evangelicalism within the United States. While I do not wish to replay the details of that controversy, it may be instructive to sketch some of its facets.

Franky Schaeffer described the book as an 'amalgam of dishonesty', containing 'coercive, leftist, and pro-abortion ideas'. He saw it as a 'noxious dish of reviving the eugenics movement of death as a solution to social problems', employing 'seductive liberal jargon'. It was, he asserted, 'a vehicle for the propaganda of the "therapeutic" abortion industry, dressed now in evangelical robes'.[1]

According to Gary North, *Brave New People* is a 'monstrous book' in that 'it imposes the satanic ethics of abortion on Christian consciences in the name of autonomous medical technology'. North claims that I am guilty of writing 'gibberish about complex moral issues', since God says 'no' to abortion. He says I espouse the ethics of sentimentality, the source of which is humanism. Moreover, he contends that my arguments lead to euthanasia, a senile person being—according to his interpretation of my analysis—'an expendable elderly fetus'.[2]

Douglas Badger[3] places considerble emphasis on my use of the concept of personhood, arguing that it is not found in Scripture and that it was devised to 'create two classes of human beings: those whose lives have value and those whose lives may be ended with impunity'. By implication this is the way in which I have used the concept. I am also said to have argued that 'God cares little for babies who are spontaneously or intentionally aborted', and he implies that I would support all abortions performed on women whose pregnancy threatens their physical or mental health. Quite specifically, he interprets my stance as suggesting that 'abortion . . . is morally justifiable under *many* circumstances', and that I believe 'that the destruction of unborn individuals is *often* the best solution to the problems of individuals who have been born' (italics mine).[4]

Badger further proposes that my arguments are indistinguishable from those used to support abortion-on-demand and infanticide. The implication appears to be that I also support abortion-on-demand and infanticide. My approach is, according to him, 'the standard fare of pro-choice apologists', and my defence of therapeutic abortion is the same as that of organizations such as National Abortion Rights Action League and Planned Parenthood.

Badger also contends that I do not regard 'unborn children as being the image of God', and that I 'would deny that many handicapped individuals are persons'. He argues that my treatment of the biblical texts relevant to the legitimacy of abortion is 'dismal', and that I fail to come to terms with the biblical admonitions against violence—admonitions that in his view rule out abortion.

The theme of a number of my critics is that someone with my position on therapeutic abortion cannot be an evangelical. Jan Dennis, for instance, states this, and also contends that my whole view of human biotechnology is open to condemnation. According to his assessment of *Brave New People,* I 'blithely endorse' a whole range of technological procedures, and espouse 'quality of life' concepts as did Hitler's eugenicists. According to Dennis, I wish 'to sanction the manipulation of a certain class of human beings (embryos and fetuses) in various unpleasant ways'. I accomplish this, he continues, by declaring 'fetuses non-persons'; in this I am compared to Hitler's eugenicists and to slaveowners in the South. Dennis describes me as being 'pro-choice', and states that my 'position inevitably leads to abortion-on-demand'. I am an example, he says, of those who have 'accommodated themselves to the world' and 'given themselves over to a reprobate mind'. In short, I have jumped 'on a bandwagon bound for hell'.[5]

## Response at a general level

These are very strongly held viewpoints, which I wish to take most seriously. I sympathize with all those who are appalled at the immense tragedy of abortion-on-demand as currently practised in many countries. The tragedy is perhaps illustrated most starkly in the United States, and some of the consequences of the present legislative situation there following the *Roe v. Wade* decision in 1973 are horrific. I understand the intensity of feeling expressed by those with a high regard for fetal life, for it is one that I share (however difficult it may be for some of my critics to believe this). I apologize if some of my statements on therapeutic abortion could legitimately be taken to read that I support a very liberal view on abortion, or that my view of the fetus is a low one. Neither of these conclusions are intended.

Nevertheless, I object to the procedures adopted by some of my critics. Ignoring the tone of my writing and also quite explicit statements about my stance on abortion-on-demand, sentences and phrases have been interpreted to mean what my critics think they should mean and not what I take them to mean. Further, on quite a number of occasions, my descriptions of other people's opinions have been interpreted as though they are my opinions. Even my attempts to show that fetuses and handicapped children should be treated with dignity and respect have been interpreted negatively, as though I believe that all fetuses and handicapped children are of no value and can be killed.

The difficulty appears to be that my critics recognize only two positions on abortion: the absolute protection of all fetal life, and abortion-on-demand. Since my position does not fit into the former category it must, it appears, fit into the latter—hence, the attempts to demonstrate that I am a typical example of a pro-choice, abortion-on-demand advocate. When I contend that this is not my position, I am accused of being superficial, inconsistent or devious.

Underlying all attempts to establish this simple dichotomy is the belief that a final solution to the abortion question must be a legislative one. My critics would, I imagine, contend that abortion should be legally prohibited since it amounts to murder. Any less-than-absolute position on abortion is seen, therefore, as a threat on these two counts: it undermines the belief that the evangelical community is politically united in its absolute anti-abortion position, and it questions the assertion that abortion under every conceivable circumstance amounts to homicide.

A repeated criticism of my position on abortion has been that many will stretch it and use it as an argument in favour of abortion for reasons of convenience. This, it is stated, is what makes my position and the book so dangerous; the effect of my views will be to support abortion-on-demand. Probably any rational response by me will not placate those who believe this. But let me make two points. First, my position differs from that adopted by the Supreme Court in its *Roe v. Wade* decision; it is therefore misleading to move directly from the consequences of that decision to the perceived consequences of my position. Second, my remarks are addressed, in the first instance, to Christians who stand before God for all their actions. Thus, my remarks need to be seen in the context of the theological principles outlined in chapters 1 and 8. My critics appear to believe that Christians (and the public at large) only need someone to suggest that abortions may sometimes be permissible, for them to clamour for abortions for any reason whatsoever. It is my hope that a careful reading of this book as *a whole* will convince my readers that it is my firm belief that the decision by a woman (Christian or otherwise) to have an abortion is one of the most serious decisions she could ever make, one that should not even be contemplated except in the most dire of circumstances. It is a decision that should always be made before God, and after much prayer and soul-searching. To have an abortion under any other circumstance is to fail in one's duty as a Christian and a human being.

In order to attempt to clarify my position—at least to some extent—I have re-written and extended parts of my discussion of therapeutic abortion (chapter 7). Due to the misunderstanding it has created in some quarters, I have set it within the broader perspective of abortion in general, and I have also devoted more space to the status of the fetus. In this way I hope that my critics will appreciate that I deplore the taking of fetal life, whatever the reason may be. Nevertheless, I am still forced to conclude that there are some *conflict* situations where abortion may have to be undertaken.

## Response to specific points

1. Objections have been raised to my use of the terms 'therapeutic abortion' and 'fetus'. They are both said to have moral connotations, which prejudge the issues. The one argument is that abortion can never be 'therapeutic' for the fetus in question; the other is that the fetus should always be referred to as an 'unborn child'. My response to these criticisms is that these are generally accepted terms in the literature. I actually discussed the meaning of 'therapeutic' abortion in the first edition of the book, where I pointed out the pitfalls of the whole concept. The term 'fetus' is a technical one and in no sense does it infer anything about the morality or otherwise of abortion. It makes no more sense to refer to a fetus repeatedly as an 'unborn child' than it does to refer to a child as an 'immature adult'.

2. Much of the critical debate surrounding my discussion of therapeutic abortion has overlooked the context of the discussion, namely, the possibility of abortion for diagnosed or suspected fetal abnormality. Chapter 7 has, as its heading, 'The ethics of therapeutic abortion'. Two of its subheadings are 'genetic abortion', and 'possible grounds for therapeutic abortion'. Where abortion is referred to outside chapter 7 it is always in the context of defects in the fetus, such as neural tube defects, phenylketonuria and Tay-Sachs disease, in the context of negative eugenics, or in a discussion of amniocentesis. Repeatedly, I refer to abortion on the grounds of fetal deformity, or to its use 'therapeutically'.

In the first edition of *Brave New People* I only dealt in passing with abortion-on-demand, and I did not deal at all with abortion in cases of rape or incest, since these were not relevant to a discussion of abortion on the grounds of fetal abnormality. Even my reference to the mental health of the mother as a possible ground for abortion was quite specifically in the context of her ability or inability to cope with the demands of a retarded or abnormal child (pp. 177–178 of first edition).

It is in this light that we have to view my statement that 'there are sometimes family situations where inadequacy, marital breakdown, financial stringency, unemployment and a host of other adverse social conditions could lead to the conclusion that abortion of an unwanted pregnancy, or of a pregnancy with a dubious outcome, is the least tragic of a number of tragic options' (p. 177). This has been repeatedly taken out of its context within a section dealing with 'abortion for genetic reasons' (p. 177). The paragraph before it states this quite explicitly, and practically every paragraph following it for the remainder of the chapter refers to fetal or genetic abnormality (pp. 177–184 of first edition).

My critics are quite unfair and are grossly misleading when they state that I am prepared to advocate abortion in, for example, situations of 'financial stringency'. This is a forced reading of the text, which ignores the context and also the whole tenor of the chapter and book. At no point do I suggest that something like financial stringency *alone* constitutes grounds for the abortion of a *perfectly healthy fetus*. Neither do I even hint that this, by itself, amounts to an 'extreme circumstance' in favour of abortion.

The point I make in that section is that where a woman and family living in appalling circumstances are confronted by the birth of a seriously malformed child, they may be unable to cope. When that is the case a remedy has to be sought—and I look at some of the possible remedies on pages 177 and 178 (first edition). Abortion may, very reluctantly, have to be resorted to. As I state later in the chapter, there will be divergences of opinion on this response, and I have very deep respect for those who would not contemplate an abortion under these or any other circumstances. What I do ask, though, is that my position is not made to appear to be something that it is not. Modifications to chapter 7 in this edition will, I hope, render it more difficult to misrepresent my position.

3. Little attention has been paid by my critics to my view that the diagnosis of Down's syndrome in a fetus does not constitute adequate grounds for therapeutic abortion. Those who believe that it does have overlooked the social significance of the condition, and unfortunately it remains the most frequently performed therapeutic abortion on the ground of fetal abnormality.

The conservative nature of my position in this instance is, perhaps, an embarrassment to my critics. Of course, my stance on Down's syndrome is a personal one; it is simply mentioned in the text by way of an illustration of how I see my principles working out in practice. I have no intention of specifying all those situations in which I think therapeutic abortion would or would not be justified. These are decisions that have to be taken, under God, by those involved—parents, family, medical advisors and concerned Christian friends.

My position on Down's syndrome should also be taken seriously by those who claim that I do, or will shortly, advocate abortion-on-demand. The gap between what I state quite categorically on Down's syndrome and the beliefs enshrined in abortion for reasons of social convenience is an unbridgeable one as far as I am concerned.

## Further considerations

1. The controversy over *Brave New People* raises theological as well as political considerations. The heresy of which I appear to be guilty is that I cannot state categorically that human/personal life commences at day 1 of gestation. This, it seems, is being made a basic affirmation of evangelicalism, from which there can be no deviation. To adopt a position that deviates from the view that the embryo is anything less than a person demanding *complete* protection under *every conceivable circumstance,* is to exclude one automatically from the domain of evangelicalism. According to some of my critics there is no room even for discussion of this point.

Differences are still allowed within evangelicalism on issues such as baptism, the charismata, nuclear warfare, the role of women in the church, divorce, on a vast range of social questions, and even on the inerrancy of the Bible. But there are to be no differences on the precise nature of the personhood of the embryo. To deviate on this matter is to court spiritual and moral disaster. No longer is it sufficient to hold to classic evangelical affirmations on the nature of the biblical revelation, the person and work of Christ, or justification by faith alone. In order to be labelled an evangelical, it is now essential to hold to a particular view of the status of the embryo and fetus.

Were this viewpoint to be generally accepted it would have profound repercussions for the nature of evangelicalism. I leave it to others better qualified than I to pursue this matter further. The question confronting us is: do we have adequate grounds for making this issue a *theological* watershed?

2. The absolute stance adopted by my critics would appear to mean that there are never any grounds whatsoever for an abortion, even when the mother's life is in danger. Whether this is the case I am not clear, except that criticisms of my position have not hinted at any exceptions to the absolute inviolability of the fetus. If this is true, the position is a more extreme one than that traditionally held in Protestant circles (see chapter 7). It has to be asked whether this stark absolutism has a biblical mandate, and also why such absolutism is not invoked by many evangelicals when it comes to divorce (on which there is ample explicit biblical teaching), or to the taking of human life, at an individual level in self-defence, or at a national level in a range of offensive and defensive wars.

The fallenness of the human condition (chapter 1) introduces conflict and strife into our world, and ensures that an absolute stance is *sometimes* impossible to maintain. For instance, this is the argument generally adopted when opposing pacificism as an option for Christians. It is argued that utopian schemes bring tragedy, and that the Bible is never utopian. Although we are on dangerous territory when arguing in favour of *any* killing, it is difficult to see why an *absolute* anti-killing stance holds in some situations but not in others; or why utopianism is acceptable in some situations but not in others.

3. Critics of my book have been unwilling to pay any attention to pre-conception or postnatal issues. They have isolated fetal considerations from all others. This attitude is understandable in a society where extremely liberal abortion laws and attitudes prevail. However, some 'pro-life' attitudes appear to concentrate so heavily on life before birth, that they may sometimes come into conflict with respect for

human life after birth. The issue confronting us is this: is it possible to have an absolute view of the sanctity of human life before birth without having an equivalent view of human life after birth? Can we be *totally* in favour of fetal life, and not also ardently committed to an anti-war stance or to concerted action in favour of the mentally retarded and underprivileged in our society, and of the poor, disadvantaged and malnourished in many other societies? Should there also not be evident a massive commitment (financial and political) to research into the causes and prevention of the enormous number of fetal lives lost by spontaneous abortion (miscarriage)?

4. I have been criticized for overlooking the biblical injunction to protect the fetus since it is weak and defenceless, and also for ignoring the violence associated with abortion. These issues are briefly dealt with in chapter 7. We have to be careful however, that we do not isolate the principles we use in this area from those we use in other areas.

It is true that the fetus is weak and defenceless, and therefore under all normal circumstances should be protected. But not only fetuses are weak and defenceless. So are children brought up in institutions, beaten at home, malnourished in Ethiopia, enticed into smoking cigarettes or drinking alcohol by sophisticated advertizing, or born with appalling physical deformities. The weak and defenceless are also young girls made pregnant by their fathers, and the men, women and children killed in modern wars, whether these be the many villagers killed in Vietnam, or the far greater number who would be killed worldwide in a nuclear holocaust.

These observations do not allow us to underestimate the horror of liberal abortion attitudes. What we need is a consistent approach to the biblical demands to protect those who cannot protect themselves, whether they are fetuses or the children and adults belonging to social systems with which we (or our society) disagree.

5. In spite of all this preamble, this book is about a range of ethical issues at the commencement of life. Indeed, my main purpose in writing it was to consider *in vitro* fertilization, artificial insemination, cloning, and some of the di-

lemmas springing from the ever-burgeoning understanding of genetics. These are discussed within the more general frameworks of a Christian appreciation of human life, and of the power and influence of modern biotechnology. Therapeutic abortion was only included because of its relevance to some of the other areas, for example, in connection with genetic counselling for some hereditary conditions, and with amniocentesis. The book is intended to be read from page 1 onwards. If chapter 7 is read in isolation from the remainder of the book, it will have been wrenched out of its context.

6. The ethical dilemmas of modern medicine will not go away; they will only increase. Since writing this book, the IVF debate has continued to explode (especially with the publication of the Warnock Committee's Report in the United Kingdom) and many more babies have been born using this technique; surrogate motherhood has emerged as a matter of immediate social concern; the debate on artificial insemination by donor (AID) has blossomed, particularly in relation to the legal status of AID children and to the anonymity or otherwise of the donor; and genetic research has continued to suggest ways in which the genetic constitution of very early embryos will be amenable to clinical analysis and even therapy.

The nagging question which remains is whether evangelicalism will provide constructive ways forward, or simply piously packaged solutions that ordinary evangelicals will ignore when confronted by difficult choices. It is my hope that this book will provide a first step towards an understanding and appreciation of the world into which we are all moving, plus some preliminary hints at the sort of responses we might make. It is presented as a discussion document, not as the final word on any of the matters raised.

## References

1. Franky Schaeffer, 'An open letter to Inter-Varsity Press' and 'An open letter to the Christian Booksellers Association and Christian Bookstore Owners and Buyers in America', 1984.

2. Gary North, 'Evangelical Ethics 1984', *Christian Reconstruction 8*, 5 (1984).

3. Douglas Badger, 'The Misuse of Scripture: Creating a Biblical Mandate for Abortion', *National Right to Life News,* 9, 13 (August 1984).

4. Douglas Badger, 'A Response to Criticism of *Action Line* Review of *Brave New People*', Christian Action Council, Washington D.C., 1984.

5. Jan P. Dennis, 'Review of *Brave New People*', privately circulated, 1984.

# BRAVE NEW PEOPLE

# 1
# Future prospects and present concerns

## Tensions and dilemmas

As human beings we are deeply concerned with ourselves: our existence, our aspirations and our future. Finite beings capable of contemplating infinity are difficult to cope with, especially when *we* are those finite beings. We are tinged with infinity and yet are limited as biological creatures. We long to be free of our all-too-fallible bodies, and yet we have to eat and sleep, earn a living and take exercise, bring up children and look after ageing parents.

This is a tension implicit in human existence. We are religious beings with thoughts of God and eternity; we feel there must be something beyond the material; we feel there is a reality to life belied by the frailty of our uncertain bodies. This mixture of the finite and the infinite perplexes us, because we find it difficult to live with the biological and spiritual aspects of human existence. We long to be free of this tension, by viewing ourselves either as impersonal biological machines or as personal ethereal spirits.

This is not a new dilemma, but it has been greatly accentuated by the challenges inherent in modern biomedical technology, especially at the commencement of life. All too easily we find ourselves dragged either into the reductionism of biology or into needless opposition to the biological endeavour itself. For Christians this is an issue of crucial significance, because modern biomedicine now affects so much of everyday existence and because it will signify whether or not we are able to relate as God's people to the world in which he has placed us.

Biology is power over the living world, and biomedicine is power over human nature. There are numerous consequences of this, and they are already the subject of daily decision-making. These decisions revolve around one crucial issue, namely, the quality of life we demand for the populations of technologically-advanced societies and for individuals within those societies. All other issues, whether at the commencement of life or at the end of life, revolve around this critical fulcrum. At the commencement of life, quality-of-life considerations lead to prenatal diagnosis of fetal defects, with its dependence on amniocentesis, fetoscopy or ultrasound, and on genetic screening for conditions such as sickle-cell anaemia or neural tube defects. These, in turn, lean heavily on therapeutic abortion as a frequently-resorted-to remedy for eliminating defective fetuses. Quality-of-life considerations also lead to artificial insemination and *in vitro* fertilization, the goal of which is to improve the quality of life of adult couples, by manufacturing embryos technologically at the commencement of life.

Underlying all these developments is the promise and the spectre of technology. They would not be serious issues for ordinary people were it not for our enormous technological capabilities in the areas of biology and medicine. It is tempting to compare the sort of genetic engineering scientists are currently engaged in, or the *in vitro* fertilization which is currently being employed in a number of countries, with the ideas of a science-fiction writer such as Aldous Huxley. How does our brave new world compare with his? How far have we gone along the road to a biologically-controlled and biologically-replicated state? Interesting as such comparisons may be, we dare not overlook one radical difference – his world was a brilliant and perceptive vision, ours is reality. His vision can be either read as entertainment, analysed as literature, or it can be ignored. Our reality cannot be ignored. No longer is it the province of academics or dilettantes; it is rapidly becoming the everyday experience of us all. We are the characters in the brave new world; we ceased being the audience long ago. It is we who are being changed and who are having to make unpalatable and unrehearsed decisions; it is we, not some interesting figment of the collective imagination, who are having to sort out the priorities.

There is no escape from the ramifications of biomedical technology. Somehow we shall have to learn to live with it and to cope with it. Unfortunately we appear to be particularly ill-prepared to do this. For so long have we welcomed every new advance of technology, that it now seems tantamount to heresy to question any aspect of it. In the biomedical realm it has prolonged our life-span, eradicated most serious infectious diseases, ushered in brilliant reconstructive surgery and given us the opportunity to live life to the full. Technology is our ally and we are in its debt.

Unfortunately, this dependence upon technology has a price-tag. Continual improvement in the quality of our physical lives is bought at a cost. Sometimes this is a financial one, because sophisticated technology is now very expensive; on other occasions it is a human cost, as values come into conflict and one life has to be staked against another life.

Some would like us to believe that biomedical technology will solve all our problems, and that there are technological solutions to all our human dilemmas. An unwanted pregnancy can be readily dispensed with by simple and safe technological means. Unfortunately, the cause of the unwanted pregnancy will remain a source of unhappiness and guilt. Even more idealistically, it is sometimes suggested that the limitations and constraints of human existence can be overcome by genetic engineering. A new type of human being is on the horizon, with new values and new abilities; an improved specimen of humanity, bred and selected by genetic means. Such a vision stems not so much from the laboratory of the geneticist as from the brain of the visionary. The danger of the vision lies in its implicit assumption that human beings can be improved morally by altering them biologically. This is a religious vision, not a scientific one. Its basis is a view of human existence far removed from that of the Christian.

There are many intertwined strands of thought in the issues raised by biomedical technology. Some of them will concern us in this book. These will chiefly be those at the commencement of human life, around the time of conception, during fetal life, at birth and shortly afterwards. And then we shall have to consider broader issues as well, including a Christian perspective on the human condition, the place of technology in human existence, and the significance of biomedical technology for the value-systems by which we live.

## Living through a revolution

It is no exaggeration to say that we are living in revolutionary times. In this, of course, we are far from unique. Most ages have, in some respects, been revolutionary. Nevertheless there is a profound difference between the present era and previous ones. Previous revolutions were principally concerned with the structure of human societies, with the physical and mental well-being of humans, and with philosophical and religious outlooks. While they increased human control over the environment and to a lesser extent over human life itself, and while some of them drastically modified our view of human existence and human society, their effect on us as biological beings was a limited one.

In striking contrast to all such revolutions of the past, the biomedical revolution currently under way has implications for human existence and human value-systems far beyond anything yet experienced. It is a crisis in human life, stemming from the control human beings are learning to exert over the lives of other humans and over the biological potential of those not yet born. It is concerned with what human beings *are*, and it has implications for what they are *going to be*.

The current biomedical revolution, with its emphasis on genetic manipulation and genetic control, *in vitro* fertilization, quality control and high technology in medicine, may well have more widespread consequences for human life than either the Copernican or Darwinian revolutions – far-reaching as they were. We now have under our control the myriad of diseases that scourged us from the environment round about us, so that we can reflect on deficiencies in our own biological make-up. We can meditate on the quality of our genetic inheritance, and we are rapidly acquiring the ability to modify and redirect that inheritance.

Already human beings have delved so deep into their genetic constitution that they can influence the course of a growing number of genetic diseases. This is but the beginning. Far more fundamental and radical steps are in the offing, and it is these that are raising extensive questions about the nature of human existence, and the extent to which our expectations of human life can and should be altered. Alongside such profound issues go more immediate ones: the status of marriage and family life, the degree of freedom individuals should or should not be allowed in the choice of a mate or in the production of offspring, and the selection of those fetuses to be born and those to be aborted.

Biomedical advances, and especially genetic ones, have these and many other theological, ethical and social issues implicit within them. Basic to them all, however, is one more fundamental issue, namely, the desire for improved biological quality. Medicine throughout the centuries has striven to improve the immediate well-being of individuals, and this has had repercussions for the quality of life of whole societies and even of whole countries. What the biomedical revolution is bringing in its wake is the conscious desire for improvement in quality. With this desire go questions on the value of human life and the nature of human expectations. These are profound questions, and alongside them are practical ones on ways in which biological control of human life may be misused.

The possible dangers of genetic and other forms of biomedical manipulation appear to have convinced many that biologists are rapidly moving out of an age of innocence.

They give the impression of being on the threshold of understanding the genetic program of living organisms, as a prelude perhaps to the creation of new programs and hence new varieties of organisms. Not surprisingly therefore, the nature of human beings has emerged as an issue of supreme importance in recent years. The world into which mankind is moving is, in a very real sense, an unknown one. It is a world in which the old frames of reference are disappearing, their places being taken by new and very uncertain ones.

We need to know where we are going, because we have at our disposal techniques for affecting what we are as biological beings. The ways in which these techniques are used will depend on us and on our perceptions for mankind. What is called for is a realistic analysis of the human condition. A Christian assessment emanates from our dependence upon God, who is seen to provide an adequate framework for our thinking and actions as human beings.

## Creatures of God

A Christian perspective starts from the foundation that human beings have been created by God. According to the biblical revelation, it was God who said: 'Let us make man in our image' (Genesis 1:26), and it was God who put this resolve into action: 'So God created man in his own image' (Genesis 1:27), or again: 'And the Lord God formed man from the dust of the ground and breathed into his nostrils the breath of life, and man became a living being' (Genesis 2:7).

There is an absolute distinction between God, the Creator, and man, the created; between God, who is the source of all that exists, and man in his complete dependence upon the sustaining power of God for his very existence. All that *is* comes from God, including the very being of man himself. Consequently there is no meaning in the universe outside of God, because it is nothing if it is not his handiwork.

It is this exalted distinction between God and everything he has made, including human beings, that characterizes the whole biblical ethos. God is self-existent and almighty; we, on the other hand, are dependent upon God and we need God if we are to express our true humanity. This dependence upon God is a strikingly one-way affair, because for us to become truly human we must recognize our creatureliness and also our utter dependence upon the One who brought us into being and who sustains us from moment to moment.

Our creation by and for God implies that it is never possible to rise to a position where we are no longer subject to him. Human beings, because they are creatures in God's universe, will never outgrow their need of God's support and direction. No matter how technologically sophisticated we, as humans, may become, we shall remain beings whose ideals and ambitions can be fulfilled only as they conform to the goals set by our Creator-God. We can never become gods, because there will always remain much that eludes our control.

A Christian framework recognizes that human beings are limited because we are creatures in a God-ordered and God-sustained world. We must operate within a particular natural and social framework, not because this is an arbitrary limitation but because it is one which is inherent within the Creator-creature relationship. We are not gods and there is no radical way in which we can transcend our creatureliness. To speak, therefore, of humans as if they had already become creators is grossly misleading, even when the context is that of genetic manipulation.

And yet it is at precisely this point that we find some writers looking forward to the day when mankind will be able to change all the biological rules and create totally new super-humans. The desire that we should transcend our creatureliness has been a frequent theme throughout the ages, although largely a vague hope rather than a practical possibility. While it would be futile to suggest that it is, even now, anything remotely resembling a practical possibility, it is increasingly being presented as such. We are frequently viewed as on the verge of controlling life, including our own lives. Hence we become the creators, creating descendents in a new image and remaking ourselves as we wish. Basic to all such longings is the expectation that we can become biologically something more than we now are, and that our original creation (and fall) can be bettered.

Before rushing too enthusiastically in that direction,

however, we should stop and think. Our present abilities are immense, and yet even these have severe limitations. There is much we can control and yet there is far more we *cannot* control. The crucial issue here is that what we cannot control will, in the foreseeable future and perhaps always, remain elusive. It is the short-term scientific achievements that are controllable, leaving the long-term ones beyond our reach. Perhaps this is a fundamental limitation built into our human finiteness. We are created beings and we shall never be in a position of stepping beyond the bounds of creatureliness. We cannot change the ground-rules of the universe; we can only understand them. And this is precisely what the scientific enterprise allows us to do; this is where its power lies and it is in this sphere that we should be exercising our responsibility as God's creatures.

From this it follows that any assessment of a technological innovation needs to take into account what it cannot influence just as much as what it can influence. All too frequently, however, no such distinction is made, on the assumption that humans are omnipotent and unlimited. Herein lies the danger of regarding mankind as possessing godlike capacities. It leads to a neglect of those areas of our existence over which we lack control and, consequently, to a neglect of our limited capacity for utilizing wisely the technological powers at our disposal. All too readily this leads to the idea that, as Helmut Thielicke has expressed it, 'instead of *man* being the measure of things, the things he has made . . . come to determine the lines along which *man* himself is to be structured'. This is a salutary reminder of the importance of distinguishing between those areas of which we are masters and those over which we have only limited control.

There is much we can do, but there is also much we cannot do. A Christian perspective on humanity accepts these two facets of our existence, recognizing our dependence upon God as well as the authority, responsibility and control bestowed upon us by God. This dual aspect to human existence is basic to our understanding of our contemporary dilemma in the face of biomedical advance. Assume we are gods, capable of doing all that is necessary for our own good, and biomedical advance becomes one of the tools of that god.

By contrast, once it is recognized that we are the handiwork and the servants of God, biomedical advance becomes a means by which God can help his creation.

Besides the gulf which separates humans as created beings from God as Creator, our creatureliness also implies that we are an integral part of the natural world. Genesis 2:7 unequivocally points to the origins of mankind in nature. We are part and parcel of the natural order, and are subject to the demands and vicissitudes of the interrelationships of the physical and material world. It is because of this that we can be understood in scientific terms, and for many purposes such an approach is a perfectly legitimate one. Our environment is that of the physical universe which we share with the myriad varieties of mammals, amphibians, fish, birds, plants, bacteria and viruses. All exist because of the sovereign will of God, and all depend upon him for their continued existence. We, like them, are finite and in a very real sense cannot live apart from them.

Human beings are in nature and must therefore live in dialogue with the remainder of nature. In many regards nature is also in us, pointing to the intimate cohesion and interdependence of human beings and the physical and biological environments. As a result the biological and physical side to human beings is an indispensable facet of what being human means, and any attempt to tear us from our biological base is a negation of what we are as created beings. This is true whether the desire is to see ourselves simply as 'spiritual' beings or primarily as 'technological' beings. The result in each instance is fragmentation of the created wholeness of human life.

We cannot understand ourselves as human beings if we overlook our place in the whole of God's creation. An assessment of the human condition and of the content of human values in a technological milieu needs to start from an acknowledgment of the many ways in which we belong to the created order of nature. And yet the biblical record makes it equally plain that our position within the natural order is a privileged and responsible one.

According to the writer of Genesis, human beings are made in the image and likeness of God (Genesis 1:26). We are made 'a little lower than the heavenly beings and [are] crowned with glory and honour' (Psalm 8:5). As a result, considerable responsibility has been bestowed upon us to rule wisely over the remainder of God's creation (Genesis 1:26, 28; 2:19; Psalm 8:6–8). Although we are an integral part of the world of nature, it was God's intention that we should exercise authority over this world. Hence we have been placed in control of everything else he has made. We have been given immense responsibility, and any misuse of this responsibility leads to our own suffering as well as to suffering on the part of the environment we despoil.

Human beings are both *in* nature as well as *over* it, continuous with it and discontinuous from it. Derek Kidner, in his commentary on *Genesis*, notes that man 'shares the sixth day with other creatures, is made of dust as they are, feeds as they feed and reproduces with a blessing similar to theirs . ...: they are half his context'. But in spite of this, 'the stress falls on his distinctness . . . man is set apart by his office . . . and still more by his nature; but his crowning glory is his relation to God'.

These are crucial principles for an analysis of our response to biomedical advances. No matter what the nature of these advances, they inevitably raise religious issues. The advances have come about as a result of human creativity and ingenuity, both God-given qualities, and the way in which they are applied will depend upon human initiative and decision making, also God-given qualities. Their application, whether good or evil, will almost definitely change human beings, sometimes in dramatic and perhaps far-reaching ways. It is hardly surprising, then, that some writers regard human beings as being capable of creating new worlds and even new people. Tempting as such vistas are, they fail to take account of human limitations and of the extent of human dependence, recognized or unrecognized, upon God.

When confronted by the extent of biomedical advances, we need to question the degree of control we have over their long-term consequences. If we are not in control, we are at the mercy of technology, and that is the antithesis of human responsibility. Human beings are then under the control of that which they have created, rather than of the One who created them. Herein lies idolatry.

This is not an argument against biomedical technology; it is an argument for the human control of such technology, and for a willingness to face up to the dilemmas inherent in biomedical advance. These dilemmas have to be faced, because we are human beings and because we are a part of the physical creation. We cannot escape our responsibilities and the control we need to exercise over the work of our hands and the products of our brains. Neither can we escape the consequences of any lack of control, because biomedical advances are capable of changing *us as people* as well as facets of the environment around us.

The intriguing question is: why have we been set apart from the rest of God's creation in this way? Why have we been given responsibility for God's creation, including that part of creation which is we ourselves? Why are we a mixture of the ordinary and the extraordinary?

## In the image of God

An answer to these questions is to be found in the biblical statement that human beings are created in the image and likeness of God (Genesis 1:26–27; 5:1; 9:6; 1 Corinthians 11:7; Colossians 3:10; James 3:9). The picture provided by this statement is of God as the original, and human beings as a perfect copy of that original. Human beings possess an abundance of God-like attributes, have the capacity of relating intimately with God, and also have responsibilities. To be made in the image of God is to be made like God.

It would be foolish to take this statement too far and conclude that we actually are gods. In certain ways we are unlike God; we are limited, finite beings and we are totally dependent upon God. Nevertheless we are sufficiently like God that we can have a personal relationship with him and he with us. This relationship is depicted in the Bible by the picture of God communicating with Adam and Eve (Genesis 1:28; 3:9ff.). He did this in quite a different way from his communication with any other created beings; he spoke to them, and they understood and responded.

Communication between God and human beings is central to the personal relationship that can exist between God and those he has created. Moreover the possibility of such communication sets humans apart from all other creatures. The startling feature of this is that it refers to a creature who came from the dust and will one day return to the dust. It refers to a finite, limited being, at home in the natural world and yet not truly at home in that world. The biological and spiritual aspects of human life are equally valid, and yet they represent fundamentally diverse levels of human existence.

The image concept and all that flows from it has many repercussions for our understanding of human existence. We are like God, in that we are *persons* who can relate to our world, to other human beings, and also to God in personal ways. As persons, we make choices and act upon them; we have values and value-systems; we are aware of ourselves and of others, of our needs and aspirations, and also of the needs and aspirations of others; we are held to be responsible for our actions. Persons are inherently creative and religious, forever longing for something, often someone, greater than themselves. Running through all these characteristics is a yearning for loving and meaningful relationships.

The world God has made is intrinsically personal. This is clearly brought out in the early chapters of Genesis with the account of Adam and Eve. God gave them responsibility and ample freedom to exercise it. They also held values and made choices. They were creative. Moreover, they related to each other as humans and to God as Creator of mankind; they were given to each other for companionship and mutual help.

For human beings to live out God's image in them entails exercising to the full these characteristics of personhood. To grow as full-orbed persons is to become more like God. To be human is, in a paradoxical way, to be like God, because Jesus Christ was fully human as well as fully God. He was the epitome of what human life should be; he was the most human of all people, beside being truly God.

The significance of this discussion for biomedical technology will become clear when assessing the status of the fetus (chapter 7). I shall argue there that the fetus is to be regarded as a potential person, its importance stemming from the fact that, if its development is allowed to continue to birth and beyond to adulthood, it will in time demonstrate these characteristics of personhood. Its creation in the image of a personal God will ultimately become abundantly clear, even if it lacks clarity as a fetus.

An alternative perspective to the status of human beings is provided by the authority God has bestowed upon us. 'Let us make man in our image, in our likeness, and let them rule . . . over all the earth, and over all the creatures that move along the ground' (Genesis 1:26). Such rule is possible only for those made in the image and likeness of God. To exercise authority over everything else created by God is a privilege and duty given only to God-like beings; it involves intellectual ability, far-sightedness, initiative, creativity, moral concern, freedom of action, knowledge of the ways of God, dependence upon God, loving-kindness towards the weak and, perhaps above everything else, an acknowledgment that all these powers come from God and are to be utilized wisely in his service.

Implicit within the idea of personhood is the morality and rationality of human beings. We are co-workers with God and, as such, are confronted with the demand to obey God. This is because relationship to God inevitably involves moral obligations. God is holy and just, and human beings created in his likeness are also to be holy and just. Time and again, the Christians of the early church were encouraged to be holy, because that is what God is like and that, therefore, is one of the goals of being made new in Christ (Colossians 1:22; 2 Peter 3:11–12).

God, in dealing with mankind in the Genesis account of the Garden of Eden, treated Adam as a morally responsible being. There were certain things he could do: work the garden and take care of it, and eat the fruit of all the trees except one; and yet there was also something he must *not* do, and that was to eat from the tree of the knowledge of good and evil (Genesis 2:16–17). What is noteworthy about this prohibition is that man was not prevented from eating of this particular tree; he was simply commanded not to do so. He was also given a reason why he was not to eat of it: it would open his eyes to evil as well as good, ushering him into a realm of God-like power, full of longings and desires with which he would be unable to cope.

God treated Adam as a being in his own image, capable of deciding issues morally and rationally. It is an awesome privilege to be treated in this way by God. There is, however, no hint in the Bible of God treating human beings in any other way, even when it would lead them into grave strife. Nevertheless this moral responsibility has limits, which have been present from the beginning of human existence and which were imposed for the benefit of the human race. No matter how great human achievements may appear to be, nor how vast human progress, we remain created beings. The desire to become gods is an abrogation of this. No matter how extensive our technological prowess, we are unable to cope with unrestricted freedom; hence the limits imposed by God in Genesis 2.

The moral responsibility characteristic of humans is an echo of the moral responsibility of God, enshrining the capacity of acting wisely and in love. Human moral obligations, therefore, are always related to the dictates of God, so that whenever God is left out of account the moral framework of human existence becomes difficult to determine. George Carey, in his book *I Believe in Man*, makes the illuminating comment that 'man needs God to protect himself from man'. Once human beings, human competence and human aspirations are placed at the centre of existence, there is no room for a view of human dignity centred on our relationship to God.

It is at this point that some of the dangers of an immensely powerful biomedical technology become evident. Since the success of this technology has been gained through human brilliance and initiative, its continued success demands further human effort. All too easily we come to adopt a humanistic outlook: technology alone matters and technology is a product of the human mind. Technology becomes an end in itself and its pragmatic success is so impressive that it comes to replace God as the centre of the everyday world. Once this movement away from God has taken place in people's thinking they have lost, not only God, but also guide-lines for making ethical decisions. The dilemma is that the success of biomedical technology, in enabling people to live longer and healthier lives, brings with it an array of startlingly difficult ethical decisions. In so far as technology is also accompanied by a loss of faith in values based on our relationship to God, the human predicament is a grave one.

According to James Houston, in his book *I Believe in the Creator*, 'Biblical man is essentially a commanded being, whose sense of requiredness provides man with dignity and significance'. God makes demands upon humans, who grow as human beings in response to those demands. In responding, we become more like God.

Individual people are ends in themselves, having a dignity bestowed upon them by God in creation and also in redemption. Accordingly individuals are to be treated as worthy of God's high estimation of them, whatever value or lack of value society may confer upon them. Human beings have a God-given dignity which stems, not from what they can *do* in social terms, but from the basic premises that they are like God and hence are moral and rational beings, and that God loved them so much that Christ died for them. All human beings are important in the sight and purposes of God.

We have been created to relate in fellowship to God and to share in friendship with other human beings. These two types of relationship are interwoven, the human-God relationship providing a framework within which the inter-human relationship can find full expression. To act humanly, therefore, means to act responsibly. Individuals, as beings of worth and value in the sight of God, are themselves responsible to God for their actions. The degree of freedom bestowed upon us by our Creator allows us to respond to God and to develop into mature, meaningful and worth-while personalities.

In terms of the Genesis account, mankind has been given dominion over the rest of God's creation and has been instructed to rule over it and subdue it (Genesis 1:26, 28). This is perhaps the ultimate responsibility, involving as it does not just human beings, but all else as well. Everything is put under our feet (Psalm 8:6), not for our own benefit but for the glory of God. The way in which human beings carry out their rule of the rest of creation is of concern to God, because it is our reponsibility to God that is at stake. We are co-workers with God in this task, and never our own master serving our own ends. Carey phrases it like this: God is still at work in his creation, and yet his work is now accomplished 'through the continuing activity of mankind to whom is delegated the task of giving it order, structure and beauty'. We are like God in the responsibility and freedom God has given us to be obedient to our Creator, and involved in this is our indispensable role in caring for and in developing the world God has made.

## Fractured humanity

The actions and motives of humans have been polluted. In biblical terms, we no longer reflect God's perfect moral character because Adam and Eve misused their freedom and sought power and knowledge independent of God (Genesis 3:6). Human beings throughout history have acted in the same way. Nonetheless, like Adam and Eve, they continue to be persons. The image of God has continued to be reflected in mankind since the fall, although our faculties of personhood are impaired. We do not always exercise authority wisely, our intellectual and moral capabilities are frequently defective, we seek to live apart from God and to become gods in our own right, we all too often exploit the weak and disadvantaged, we love ourselves at the expense of others. Yet, in spite of all this, we are persons who continue, in some measure at least, to be like God. Fallen humanity is still the image of God, although it is often a distorted and forlorn image.

The biblical picture of Adam and Eve portrays them turning their backs on God's dictates, choosing the path of worldly wisdom and elevating human reason to a godlike status. They made self-fulfilment their goal by seeking material, aesthetic and mental enrichment at the expense of submission to the wisdom of God, their Creator. For them, there was no room for either God's word or the response of faith. They were forced to rely on their own efforts for an understanding of both themselves and their role in the world.

This is demonstrated by the evocative phrase in Genesis 3:7 where, after the act of disobedience, the eyes of Adam and Eve 'were opened, and they realized that they were naked'. Kidner describes this as a grotesque anticlimax to the dream of enlightenment. The familiar world was still there, and yet evil had been projected on to innocence; and they reacted to good with shame and flight.

The plight of contemporary mankind epitomizes the effects of the fall. There is no paradise, because the harmony of the original creation has been lost. We *know* evil, which is precisely what Adam and Eve sought by disobeying God and eating the fruit of the tree of knowledge of good and evil. We indulge in evil, because it is an integral part of our perception of reality; we ourselves are evil as well as good. We are subject to hostility as well as harmony, to ugliness as well as beauty, to the misuse of God's creation as well as its right use, to the dehumanization of human beings as well as their humanization, to manipulation of our children as well as their education, to disease as well as health. So often creativity turns sour, actions are irrational, desires are self-centred, and human achievement serves the base elements in human nature rather than directing honour and glory to God.

In so many respects, we are now lost; our life is one of confusion and mixed motives; we are filled with fear in the face of an uncertain future, instead of with joyful anticipation by being in the purposes of God. We long for good things, and yet so often we pervert that which is good. Envy, jealousy, suspicion and lovelessness repeatedly intrude into relationships, debasing them and alienating humans from each other.

So much of the human predicament, therefore, is a spiritual one. We are separated from God; our lives are characterized by our hiding from God (Genesis 3:8–13), a fear of God (Genesis 3:10) and a running away from the extent of our responsibilities as human beings (Genesis 3:12–13). Our spiritual plight is a consequence of deliberate disobedience and a wilful assertion of human autonomy, so that we stand guilty before God.

We are anomalies in God's creation, in that we are like him and yet we want to live as though he does not exist. We have become like God in a wrong sense: we know 'good *and evil*' (Genesis 3:22). We are capable of both, and in most situations both are present.

It is important to realize that, to some degree, we shall always misuse the possibilities opened up by biomedical technology. This is not an all-or-none phenomenon, since the good and evil uses to which it will be put are intermingled. Techniques for bypassing infertility and enabling an infertile married couple to have a child of their own may also give rise to surrogate motherhood and even, in futuristic terms, to human-animal hybrids. The technology itself opens the way to a wide diversity of possibilities, all of which will probably be advocated by one group or another.

Similarly, the decreases in the neonatal mortality rate and the ability to carry out heroic surgical feats on malformed babies have been accompanied by a dramatic upsurge in abortion on demand. The technology underlying these developments is similar, and may be put to life-saving or life-destroying uses. The benefits and the hazards of biomedical technology exist alongside one another, reflecting the wonder and the tragedy of human life, with its God-likeness and its rebellion against God's authority.

The limitations and the sinfulness of human beings also manifest themselves in the 'one-way character' of human decisions, many of which have permanent repercussions. Decisions have a logical end-result, which subsequent actions can only modify or postpone. It is tempting to think that biomedical technology can overrule this one-way movement of events. Frequently, however, this is an illusion. The abortion of an unplanned and unwanted pregnancy is a technological answer to an action with undesirable consequences. It appears to negate the one-way character of decision making, and yet it has no effect on the feelings and relationships that led to the pregnancy. It cannot eradicate the early stages of the pregnancy and their consequences. Moreover, the abortion itself has its own consequences.

To expect too much of biomedical technology is to underestimate the effects of human sin and rebellion, and to ignore the limitations of a created being. Although technology in this and other spheres has made an immense contribution to human welfare, it has not altered the basic human condition. The extent to which it is used for good or evil depends upon the motives and aspirations of human beings, and these in turn reflect the creatureliness and fallenness of mankind.

## Redeemed humanity

Biomedicine has a part to play in the life of humanity – both fractured and redeemed. It is not the prerequisite of either Christians or non-Christians; neither is it the epitome of good or evil. It may not be the road to the perfect future; but neither is it the path to self-destruction. Biomedicine has to be viewed within the context of the hopes and longings, aspirations and deceit of human beings.

In reminding us of our humanness, it also reminds us that the purpose of the Christian life is the recovery of the original image of God; it is the recovery of the kind of human experience God intended for mankind. The Christian life, therefore, is intended to be an affirmation of all that God has made. Ranald Macaulay and Jerram Barrs, in their book *Christianity with a Human Face*, write: 'To be human is to be a reflection, as a finite and physical person, of the experience of the infinite Person who made us.'

Neither biology nor medicine poses a threat to Christian ideals when seen as means of understanding and appreciating human life. They have the potential for helping us rejoice in the humanness of human beings and in their God-likeness. To appreciate this, however, we need to understand the implications of Christ's own human life and subsequent death and resurrection.

Christ became fully human in order to redeem human beings. In the Bible Christ is described as the last Adam (1 Corinthians 15:45). Like the original Adam he was human and truly physical. This was essential, if he was to turn the course of human history. As a human being, he perfectly fulfilled the requirements of God. God was pleased with his free obedience, because in Christ he saw what human beings were meant to be.

Christ transforms human lives, because he was a genuine human being. He was subject to all the experiences that make up human life, except that he did not disobey God. He lived as part of a normal family, enjoying its demands, festivities, friendships and aspirations. He learned a trade; he felt compassion for those in need, for the sick and the bereaved; he rejoiced with those who were glad; he could be anxious and distressed. He was tempted to assert himself, to demonstrate his power, and to show himself as God. He was a human being like us, and yet was without sin.

Christ had to become human in order to be the Saviour of mankind. The incarnation was essential, because through it Christ made possible the recovery of full human experience. The model of the Christian life, therefore, is the recovery of ordinary human experience; ordinary, that is, in terms of God's original creation and Jesus' perfect example. To be 'in Christ' is to be 'renewed after the image' of one's Creator; it is to become more like God.

The perspectives opened up by biomedical technology, therefore, are to be welcomed by Christians, for whom human life is to be cherished. Improvements in the quality of human existence, including the quality of physical and mental health, of human relationships, of the environment, and of the culture, are important goals. While they do not depend solely on technology, the technological contribution cannot be ignored. On the other hand, the values and dangers of the technological contribution are closely interwoven with the grandeur and tragedy of human existence. Secular society must learn to accept its own limitations and to recognize biomedicine as a useful, but tainted, tool.

# 2
# Biomedicine and technology

## The dilemma of science

The specific biomedical issues to be discussed in the coming chapters need to be seen against a background of science and technology. Modern medicine is an illustration of the power of contemporary science, and its exploitation owes much to technology. To understand medicine better, therefore, we need to explore the way in which science functions, and to confront the dilemmas facing a technologically-based world.

The triumphs and pitfalls of contemporary science are poignantly illustrated by the following quotation of geneticist Leon Kass.

> I was conceived after antibiotics yet before amniocentesis, late enough to have benefited from medicine's ability to prevent and control fatal infectious diseases, yet early enough to have escaped from medicine's ability to prevent me from living to suffer from my genetic diseases. To be sure, my genetic vices are, as far as I know them, rather modest, taken individually – myopia, asthma and other allergies, bilateral forefoot adduction,

> bowleggedness, loquaciousness, and pessimism, plus some four to eight as yet undiagnosed recessive lethal genes in the heterozygous condition – but, taken together, if diagnosable prenatally, I might never have made it.

No longer is it possible to accept uncritically the material benefits of the scientific endeavour. We know only too well that these benefits cannot be viewed in a social vacuum; they have repercussions which, regardless of our immediate reaction to them, will force us to make decisions that would otherwise not have arisen. And this is precisely what Kass is envisaging. According to his speculation, had he been conceived fifty or so years later than he was, he may never have been born. He may have been therapeutically aborted, on the grounds that he was genetically unfit for human existence. I imagine that in Kass's case this would have been unlikely, but the speculation pinpoints a dilemma: advances in genetic research raise profound issues in values. And what is true of genetic research is equally true of research in most other scientific domains.

Scientific discovery alters human life, because it confronts us with questions that would not otherwise have existed, and it forces us to give answers to these questions, answers which may not satisfy and yet which must be given. The questions and answers may take us into areas not previously explored, and where traditional value-systems have no ready-made responses. Science therefore, besides altering the physical world, also introduces moral conundrums. It affects us as human beings – in our relationship to the environment, to other human beings and to God. It forces us to question our role in the world; hence its religious dimensions.

For too long it was assumed that scientific research and the whole technological superstructure emanating from its application had effects only on the material world. Its material benefits were gratefully accepted, the diseases that could now be cured or, even better, prevented were assiduously ticked off, and we gloated with incredulity at the extraterrestrial feats of mere mortals. Of those who contended that humans had become gods, only some realized this bestowed on us an onerous degree of responsibility.

Gradually it dawned upon scientists, politicians and philosophers alike that the scientific enterprise is not as impersonally objective or morally neutral as once thought. While scientists strive to be as objective as possible, they are still human beings working within specific social, political and religious contexts. We cannot escape these influences, neither can we escape our own presuppositions.

The distinction once made between basic scientific knowledge and its application has become increasingly hazy over recent years. There is still a distinction, but the almost absolute distinction once in vogue was rudely shattered by the atomic bomb. Once that was exploded it became all too clear that scientists themselves were implicated in much that it stood for. Robert Oppenheimer picturesquely remarked that, with the atomic bomb, physicists had known sin. Never again could scientists claim complete moral neutrality in their investigations. They are not merely robotic technicians carrying out the whims of despotic masters; they are responsible human beings and citizens acting creatively and imaginatively to unravel the secrets of the natural world. This, in turn, leads to ways of applying that information to control the world. These two facets cannot be completely separated from each other.

This was true for those Christians who were involved in the foundation of modern science in the sixteenth and seventeenth centuries. They longed for a truly reliable science, because only a reliable science could serve human beings by restoring their rule over nature. This fitted in admirably with their Christian aspirations, and provided a means by which they could overcome the continual fear of the powers of nature, particularly of uncontrolled disease.

Theirs was a religious and moral crusade against the philosophical traditions of bygone eras. They wanted a science that worked, a science that helped alleviate disease, and a science that helped them to unravel the secrets of their world. For them, such a science emerged from their Christian view of nature; it was as objective as possible; it was concerned with basic questions, but it was also motivated by social and human concerns. The theoretical and the applied are not unrelated spheres.

This is also brought out by the negative results of some scientific endeavours. The material and social benefits of scientific advance are amply matched by a plethora of unbelievably destructive weapons, environmental despoliation, overpopulation and technological overkill. As we ponder the advantages and disadvantages of modern science, therefore, we are confronted by a crisis in values, to which there are no easy answers and from which there is no ready escape.

## Science and values

Science aims at as much objectivity as possible, realizing that absolute objectivity is an unattainable ideal. The search for scientific truth does not have the infallible, impersonal objectivity sometimes attributed to it. Science is always undertaken by scientists, and it is scientists as human beings who are the ones to formulate the ideas, set the goals and make the observations. There can never be science without scientists, because however much we may talk about 'Science' with a capital 'S', it is not an autonomous monster. It is the outcome of human endeavour and it manifests human aspirations and human longings.

Science, therefore, has an essential human and personal element to it. It is not unknown for scientists to be swayed by aesthetic concepts, the dynamic of which stems from their simplicity and beauty. Michael Polanyi, who has stressed the human element in science, argues that a scientist assesses a theory not only for its empirical validity, but also for its rational appeal to him personally. This does not downgrade the necessity of empirical observation; rather, it stresses the role played by personal, non-objective factors in scientific discovery.

Even in the relatively objective world of science, ideas and hypotheses encompass values. These ingredients are unavoidable, and sometimes are even beneficial in constructing useful hypotheses. Scientific investigation is a *human* activity, carried out by human beings who live by certain value-systems, and have obligations, aspirations and concerns as individuals. There is an ethical dimension, therefore, both to the search for scientific truth and to the application of the results of scientific research.

Over recent years it has become increasingly obvious that the application of scientific knowledge requires ethical guide-lines. One has only to look at ecological, nuclear, medical and genetic issues to be convinced of this many times over. The difficulty is that ethical guide-lines do not arise from within science itself. They have to be imposed from without, and their nature will depend on a host of religious, political and social presuppositions.

Ethical directions are crucial for the scientific endeavour, because science aims not merely to describe the world but also to control it. Power over the physical and biological worlds is central to science. Without this power, mankind would still be at the mercy of natural forces, hostile animals and rampant diseases. But power demands direction, and it is here that ethical presuppositions and goals become critical, all the more so as the power becomes greater and potentially self-destructive.

Christians have, at times, feared science because they have sensed it to be at odds with Christian concerns, perhaps even directly at enmity with God. This fear has stemmed from the apparently autonomous nature of science, and from its immense ability to unfathom the secrets of the world without recourse to God. It has given the impression of being as big as God, and a rival for our worship and loyalty.

Such opposition to science has not been entirely without justification, and yet what is now emerging is that science needs direction. It must be governed by ethical principles, so that it is used for the benefit rather than the detriment of human communities. Christians should recognize in this an opportunity to develop biblical principles, which will express the significance of human life and the importance of personal relationships. This is particularly so in the biomedical field, where human concerns are at stake and where the rapid development of scientific expertise is posing a plethora of problems.

## Technology and human life

It is impossible to speak about science in contemporary society without referring to technology. The reason for this is not simply that Western societies are dominated by technology, but because science itself has been revolutionized by technology.

The fusion of physical science and technology is an accomplished fact. What we are currently experiencing is the fusion of biomedicine and technology. However great may have been the implications of the physical science fusion, the implications of the biomedicine fusion are infinitely greater because the nature of the human person is directly implicated in this latest development.

*We*, rather than our environments, are being moulded by technology. *We* are being changed, and it is at this juncture that technology has religious and philosophical overtones. The fusion of science and technology brings to the fore the fact that scientific understanding is a source of power. Once this fusion has taken place, power dictates the relevance and value of scientific understanding. This is because the scientific endeavour is being funded and promoted for quite specific purposes within society and industry. These purposes may or may not be legitimate; the point is that science has become an offshoot of government and commercial enterprises. It has lost its inherent freedom to investigate whatever it wishes and to publish the results freely and universally. All too easily we may find ourselves in the position of seeking only that truth which fits the purposes of certain interest groups within society.

This may sound a harsh judgment, and the limitations imposed by technology are not confined to technology. Freedom of scientific enquiry may be restricted by governments for political reasons or by the church for religious ones. Hence this is not a criticism of technology *per se*. Nevertheless it would be folly to think that we can readily escape the pervasive influence of technology. Political ideologies can be overthrown and replaced by alternative ones in which respect for individual freedom of enquiry is maintained. Religious reasons for circumscribing scientific freedom are, from the perspective of biblical Christianity, a negation of fundamental Christian tenets, according to which freedom and responsibility are mutually interacting characteristics of human life. Any form of vigorous Christianity, therefore, will strive to extend scientific freedom rather than limit it.

I am not arguing that technology always restricts freedom or that it is of necessity evil. What is important is that we ensure that we can make use of technology and direct it for our purposes, rather than find ourselves and our science being directed by it. Scientific freedom is important and should not be traded in for the dubious advantages of technological efficiency.

The science-technology fusion is also of profound significance, because it has revolutionized human existence. Technology is a product of human creativity and enables us to exercise control over the natural and physical world. Unfortunately, human societies have become so dependent upon technology that their existence is rapidly becoming impossible without it. The means of liberation from the tyrannies of the natural world is also a means of enslavement. The question facing us is whether it is possible to have the liberation without the enslavement. This is a religious question, because if enslavement is a necessary accompaniment of liberation, we have to ask what price we are prepared to pay for liberation from the impediments of disease and physical disorder. Perhaps it is a question of gaining a world of painless ease and losing the freedom to be oneself and to fulfil one's own capacities.

This is a predicament of values, and technology itself is incapable of providing us with the necessary answers. Its value-systems have been predetermined by society, and now society could be held captive by technology. We cannot retrace our steps to some idyllic pre-technological era; we have to live with our creation, because we are now technologically-dependent beings. *We* have been changed; we are part of a new reality, with new attitudes to space and time, with new expectations of work and leisure, and even with new aspirations for body and mind.

For Christians the challenge is to determine what constitutes human values and how these values are related to the precepts of Jesus. These are issues I shall tackle in later chapters. It is vital, even at this stage of the book, to realize that whatever our values may currently be, they are liable to be radically transformed in a technological society. Technology is characterized by attitudes which are implicitly *materialistic*. Every facet of technology affirms that the immediate and physical – things and possessions – are important. From here, it is a short step to the affirmation that they are of *ultimate* importance. This is a religious statement, which underscores the challenge, perhaps the threat, of technology to Christian values.

In the biomedical area, the materialism is just as evident, although we may not generally use this term in a medical context. When dealing with human life, the materialism of technology manifests itself as naturalism. Reliance is now placed on the natural and physical and, when this is done at the expense of the supernatural and of human relationships and aspirations, technology becomes a threat to human and spiritual values.

To some, such as Jacques Ellul, technology is autonomous; it has become an end in itself with values antagonistic to human values. This need not be the case. It need not be dehumanizing, and yet if it is not directed by other value-systems, it may run out of control and become inimical to the human good. Technology must be controlled and must be put to the common good. It must never be allowed to become an end in itself.

## Technology and biomedical ethics

It is often claimed that the underlying assumption of modern medicine and health care is the biomedical model. While this model may not be accepted by all involved in health care, it deserves serious consideration. According to it, lack of health is primarily due to disease which, in turn, reflects an abnormality in some aspect of the body's normal mode of functioning. The diagnosis of this abnormality and its subsequent treatment constitute a cure because, by definition, normality has replaced abnormality.

The biomedical model is essentially a technological

model. Its rationale stems from viewing human beings as physical machines. When these machines cease to function adequately, they can be repaired by technological means. It requires only a brief glance at modern medicine to realize how extremely powerful and eminently successful this model has proved. And yet its success has been bought at a cost, and this is the necessity of regarding human beings as little more than physical machines. The end-result has been the almost inevitable tendency to reduce human beings to impersonal dimensions; the seriousness of this trend is accentuated as technology itself becomes ever more expensive.

Most societies can no longer afford to dispense high biomedical technology to all who, in terms of the biomedical model, could benefit from it. Consequently choices have to be made between one individual and another, all of whom expect to benefit from the technology, but cannot. If human beings were nothing more than physical machines, there would be no problems, since impersonal criteria could always be devised to solve conflicting interests. But human beings are much more than impersonal machines; they have expectations, wishes, desires, feelings and beliefs. Unfortunately it is sentiments and feelings such as these with which the biomedical model is unable to cope. Technology, by its very nature, is ill-equipped to solve the profoundest of our biomedical problems.

A pure technological approach to biomedicine is good at tackling disease, but is weak at promoting health in a positive way. It cannot take account of environmental, emotional, sociological and spiritual factors which, together, constitute the uniqueness of each person.

It is here that Christianity impinges on scientific answers. Christianity asserts that human concerns are significant and cannot be relegated to the demands of the technological juggernaut without grave consequences for the future of humanity. Human beings, therefore, must control technology rather than be controlled by it. This reflects the Christian contention that humans demonstrate many of the moral qualities of God himself, including responsibility for their own actions and for the outcome of creative human endeavours.

Whenever choices have to be made between technological and personal considerations, the personal concerns must as a principle be placed first. This is because, from a Christian standpoint, individuals are important in the sight of God. They are to be respected, because they are human beings endowed with God-like characteristics. They are ends in themselves.

For Christians, human beings possess a dignity beyond that placed upon them by society; it stems from the value placed upon them by God. This value is reflected not in what we can do, but in the fact that God loves us and Christ died for us. Those who have no functional value in society – the genetically-disadvantaged and the mentally-retarded – still have an 'alien' dignity. They are important in the sight and purposes of God.

Another issue concerns our changed expectations of health and what we regard as 'normal'. Technical advances in biomedicine have dramatically altered our expectations of what constitutes normal human experience. Many of us now feel we have a right to live lives free of headaches, illness, depression, stress, tension and any sort of deformity. Normal life has, by definition, come to exclude such experiences, because we have come to equate human well-being with biological well-being. We have a different view of what 'normal' existence is, and this change has been brought about by the successes of biomedical technology.

There is no way out of these changed expectations; what we must realize is that they are posing immense challenges to our value-systems. Biomedical technology has made possible biological quality control, since measures can frequently be taken to improve the biological quality of human life. This is where the thrust of genetic engineering and genetic counselling comes in, and it is where prenatal medical care has made immense contributions. Unfortunately the goal of improved quality may come into conflict with considerations such as individual freedom of choice, or differences of opinion over therapeutic abortion. Quality control, as an end in itself, is based on the premise that healthy, normal individuals are preferable to unhealthy individuals.

It is difficult to escape from these issues, because so much of what we have done for so long has been in this direction. We have gradually been increasing our control over our environment and ourselves, until it is difficult to leave anything to chance. In many respects this movement has been in a desirable direction, because apart from it we would still be engulfed by a myriad diseases that have almost disappeared into oblivion. Nevertheless we need to resist the technological imperative of concluding that only the biological quality of our lives matters. Quality control needs to be viewed within the broad framework of the hopes and aspirations of individual persons or patients. Christians, in particular, need to place material progress and human happiness within the context of the well-being of people in their wholeness.

Technological advance raises issues of perplexing complexity for society, because it has revolutionized our relationship to society. Biological normality is no longer a private matter, of concern only to individuals. It is attained by technological means and, if lost, may be recovered by technological means. But society has a stake in this technology, and increasingly is insisting that it makes decisions about whether these means are, or are not, employed. Hence, the growing conflict between freedom of choice by the individual and coercion by the state. Technological resources are limited, and yet our biological well-being is becoming increasingly dependent upon such resources.

At present, for instance, we can still debate whether deformed children should be allowed into the world. And yet, in a technological society, will the time come when such children are denied human existence on the grounds that biologically inferior children are too expensive to maintain? This is an inevitable outcome of technological control, unless we argue persuasively that human beings must be viewed in a broader context than that of the biological alone. We need to take seriously the humanness of human beings, the inherent value of human beings, whether or not they are of functional value to society, and the importance of human relationships within society and for society.

A possible danger of technological advance in the biomedical realm is that it opens the door to a divorce of humans as biological phenomena from humans as people. This is the essence of dehumanization. We can live more of our lives on a purely biological plane, having little fear of imminent death, often having little fear of illness, knowing that our needs can be controlled and even manipulated by biomedical techniques. As our future characteristics also come under the aegis of these techniques, and as we gain increasing control over the characteristics of future humans, the possibilities for further dehumanization grow. Technological solutions to human problems are all too easily dispensed, and yet are notoriously short-term solutions, leaving the social and human predicament untouched. Here again, the danger comes when reliance upon the technology edges out human and personal considerations. There is a place for technology, controlled and directed by human values. There should be no place for rampant, directionless technology.

If dehumanization is one side of the coin of technological medicine, the other side is reductionism. When medicine is viewed solely as a scientific exercise, and hence only as one of the wonders of advanced technology, it is committed to reducing complex human beings to a set of functioning parts. Attention is paid to one or more of these parts, with the consequence that treatment is directed at these parts rather than at the whole person.

I am not arguing that this approach has no validity. If an appendix or gall bladder is diseased, it is to those organs that attention must be primarily directed. Very often, however, life is not that simple. Lack of health may not stem from one discrete, well-defined source. It may not have a neat biological cause; rather, it may be a manifestation of a complex interplay of social and psychological factors, with nutritional, environmental and behavioural components.

When this is the case, as it is in a large percentage of patients seen by the family doctor, the biomedical model is inadequate. The limitations of any purely technological approach stem from its lack of concern with health and its inability to deal with it.

And yet, from a Christian perspective, there is still hope. In a technological world, the possibilities for alienation are legion; dehumanization is an ever-present possibility; human activities are all too readily reduced to inhuman, impersonal techniques. Nevertheless biomedical techniques can still be utilized to enhance the meaning of human existence by reducing the burden of illness and by increasing the opportunities for deepening the richness of human experience. We should not succumb to the allures of biomedical technique for its own sake; rather, techniques of this type need to be seen as implements to be used within a person- and human-centred framework.

Christianity reminds us of the enduring significance of human beings. To allow humans to be swamped by impersonal techniques is to do them a grave injustice. Humans are, and will continue to be, of immense significance, as demonstrated by their relationship to God and by his deep concern for their welfare. This concern was irrevocably demonstrated in Jesus Christ, and is of equal poignancy and relevance for a scientific and technological age as it was two millennia ago.

## Health and disease

To look further into the consequences of relying heavily on biomedical technology, we need to pursue the meaning of health and disease. Perhaps the best-known definition of health is that put forward by the World Health Organization: 'Health is a state of complete physical, mental and social well-being and not merely the absence of disease and infirmity.'

There can be few definitions that have come in for more criticism and even ridicule than this one. Without question it is an unattainable ideal. It also leaves itself open to the criticism that it equates social and health problems, thereby leading to a potential loss of patient responsibility and to defining all human disorders as forms of illness. Nevertheless it serves as a reminder that health, if it is to have any meaning, must encompass more than the mere absence of illness. Health must tell us something about the ability of individuals to function acceptably in society, and in ways which fulfil their aspirations and expectations.

Once health is viewed in anything like this way, however, it introduces difficulties. It has moved away from the biological towards the social, and with this it may have lost hold on hard data. It is also as vague as ever. Valid as these comments are, however, health as a sociological phenomenon cannot be totally dismissed. Its positive aspects are needed if people are to be viewed as whole persons rather than as mere collections of parts. It must be concerned, in part at least, with the prevention of disease and the promotion of fitness, with housing conditions, sanitation, nutrition, job satisfaction, employment opportunities, road safety and atmospheric pollution.

By contrast, technological medicine is primarily concerned with disease. This brings us back to the biomedical model, with its emphasis on the recovery of health by the elimination of disease. Remove a disease process, and health is attained. The more disease processes that can be eliminated in this way, the more successful medicine is seen to be. And this is where technology comes to the fore: technology is being used increasingly to combat disease processes. Indeed, the only way forward appears to be with technology. But this, as I have already attempted to show, has its drawbacks – both financial and philosophical.

And so it becomes imperative to ask whether modern medicine has placed itself in a technological strait-jacket, because of an over-emphasis on disease. Has medicine, and the public at large, been misled by some of the startling successes of the medical enterprise, particularly by the eradication of many infectious scourges? Is it legitimate to expect that the technological sophistication of modern medicine will eliminate cancer or heart disease, congenital disorders or senility as dramatically and effectively as TB, cholera, diphtheria, typhoid, smallpox, whooping cough and scarlet fever were eliminated? The assertion is even being made by some, such as Ivan Illich, that the disappearance of these infectious diseases was due in no small measure to improved housing, sanitation and nutrition; prophylactic measures certainly had their important part to play, but they do not constitute the whole of the story.

Illness, therefore, is not to be seen simply as a straightforward scientific concept. It amounts to more than just the diagnosis of disease-entities, and hence is not just a matter of technological wizardry. Illness is also a status, in that it is a socially acceptable form of deviance. Once a doctor defines an individual as ill, society confers upon that individual freedom from any blame for his or her condition.

It is not my intention to follow this argument any further. Nevertheless the social power bestowed upon the medical profession is an important one, and it should convince us that contemporary medicine is more than merely a scientific enterprise. We are more than machines, and doctors are more than technicians. As we consider modern medicine, therefore, we need to place its social and moral obligations alongside its technological prowess.

What I am arguing is that, if modern medicine is seen as nothing more than technology writ large in human form, it will also be seen as nothing more than a means of dispensing cures for diseased states. In these terms cures will have to be provided for everything, because everything from pregnancy to dying, and from frustration to unhappiness, will be seen as an illness. In a technological paradigm, once something is called an illness it has been converted into something which is amenable to treatment. Even death presents itself as a state to be prevented, even cured, at all costs. Once death has been medicalized, it becomes necessary to cure it.

The over-medicalization of life is well and truly with us; it is a symptom of the technologization of medicine. Once we do things for no better reason than that they can be done, technology has commenced its rule over us. We have become its captive, and have ceased to control it and use its powers wisely and humanely.

The challenge facing medicine and society today is to keep technology in perspective, to use it where it is valuable and to refrain from using it where it is misleading. Of course, we have to decide under what circumstances and in what medical conditions the use of our technological skills is justified. This is a value-judgment, but so are many other decisions in medicine.

Some of our guiding criteria need to be recognition of the personhood and dignity of human beings, the role of poor or unsatisfactory social conditions in many illnesses, and the crucial place of caring as well as curing in medical practice. These criteria are implicitly Christian; they can, however, be worked out in more explicit Christian terms.

A principle to which increasing attention is being paid is that God takes the side of the weakest and poorest. Chris Sugden, in his book *Radical Discipleship*, writes: 'The biblical commands to defend the widow and orphan are commands to side with those who are vulnerable.' From this we can conclude that God is concerned for the ill, the retarded, the malformed and those in desperate pain. This is ample justification for taking medical care seriously and for giving it high priority in a community's scale of values. This principle was also illustrated in a very practical way by Christ, many of whose miracles were healing miracles. In these, Christ demonstrated who he was by helping those in physical and mental need. His miracles, far from being exercises in bravado, underlined his deep concern for those whom society could not or would not help.

The complementary principle, however, is that the healthy should not seek security in their good health. Jesus repeatedly warned that riches are dangerous, because they lead to an undue dependence upon the obvious and the temporary. In similar fashion we should not rely upon good health. It is a blessing to be thankfully received and gratefully made the most of; but, like wealth, it is ephemeral. To make health an end in itself is to make it a rival to God; it is to get our priorities wrong. An undue dependence upon physical fitness may even blind us to the plight of the physically unlovely – those whom we are to help and support.

God's concern is for all, especially those in need. These are to be our concerns as well. Such an attitude is, however, possible only as long as we recognize that all human beings should be able to enjoy the basic necessities of life. While these necessities may not include perfect health, they encompass the availability of basic medical care. Excellent health for *some* should not, therefore, take priority over reasonable health for *all*.

This is a principle with immense repercussions. It calls attention to God's love for all, and the ease with which those, who have access to high technology medicine, slip into selfish excesses. Improved standards of health for one sector of a society, perhaps at the expense of adequate health for another sector, is unjust. Adequate standards of health should be made available to all within a community; otherwise interpersonal relationships are abrogated and God's intentions are thwarted.

Injustice in health matters will continue as long as health is viewed as a right for only some, and therefore an expression of privilege and wealth. In Christian terms, health needs to be seen in the wider context of just social relationships and human dignity. Health, as an isolated commodity, does not lead to the development of a sense of dignity and self-worth. Relationships within a society should be such that all the members of that community can come to see themselves as valuable human beings, whatever degree of biological health they do or do not possess. When the physical health of some is attained by exploiting others, the overall result for society is disharmony and fragmentation. By contrast, a community based on human dignity, reconciliation and social justice is capable of ministering to the sick and feeble.

Biological health has been seen far too much in individualistic terms. When viewed in community terms, we begin to realize that 'health for all' demands the sharing of resources. We begin to see that God is central to health, and that right relationships with others are also critical. Living for others, and not for biologically perfect bodies, is at the heart of wholeness, which reflects healthy mental and physical attitudes and aspirations. I am not denying the significance of biological fitness, but I am placing it in a context of right relationships with God and our neighbours.

A Christian perspective on biomedical technology also emphasizes simplicity of life-style. Technology is capable of removing from us control over our own health. The danger of this trend is that it leaves us open to exploitation by others. If all decisions regarding our health fall into the hands of professionals, we become entirely dependent for our physical well-being upon them and the technology at their disposal. A crucial area of control over our lives has passed into the hands of others. They control us, the nature of the control depending upon their beliefs, attitudes and concerns. A point may be reached where we abdicate responsibility for crucial decisions in our own lives. This is a danger implicit in all forms of technology, a danger that may result in Christians indulging in actions they would normally consider unethical. A case in point is the termination of pregnancy for predominantly social reasons. Recommendation of termination by a doctor may be accepted by a Christian couple, simply because it is made by an 'expert'. On reflection, the couple may soon realize that the grounds for the termination are non-medical and pay no regard for human life or human relationships.

Ordinary people should make as many decisions as possible about their own health and that of others in society. Medical services should be structured to allow for lay participation in decision-making, especially where ethical issues are at stake. When such participation is not allowed, there may soon be little opportunity for the expression of Christian principles. This is because societies without a firm religious base, whether Christian or not, are at the mercy of technological trends. These trends reflect professional expertise and the advocacy of short-term technological solutions to human problems; they have no room for human concerns nor for non-mechanical directions; neither do they show concern for the deprived and the powerless within society.

Jesus emphatically stated that we cannot serve God and Mammon; God and self-interest; God and Money. It has now become eminently clear that we cannot serve God and untethered technology. We can use technology and we can direct it to useful ends; but to lay too great stress upon it is to serve it, and to allow it to displace the worship of God in our lives.

## Levels of biomedical technology

Medicine today is in a transitional state. Application of genuinely high technologies, such as recombinant DNA technology, genetic manipulation and neurobiology, lies in the future. By contrast, our knowledge of many disease mechanisms has a nineteenth-century ring about it. Nevertheless we are becoming increasingly dependent upon technology.

To make sense of this state of affairs, a distinction can be made, as Lewis Thomas has expressed it, between three levels of technology within medicine – high technology, half-way technology and non-technology. Although these levels are arbitrary, and while there is overlap between them, they provide a general framework for thinking about technological procedures in medicine.

*High technology* is the genuinely decisive technology of modern medicine, including immunization against infections such as diphtheria, typhoid and whooping cough, the whole range of antibiotics and chemotherapy for bacterial infections, and the capacity to deal effectively with conditions such as TB and syphilis. Besides these examples, others might include contraception, the treatment of endocrine disorders with appropriate hormones, perhaps the treatment of diabetes with insulin, the prevention of haemolytic disease in the newborn, and the treatment and prevention of a range of nutritional and allied disorders.

Underlying all such instances of high technology in medical treatment is an understanding of the disease processes and an ability to rectify or alleviate the disorder in a specific way. High technology marks the zenith of medical technology, combining as it does understanding and effectiveness. Unfortunately, examples of high technology are less numerous than many imagine, and they do not usually appear overnight.

*Half-way technology* is by far the most common form of technology in contemporary medicine. It is designed to compensate for the incapacitating effects of disease, in the absence of any more fundamental form of effective treatment. On occasions, it may serve simply as a means of postponing death.

Examples of this form of technology include organ transplantation, renal dialysis, much of the management of coronary heart disease following heart attacks, the surgery, irradiation and chemotherapy for many forms of cancer, and *in vitro* fertilization.

It is not that there is no value in such treatments; rather we need to recognize that this kind of technology is of a makeshift variety. Half-way technology is a mixture of technological sophistication and primitive understanding, the sophistication lying in the technological gadgetry rather than in the level of medical understanding.

For instance, kidney transplants are carried out because something has gone profoundly wrong with an individual's kidneys and this cannot be rectified in the individual's own kidneys. Hence the need for a transplant. Even when tissue rejection problems are overcome, and transplantation becomes a much more successful procedure, the basic ignorance necessitating transplantation will remain. Similarly with *in vitro* fertilization. Even the stunning success of coronary bypass surgery cannot hide our ignorance of why people are subject to heart attacks; the numerous conflicting opinions on their causation bear ample testimony to this ignorance. The surgery is, and will always remain, second-best. The treatment of cancer also falls into this category, simply because it is an acknowledgment that we still do not fully understand why cells on occasion become malignant.

Half-way technology is not to be despised; far too often it is all we have. It is important, however, that we see it in its rightful context. It is a temporary expedient, which will be surpassed when understanding of the disease processes in question opens the way to a totally different form of high technology therapy.

All too frequently half-way technology is a last-ditch stand against disease. Prevention has failed; the disease process in a muscle, valve or organ cannot be reversed, and so replacement, removal, or some form of alleviation is demanded. It is at this junction that technology with all its stunning virtuosity takes over – automated tests galore, much exceedingly expensive equipment, and a galaxy of human expertise. Again, such technology is not unimportant, as long as it is placed in perspective. It represents in many instances an investment of thousands or millions of dollars, and yet what it is saying all the time is that we do not understand the basic biological problems giving rise to its use. Perhaps we have to live with this ignorance, and yet alongside this must be placed an anomaly: the more successful this technological expertise proves, the more it will be required. It goes on multiplying, the costs continue to escalate, and medical care becomes an ever-greater burden on society. This is inevitable and it will continue as long as half-way technology has to be employed.

We need to realize that more and better technology of the half-way variety does not solve the problem; it is still directed at the end-results of disease processes rather than at underlying mechanisms. Furthermore, the enormous financial outlay ensures that less money is available to other medical areas and perhaps also to other areas within society. It is also accompanied by a host of ethical dilemmas. The medical profession finds itself in a dilemma. Any new technology must be used if it will benefit only a few patients, even at inordinate expense. If it is available, there will be a demand for it. The only long-term escape from this dilemma is new knowledge and hence a means of moving from this level of technology to high technology. Fundamental research is essential, and yet there is no knowing how long it will take for the required major breakthroughs to occur. A clear illustration of these tensions is provided by the use of *in vitro* fertilization in the alleviation of infertility (chapter 5).

In the meantime it is essential that half-way technology is not allowed to devour all our resources, and that we do not ascribe to it a higher status than it deserves. Basic research is a prerequisite, because totally new concepts and ideas are the only ultimate way out of the financial ruin and ethical nightmare world of rampant half-way technology.

The third level of technology is best termed *non-technology*. It is the realm of supportive therapy and caring, when there is little any form of technology can be reasonably expected to achieve. This is the physician's response to intractable cancer, strokes, multiple sclerosis and some forms of mental illness and severe congenital malformation, although even here technological back-up in the form of appropriate drug regimes may be important. Non-technology is expensive, requiring hospitalization, nursing and the time of medical and paramedical personnel. Nevertheless it is an indispensable, if unglamorous, aspect of health care. Again the solution, to the extent that there is one, lies in the direction of fundamental research.

## Limitations and hazards of biomedical technology

Biomedical technology, both in the guise of high technology and half-way technology, has made impressive advances. And yet the successes of modern medicine cannot be ascribed solely to recent technology. They must be seen alongside major improvements in public health and nutrition. It is also sobering to realize that life expectancy in the technologically-advanced societies has changed relatively little over the last thirty years or so, although considerable gains were made in the first half of this century. This is because of the limited effectiveness of modern medicine in preventing, or even, in some instances, substantially prolonging the lives of many suffering from, today's main causes of death, namely, violence, coronary heart disease, cancer and chest conditions such as bronchitis and emphysema. Whether or not modern treatment improves the quality of life of patients with these conditions is another matter. It is on these grounds that critics of biomedical technology such as Ivan Illich, Ian Kennedy and Richard Taylor argue against many facets of modern medicine.

The risks and side-effects of biomedical technology are inevitable, and yet they are also worrying. Drug reactions and side-effects are common, particularly when multiple drugs are prescribed. Many of these are more a nuisance value than anything else, and yet the thalidomide tragedy is not the only drug-related tragedy of recent times. While stringent regulations and considerable care on the part of the medical profession prevent many untoward occurrences, it must never be forgotten that risks are inherent to technology. It is sometimes all too easy to adopt a seemingly neat technological solution rather than a cumbersome natural one, without realizing that the social and long-term consequences may be considerable. Perhaps the replacement of breast-feeding by bottle-feeding, especially in developing countries, aptly illustrates that point.

The risks of technology are also evident in modern diagnostic technology. X-rays are a well-known example, emphasizing once again the importance of caution in their use and the dangers of over-investigation. This latter issue is coming more and more to the fore with the escalating potential of automatic analysers for providing larger and larger amounts of random data. This, in turn, makes possible the rapid screening of people for potential abnormalities and hence makes them liable to being labelled as ill, even in the absence of any symptoms or signs.

The question which needs to be faced is: What can be done with the data? If it leads to a cure for the diseased state, there is no problem. Often, however, this is not the case: diagnosis as an end in itself hardly justifies the use of expensive, and sometimes dangerous, technology. Care must be taken that technological procedures are not used simply because they are available. They need to be adequately evaluated, they must not create more problems than they solve and, as far as possible, there must be reasonable assurance that they will benefit the patient in question. The availability of such technology presents the medical profession and the community at large with decisions and choices, not the least of which are knowing when to say 'no' to technology.

Just as technology enables us to exercise control, so we have to exercise control over the use and application of the technology. Our quality of life has quite clearly been improved by biomedical technology and yet that same technology can be used, undoubtedly inadvertently, to place quality of life in jeopardy. We only have to think of the use of life-support systems on a moribund patient, when there is no realistic expectation of anything approaching independent life again, to realize that the value of existence can be placed above the dignity and quality of human life. Medical problems should never be seen solely as exercises in logistics and technical prowess; if they are, the psychological repercussions may outweigh any benefits of the technology itself.

A final consideration is the danger of using biomedical technology to convert the entire population into patients. This has been referred to as the patientization of the population; it is the over-medicalization of life. This stems from an over-emphasis on disease, and from an ever-increasing ability to measure an endless range of parameters with ease and rapidity. The availability of blood-pressure measuring-devices outside some pharmacies is an extreme example of this.

In this instance, as in previous ones I have examined, the danger lies not in these capabilities, but in viewing them in the wrong context. It is difficult for many people to realize that variation from a biological norm does not, in and of itself, signify abnormality or illness. People must not be converted into patients simply because they differ in one or two respects from other people, and these differences must not make them liable for further investigation and 'treatment'.

It is imperative that we do not use our technological skills to convince people that they are living on the edge of mortal disease, constantly in need of medical support and sustenance. We must ensure that our technological expertise is not employed to produce a population of 'worried well'. Health is more than being convinced one has a 'non-disease', and a healthy society amounts to more than a population of non-patients.

Nevertheless, in a technologically-dependent society, it is difficult to escape completely from these trends. The availability of a piece of technology predisposes the medical profession and society towards its use to demonstrate the non-existence as well as the existence of some pathology. From here it is but a short step to the more general belief that equipment of this nature must be used to demonstrate the health of individuals. Once this happens, they have been patientized and all their problems henceforth will be seen primarily in medical terms.

We find ourselves *in* a technological world, living by technologically-inspired values. It is hardly surprising, therefore, that we have vast expectations from the new technologically-based medicine. We need to beware, however, lest our expectations are quite unjustified and place upon the medical profession an intolerable burden. Biomedical technology does not provide us with miracles, in spite of the occasional spectacular result. We should not, therefore, make of it insatiable demands.

Aware of these things, we should strive to make the most of this technology, seeing it always within a human framework. It must be used to serve us and our needs, and must not be allowed to become an end in itself. The way ahead will not be easy, because the problems are complex and emotionally charged: after all, the quality of our lives and our dignity is at stake. The issues are vital ones for Christians, in terms of their own responses to God and also of their role within society. Our perception of ourselves is at stake, and this is a profoundly religious issue.

In this chapter I have remained at the level of general principles. Nevertheless they are principles of immense relevance for a discussion of the impact of technology on our attitudes towards the commencement of life. Our dependence upon technology at the time of conception, throughout fetal life, and at birth, surpasses our dependence upon it at any other stages of life. Throughout the succeeding chapters, therefore, we shall have to return repeatedly to issues raised by technology.

# 3
# Improving the quality of life

## Quality-of-life decisions

Decisions in medical areas, both at the beginning and end of life, are focusing increasingly on a single element – the kind of life a person has, or will experience. The crucial role of quality-of-life decisions is being forcefully advocated on all sides, to the exclusion sometimes of other considerations. While these decisions are usually extensions of those traditionally made in medicine, some current means of attaining quality may be at variance with traditional means, and may on some occasions place in jeopardy traditional values of care and compassion. An exploration of issues raised by this possibility will occupy our attention throughout the remainder of this book. In the present chapter we shall begin our exploration by looking at genetic diseases and their implications.

A few years ago Joseph Fletcher, the American theologian and ethicist, wrote a book *The Ethics of Genetic Control*, with the enticing sub-title: 'Ending Reproductive Roulette'. In this he wrote: 'To repair and prolong lives, indiscriminately, may be a kind of technical virtuosity but it is not control. To control means to choose, and therefore any absolute morality about always keeping life going, before or after birth, regardless of quality considerations, is the very opposite of control and a denial of quality.' Fletcher argues that, since control is human and rational, humans should exert as much control as possible over everything. It is time, therefore, that we accepted control of heredity, with an emphasis on quality.

I do not wish to follow Fletcher's arguments any further or even to comment on them at this juncture. What is significant is that quality control, which is foundational to his position, is one of the most pervasive influences in modern medicine, so much of which is directed towards either producing individuals of better quality or improving the quality of existing individuals. The natural means of choosing mates and of producing children are, in biological terms, haphazard and uncontrolled. Quality control, by contrast, recognizes the desirability of healthy individuals against the undesirability of unhealthy individuals. This can readily lead to the point of view that, given the technical means of producing healthy offspring, we are obliged to strive for such offspring, even if this is at the expense of unhealthy ones. This is what Fletcher terms choice ethics, as opposed to chance ethics. According to him, the adoption of choice ethics will increase human happiness.

Control is at the heart of all modern medicine. Consequently it has not become a new phenomenon with the onset of such procedures as the prenatal diagnosis of genetic diseases or *in vitro* fertilization. What is changing is its degree and precision. The resultant dilemma is that, logically, such control reduces human beings to biological dimensions and little more. If this reductionism is to be avoided, quality control will have to be viewed within the broader framework of the needs, hopes and desires of individuals. This is a question of values. Unfortunately, values are also being placed in jeopardy by modern biomedical procedures.

Living as we are in societies dominated by technological medicine, we cannot escape the quality-of-life decisions. The biological quality of our lives and of those around us, children, parents, relatives, patients, is important. We cannot escape having to make decisions about fetuses and children with Down's syndrome or a myriad other conditions, whether these be the mentally-retarded or the senile. They are a part of our world, and pressures in favour of quality control could have major repercussions for them.

## Genetic diseases

The importance of genetic disease at the commencement of life can be illustrated in many ways. About 3 per cent of all children at birth have some genetic defect resulting in an easily diagnosable anomaly. When other diseases identified later in life are also taken into account, the actual frequency rises to about 5 per cent. Approximately 0.5 per cent of liveborn children have chromosomal aberrations. Such abnormalities account for at least 20 per cent of all spontaneous abortions, and also a significant amount of infertility. About 1,600 human diseases have a genetic origin, including relatively common conditions such as cystic fibrosis and sickle-cell anaemia. Of chromosomal abnormalities, Down's syndrome is by far the best known, with an incidence of one in 600-900 live births.

The major causes of genetic defects are deleterious genes and chromosomal abnormalities. About ten per 1,000 live births in European populations carry harmful single genes (dominants plus recessives) responsible for genetic disease, and five per 1,000 suffer from chromosomal abnormalities. Of the large number of genetic defects, some are relatively common and can be detected by genetic screening. The principal such defects are Down's syndrome, cystic fibrosis, phenylketonuria (PKU), sickle-cell anaemia and Tay-Sachs disease. Of the metabolic diseases caused by deleterious genes, glucose-6-phosphate dehydrogenase deficiency is a notable example.

Down's syndrome is due to an excessive number of chromosomes, most cases having three number 21 chromosomes in each cell, instead of the normal two. The social importance of this condition stems from its relatively high incidence and the fact that it is far more common in older mothers than in younger ones. For instance, one in 2,000 women under the age of 25 give birth to Down's syndrome children, whereas the incidence rises to one in 290 for mothers in the 35–39 age-bracket, one in 100 for the 40–45 age-group, and one in 40 for mothers over the age of 45. Unfortunately, most children with this condition are severely mentally-retarded and frequently require institutional care. Even those who are less severely retarded are still definitely retarded. In the United States, 7,000 children suffering from Down's syndrome are born each year, with these children comprising as many as 30 per cent of those school-aged children having some form of severe mental handicap.

The ethical realm enters into discussions of Down's syndrome because affected fetuses can be detected during pregnancy. This detection is accomplished by the procedure of *amniocentesis*, which will be described later in this chapter in my discussion of the prenatal diagnosis of genetic diseases. A positive diagnosis of Down's syndrome at 18–20 weeks of pregnancy opens the way for a therapeutic abortion, which is the only means currently available of circumventing the birth of a child with Down's syndrome. There is no treatment of the condition, in the conventional sense. Whether or not an older woman (35 plus) who becomes pregnant should be encouraged to undergo amniocentesis will depend on a number of factors, including her attitude towards therapeutic abortion.

Other genetic conditions involve defects, not of chromosomes, but of particular genes making up the chromosomes. For instance, *haemophilia* and *muscular dystrophy* are caused by abnormal genes on one of the sex chromosomes, and hence are sex-linked diseases (X-linked recessive disorders). In general only males suffer from them, although they are transmitted through females. Important as these two conditions are, they are relatively uncommon. For instance, in Britain where there are of the order of 800,000 births a year, approximately 160 cases of Duchenne muscular dystrophy occur and only 80 cases of haemophilia. One reason why these conditions are significant is that, because of the manner in which they are inherited, their incidence can be lowered by careful genetic counselling.

Other genetic diseases are linked, not with sex chromosomes, but with one of the 44 other chromosomes in the nucleus of a normal human cell. These fall into two general classes, *dominant* and *recessive* conditions.

A well-known disease caused by a dominant gene is *Huntington's chorea*, which commences in the third or fourth decade of life and leads eventually to severe mental deterioration and finally death. Whenever the offending gene is present, the disease emerges. Each afflicted person has a 50 per cent chance of passing the condition on to his or her offspring, with men and women being equally affected. The high probability of passing on the condition to one's children and the inevitability of serious dementia followed by early death when afflicted constitute dimensions of tragic proportions.

Far more common than this type of genetic disease, however, are the *recessive conditions* of which some 800 are currently recognized. Fortunately most of these are rare. In these conditions the two genes responsible for the disease must be present, one coming from the mother and one from the father. But, even when both parents carry the particular gene, on an average only one in four children of such a union will actually have the disease. Each child born to such parents will have a one-in-four chance of carrying the two genes responsible for the genetic defect.

A common example of a recessive disease due to one particular gene is *cystic fibrosis* of the pancreas, with an incidence of one affected child in every 2,000 births in most Western countries. This disease has a heterozygote frequency of 4–5 per cent. The incidence of cystic fibrosis is thought to be too high for a recessive lethal unless heterozygotes have some undetected advantage. The frequency is much lower in non-European populations.

In cystic fibrosis the body's mucus-secreting glands function abnormally, a thick viscous mucus being produced in the pancreas, duodenum and lungs. As a result the digestion of food is impaired, pneumonia is a frequent occurrence, and chronic lung disease may develop. An excessive amount of salt is produced in the sweat, and this provides a means of diagnosing the condition. Death generally occurs during childhood or in early adult life. Since the basic biochemical defect in cystic fibrosis is still unknown, no satisfactory means of detecting carriers have been found.

Another example of a recessive genetic disease is *sickle-cell anaemia*, in which individuals carry two abnormal genes and suffer from an abnormality of haemoglobin, dying in most cases before the age of 20. In parts of West Africa, one child in 64 is affected, with one in 500 black children similarly affected in the United States. Besides these affected individuals, about two million people carry just one abnormal gene. These are the 'carriers', who are clinically normal and who, in parts of Africa, manifest an increased resistance to malaria.

The intriguing situation here is that those who are carriers of the disease, but do not themselves suffer from it, can be identified by suitable screening or detection programs. Sickle-cell anaemia can now be prenatally diagnosed either by fetal blood sampling or sometimes by amniocentesis. Many of those at risk, however, may not want this.

*Phenylketonuria* (PKU) is another recessive condition which, in European populations, has a frequency of between one in 10,000 and one in 20,000. PKU represents an extremely interesting condition from a medical standpoint because, although it cannot be cured, its clinical manifestations can be controlled. The genetic deficiency in this instance leads to the body's inability to produce an essential enzyme, with the result that toxic products (phenylalanine) accumulate in the body, leading to mental retardation. These consequences can, however, be prevented provided the disease is detected within the first few weeks of life and the individual is subsequently kept on an appropriate diet. Screening for PKU is now carried out in the majority of births in a number of countries.

In this case there is little conflict, since the costs of wide-scale screening programs are generally outweighed by the costs of keeping affected individuals (assuming no screening and no early dietary treatment) in mental institutions for the rest of their lives. The cost of screening and treatment per affected individual is only about 16 per cent that of the lifelong maintenance of an untreated individual in an institution. It may seem callous even to raise the question of money when a method of successful treatment is known. This may be so, but the cost-benefit ratio advantage for a screening program decreases as the frequency of the disease decreases. A point must be reached, therefore, where the potential benefits of the screening can no longer justify the financial outlay. This is not the case with PKU, but it is in some other instances. Even when screening is used, as for PKU, some apparently positive results are not, in fact, due to PKU. The possibility that then has to be considered is whether these 'false-positive' individuals will suffer from being 'treated' with the special diet.

*Tay-Sachs disease*, like PKU, is an inborn error of metabolism – being caused by a recessive gene and having a one-in-four chance of appearing in children of carriers. It has a frequency of one in 2,000 among Askenazi Jews, but a very much lower frequency in other populations. Infants suffering from it develop progressive mental deterioration, followed by blindness and paralysis, and death by the age of about 3 years. Because both carriers and affected fetuses can be identified, normal children can be guaranteed to matings between carriers by aborting affected fetuses. Screening programs involve wives, husbands, and finally fetuses, and there can be no doubt that, in cost-effective terms, they are highly successful among the Askenazi Jews in the United States. The one proviso is that *in utero* detection of the disease must be followed by therapeutic abortion if the programs are to be of any avail. An unwillingness to go through with subsequent abortion negates the rationale of the schemes, raising yet again the crucial significance of therapeutic abortion for their success and highlighting its pivotal position as an ethical question.

These examples confront us with the challenge of biological quality, and with a plethora of questions. Is it the paramount right of every child to be born with a normal hereditary endowment? Is a society justified in denying existence to individuals likely to develop a genetic disease? If decisions are taken to prevent such individuals coming into the world, in whose interests are these decisions? If individuals should not be born on the basis of the cost of their future upkeep or on the grounds of the genetic fitness of the human race, whose interests are uppermost – those of society or of the future individuals?

The approach to genetic problems epitomized by these illustrations and questions is the province of *prenatal control* or *negative eugenics* – negative because it involves the elimination of defective genes (and hence the prospective possessors of these genes) from the population. While negative eugenics is not a radical approach to the genetic constitution of man, and while it does not actually change individuals, its impact on society is an important one and its potential for changing the genetic make-up of a community is far from negligible.

The challenge of negative eugenics has been provocatively expressed by Professor Bentley Glass. According to him, 'the right of individuals to procreate must give place to a new paramount right: the right of every child to enter life with an adequate physical and mental endowment'. The consequence of such a position is that the diagnosis of genetic disease in a fetus carries with it the moral responsibility to minimize the birth of defective children. And so emerges Glass's now-famous remark that advances in human genetics should usher in the day when the paramount right of every child is to be born with a normal, adequate hereditary endowment. Such a stance assumes that biological quality is the paramount goal of genetics, and hence is to be the overriding directive of human endeavour.

The complexity of the decisions that have to be taken by parents before consenting to fetal diagnosis and consequent abortion has been outlined by a 1974 report of the Church and Society sub-unit of the World Council of Churches. This assessment, while a helpful guide to the issue, accepts the legitimacy of therapeutic abortion and, therefore, mirrors an approach incorporating abortion as an indigenous part of the procedures. According to this outline, abortion should be considered only when any detriment resulting from the birth of the fetus outweighs the potential benefits. The criteria suggested include: i. the severity of the genetic disorder and its effect on the possibility of a meaningful life; ii. the physical, emotional and economic impact on family and society; iii. the availability of adequate medical management and of special educational facilities; iv. the reliability of diagnosis; v. the recognition that an individual genetically defective in one respect may be superior in others; vi. the increase in the load of detrimental genes in the population that may result from the reproduction of carriers of genetic diseases.

At this stage of the discussion I do not intend to prejudge the question of therapeutic abortion. That will be discussed in chapter 7. Nevertheless, negative eugenics cannot be ignored and, as these guide-lines indicate, the biological health of a prospective child should not be used as the sole guide to the course of action to be taken. Negative eugenics, therefore, opens up a range of ethical considerations.

*Positive eugenics* or *preconceptive control* has far more radical vistas than negative eugenics, and yet any approach to it depends heavily on present experience with negative eugenics. Control in this instance precedes conception, the intention being to produce an individual who differs in some important respects from the individual who would have resulted without this intervention. In other words, a deliberate effort is being made to produce an individual with 'new' specifications. Hence this is the realm of genetic engineering proper, illustrating as it does positive – as opposed to negative – eugenics.

Genetic engineering has been defined by the American Medical Association in these terms: 'It might be considered as covering anything having to do with the manipulation of the gametes or the fetus, for whatever purpose, from conception other than by sexual union, to treatment of disease *in utero*, to the ultimate manufacture of a human being to exact specifications.'

Preconceptive control invites a great deal of idealistic support, with visions of rectifying genetic and chromosomal aberrations prior to conception. Utilizing these techniques it is envisaged that the amount of human misery will be reduced, and that the struggles of postnatal or traditional medicine will be diminshed. According to Joseph Fletcher, 'the ultimate goal of genetic engineering is not to ameliorate the ills of patients prenatally or postnatally, but to start people off healthy and free of disease . . . It aims to control people's initial genetic design and constitution by gene surgery and by genetic design.' This is the essence of *quality control*, the goal of which is to be able to choose who shall live as opposed to who shall not, those selected to live possessing characteristics of which the controllers approve. For Fletcher, whose situation ethics reach unprecedented levels of optimism in the genetic realm, quality control in birth technology should select for intelligence, on the ground that control is human and rational and is, therefore, to be espoused.

Positive eugenics, however, has a very much longer history than genetic engineering, and yet the intentions of the two have much in common. Francis Galton invented the term 'eugenics' in 1883, the essence of which was to encourage the reproduction of the select. The difficulty has always been to identify the select, and having done this to promote only those genes considered to be desirable. In order to accomplish this, it would be necessary to be very restrictive in the selection of partners and the lethal genes carried even by the select in the population would have to be eliminated.

Positive eugenics has always had to face the objection that it would not succeed in eliminating all known genetic diseases. Therefore, even if it was considered worth sacrificing much individual freedom of choice in the cause of positive eugenics, it would amount to a hollow achievement. It would not achieve enough. We would still be left with the uneasy knowledge that we do not know what will be best for mankind centuries or millennia hence. We cannot speak about 'good' heredity, as if this is some package that can be isolated from the environment.

As if this criticism of positive eugenics were not enough, there remains the practical problem of knowing which characteristics to choose. Even if agreement should be reached on qualities such as loving-kindness, compassion, generosity and courage, the issue then resolves itself into the genetic basis of such qualities. Professor R. J. Berry argues that it would be impracticable to select for two or more such attributes, since any responsible genes will be distributed throughout the genome and could only be concentrated at the cost of other developing systems. If, therefore, it proved possible to improve certain characteristics, this may be achieved only at the expense of other systems. The end result may be unwanted features such as mental deficiency.

Another way of highlighting the limitations of positive eugenics is to consider what might actually be accomplished by it. For instance, if one per cent of females with an IQ of 100 had 50 per cent of their children by donors with an IQ of 115, the mean IQ of the population would rise by as little as 0.04. It is not difficult to see why positive eugenics, as traditionally conceived, has failed to open up the revolutionary vistas once imagined. Nevertheless, the hope enshrined in it lives on in modified form, especially in genetic engineering but also in negative eugenics.

## Prenatal diagnosis of genetic diseases

Increasing knowledge of the characteristics of genetic diseases can have an impact in clinical terms only if these diseases are detectable prenatally. Prenatal diagnosis of an increasing number of these conditions depends on the use of the techniques of amniocentesis, ultrasound and fetoscopy. Of these amniocentesis is the primary tool for prenatal diagnosis, and can be used for the detection of almost all the chromosomal disorders and about 70 inborn errors of metabolism.

*Amniocentesis* is performed as an outpatient procedure between the 14th and 16th week of gestation. A sample of the amniotic fluid is removed from around the fetus, through a needle inserted through the anterior abdominal wall into the uterine cavity. At this stage of gestation, approximately 200 ml of amniotic fluid is present, of which 10–20 ml needs to be drawn off for diagnostic procedures. Amniotic fluid contains epithelial cells shed from the skin and from the gastrointestinal and respiratory tracts of the fetus, and it is these cells that are required for the detection of defective genes or of abnormalities in the structure or number of the chromosomes.

A single tap is sufficient to obtain adequate quantities of fluid in about 95 per cent of women. It has to be repeated, however, in about 5 per cent of instances, not only because of an inadequate volume of fluid, but also due to poor cell growth and inconclusive results. Once obtained, the fetal cells are prepared for cultures, which are subsequently used for biochemical or cytogenetic tests. The levels of alpha-fetoproteins can be measured, and these serve as important indicators of severe structural defects of the brain and spinal cord.

Amniocentesis is associated with some degree of risk to the fetus, although this appears to be low. According to a major study carried out in 1971 by the Institute of Child Health and Development at the National Institutes of Health (NICHD), there was no significant difference between the number of subsequent fetal deaths in the amniocentesis and control groups, the groups having death rates of 3.5 and 3.2 per cent respectively. A more recent American study reports a rate of spontaneous abortion after amniocentesis of 1.5 per cent, and a 1978 British study reports a 2.6 per cent rate of fetal loss compared with 1.1 per cent for controls. When all theoretical risks are taken into account, the overall risk figure for morbidity is of the order of 1 per cent. The rate of maternal complications is probably low, although haemorrhage, infection, and blood group sensitization are all possible risks.

Amniocentesis is a very reliable procedure in detecting genetic and chromosomal abnormalities. In the NICHD study, the overall accuracy rate was 99.4 per cent. Of the 1,040 patients studied, three errors were made in sex determination, one enzyme determination gave a false-positive result, and two children with Down's syndrome were diagnosed as normal. In another series of 1,600 amniocenteses carried out in the mid-1970s, seven errors were made in sex determination; 14 diagnostic errors were made in 3,000 amniocenteses in a 1979 study.

In spite of these impressive figures, caution is still required. These studies were undertaken in specialized laboratories, and the amniocenteses were performed by people with a great deal of experience. These figures should not be used, therefore, to argue for the routine or indiscriminate use of amniocentesis.

*Ultrasound* can be employed in the estimation of gestational age, location of the placenta prior to amniocentesis, diagnosis of twins, and detection of major structural defects in the fetus. This technique, which has minimal risks for both mother and fetus, is of especial value in the diagnosis of hydrocephalus and neural tube defects.

*Fetoscopy* is the direct visualization of the fetus, by the introduction of an optical system into the uterine cavity through the abdomen. It is an experimental procedure, which may lead to fetal damage or spontaneous abortion. There may also be fetal or maternal blood loss, infection and emotional disturbance.

While fetoscopy is currently limited by numerous complications, it could open the way in the future to the biopsy of fetal skin, to obtaining blood from the umbilical cord, and to the detection of external structure anomalies of the fetus. These would prove useful in the prenatal diagnosis of a number of genetic conditions, including thalassemia, sickle-cell anaemia and neural tube defects. Its potential, therefore, is considerable, although it is the sort of technology which will not unfortunately be readily available in the foreseeable future in poorer countries.

*Radiography* has the potential to detect conditions such as limb and neural tube defects and general disturbances to bone growth, at around 20 weeks' gestation. The realization of this potential, however, requires the injection of dyes into the amniotic fluid to delineate the fetal outline. This procedure, therefore, is associated with a combination of hazards stemming from amniocentesis, X-irradiation and the contrast media themselves.

The medical indications for prenatal diagnosis can be classed under the following headings: chromosomal abnormalities, X-linked recessive disorders, inborn errors of metabolism, and neural tube defects.

In the case of suspected *chromosomal abnormalities*, the main consideration is Down's syndrome. In the major surveys of amniocentesis undertaken up to the present, approximately 50 per cent of women have been over 35 years of age. This is because, as we have already seen, advanced maternal age is closely correlated with an increased incidence of Down's syndrome. The next most frequent indication for amniocentesis is the previous birth of a child with Down's syndrome, the risk in this instance being 1–2 per cent. Still in this category other indications for amniocentesis are the birth of a previous child with congenital anomalies, and a history of three or more spontaneous abortions. In the former instance, if the congenital anomalies result from an unbalanced translocation, there is a 20 per cent risk of a second abnormal fetus. A history of spontaneous abortions may well be associated with a greatly increased incidence of chromosomal abnormalities.

With *X-linked recessive disorders*, such as haemophilia and muscular dystrophy, amniocentesis is aimed at detecting the sex of the fetus. For families in which the wife is a known carrier of one of these conditions, a male fetus has a 50 per cent chance of being affected. As long as there is no means of distinguishing affected from unaffected male fetuses the only means of preventing the birth of an affected child is to abort all male fetuses. However, the situation in regard to haemophilia is changing, since it can now be detected using fetal blood sampling. The problem of aborting all male fetuses need not arise with haemophilia in a developed country.

*Inborn errors of metabolism* affect about 0.8 per cent of newborn babies and are characterized by the absence or deficiency of an enzyme. A well-known example is Tay Sachs disease. When both partners are carriers there is a 25 per cent chance that each pregnancy will result in an affected child. An increasing number of these conditions can be identified prenatally by detecting the enzyme deficiency in cultured fetal cells following second trimester amniocentesis.

*Neural tube defects* are common malformations of the central nervous system, and include anencephaly, encephalocoele and spina bifida. Anencephaly is the absence of the vault of the skull, associated with complete or partial absence of the brain. Fetuses with this condition are frequently spontaneously aborted or stillborn; if these do not occur, life is confined to a matter of hours or days. Encephalocoele is a condition in which the brain protrudes through the skull. The severity of the condition varies widely, although the neurological defects are generally major and mental retardation is frequently present. In spina bifida, the neural arches fail to close in the lower part of the vertebral column leaving the protruding spinal cord covered by skin (closed spina bifida) or by a membrane (open spina bifida). Spinal cord damage is a frequent accompaniment of spina bifida, although its severity varies considerably.

Neural tube defects probably have a genetic component. After one affected child the chance of a second with one of these defects is about 5 per cent, and after two affected children it is 12–15 per cent. Prenatal diagnosis depends on the measurement of elevated alpha-fetoprotein levels in the amniotic fluid. A complicating factor is that fetuses with closed spina bifida have normal alpha-fetoprotein levels, while the gestational dates must be known with considerable accuracy. False negative results may be as high as 10 per cent, although false positives are as low as 0.1 per cent. False positives can now be virtually eliminated by testing the amniotic fluid for the enzyme acetylcholinesterase.

An ethical assessment of amniocentesis immediately confronts us with the issue of therapeutic abortion, since the only way at present of preventing most of these genetic and chromosomal abnormalities is by bringing the lives of those who would have been afflicted by them to a premature end (chapter 7). For those with few or no reservations about therapeutic abortion, amniocentesis is proving a major addition to medicine's therapeutic armamentarium. For those with reservations about the ethical acceptability of therapeutic abortion, amniocentesis is morally ambiguous.

Its status as a diagnostic procedure is ambivalent, since a positive diagnosis may be a prelude to death rather than life. Instead of opening the way to the application of therapeutic regimes in the conventional sense, it is frequently used as an indication for termination of pregnancy. In practice, therefore, amniocentesis is not a neutral procedure. It is closely allied to induced abortion, which is regarded as the therapy for the defect uncovered by amniocentesis.

Would the justification for amniocentesis disappear if the possibility of therapeutic abortion disappeared? In that instance amniocentesis would only provide information, about which nothing could be done. Although negative findings may prove consoling, can such findings alone justify its use, especially when there is a risk attached to the procedure? The intimate link between amniocentesis and therapeutic abortion is highlighted by those medical practitioners who are prepared to carry out amniocentesis only if there has been prior agreement to abort a defective fetus. Implicit in any such agreement is the worthwhileness of a healthy fetus and the lack of worth of a defective fetus. Unfortunately, even within this narrow compass, there is a difficulty. Amniocentesis does not guarantee a normal fetus, since it is concerned with the diagnosis of only a limited range of genetic and chromosomal conditions.

A further example of the uses to which amniocentesis may be put is in sex choice, where the prospective parents wish to select the gender of their next child. Although this does not appear to be a frequent occurrence in Western societies, it does occur. It is not viewed as a practical option by many couples, however, because it would lead to a midtrimester abortion, and also because most prenatal diagnostic clinics oppose it under normal circumstances. Nevertheless it illustrates how amniocentesis can be used against a fetus considered undesirable on purely social grounds.

The dangers of this type of application of amniocentesis are that it regards the 'wrong' sex as a disease, treating unwanted males or females as disease entities. It may also contribute to social inequality between the sexes with, in most instances, males probably being preferred to females. This trivial and morally reprehensible use of amniocentesis is perhaps the gravest consequence, with social flippancy being accepted as a legitimate reason for destroying human life and wasting scarce medical resources.

The major argument put forward in favour of amniocentesis for sex choice is that any abortion law which protects the absolute right of women to control their own reproduction, must also allow them to have an abortion for any reason, including this one. This argument is framed in terms of the United States Supreme Court decision of 1973 on *Roe v. Wade*. This, once again, demonstrates the intimate link between amniocentesis and abortion. It also demonstrates the inexorable logic of a technological innovation, from the use of amniocentesis in the context of a serious genetic disease, to its use where there is a statistical risk because of age, to its use to circumvent having a child of the wrong sex. The original purposes of the diagnostic tool have been radically altered. The question is: were the original purposes justified?

Is amniocentesis ethically justified, if doubts are entertained about the ethical acceptability of therapeutic abortion? Why undergo the risks associated with amniocentesis, if little or nothing can be done to alleviate the condition of the diseased fetus? Although there may be no simple answers to these questions, the act of asking them suggests that amniocentesis should not be undertaken as a routine measure. Whenever an amniocentesis is considered, a balance-sheet should be drawn up of the anticipated benefits to the fetus and mother, against the potential risks to the fetus. This exercise needs to take account of the nature and prognosis of the disease in question, and of the acceptability or otherwise of an abortion to the couple.

An amniocentesis should always be undertaken with a specific goal in view. If corrective measures can be undertaken to alleviate a disorder during fetal life, amniocentesis is justified whatever the prevailing view on therapeutic abortion. Unfortunately, such instances are relatively uncommon at present. For some couples, the knowledge that a fetus is defective may help them adjust to the prospect of the birth of a defective child. This possibility, though, needs to be thought through before proceeding with an amniocentesis. The ease with which amniocentesis can be carried out is never adequate justification for its use.

## Genetic screening

Genetic screening programs have as their goal the diagnosis of defects either before or after birth. Hence some of the issues surrounding them will be similar to those already discussed in relation to amniocentesis. Both prenatal and postnatal screening, however, involve very large numbers of people in the community, and may raise further ethical issues such as freedom of choice, confidentiality, and the role of the doctor-patient relationship.

Mass screening programs acquire genetic information from large numbers of normal and asymptomatic individuals and families. This information is obtained after only brief medical contact, which does not come within the ambit of the usual patient-initiated doctor-patient relationship. Large-scale genetic screening programs are carried out, or have been attempted, in various countries for conditions such as neural tube defects, sickle-cell anaemia, Tay-Sachs disease, PKU, maple syrup urine disease, and galactosemia. In order to illustrate some of the issues involved in mass screening, I shall concentrate on screening for neural tube defects.

Tests for neural tube defects have been used in parts of the United Kingdom since 1974. In the first five years of their use there, about 700,000 pregnancies had been screened, with 50 per cent of all pregnant women being tested. Screening tests are carried out at 16 weeks' gestation, when the mothers' blood is tested for alpha-fetoprotein. This protein leaks out of the fetal spinal cord if it is open at that stage, and subsequently enters the maternal bloodstream. Positive tests are obtained in about 50 out of every 1,000 women; on a second test, there are about 30 positive results. These 30 women are then referred for ultrasound sonography, which eliminates about 15 of them. These remaining 15 women are subject to amniocentesis, and 1–6 of these are found to have high alpha-fetoprotein in the amniotic fluid and therefore, in all probability, are carrying fetuses with neural tube defects.

Of the neural tube defects, spina bifida presents the greatest ethical problems. Closed spina bifida accounts for 20 per cent of children with spina bifida. The prognosis is good, the children having few physical handicaps and normal intelligence. In contrast, the remaining 80 per cent of children with spina bifida, those with the open variety, have a range of physical incapacities, including lack of bowel or bladder control and some lower limb paralysis. Approximately 70 per cent of those with the open condition have hydrocephaly, 50 per cent die by the age of two years, and 25 per cent are mentally retarded.

The information provided by the genetic screening procedures presents physicians and parents with decisions they would not otherwise have had to make. Should parents be informed of the results of the tests if they are positive and, more importantly, the implications of the results? Anxiety is bound to be generated by a positive blood test, even though 95 per cent of women with an initial positive result have a normal fetus. Some women may opt for an abortion following two positive blood tests, although this is very rare.

Spina bifida, if undetected during fetal life or detected but allowed to continue to term, presents problems of a different kind at birth. The severe disabilities of children with open spina bifida, coupled with the costs of medical care, have led to a variety of therapeutic regimes by paediatricians. The divergence of opinion can be illustrated by the approaches of two paediatricians from Sheffield in England.

Dr R. B. Zachary does not operate on two groups of spina bifida babies. The first group consists of babies who will in all probability die within a few days. Zachary does not operate on this group because an operation would not affect whether these babies lived or died. The second group comprises severely afflicted babies which may live for many months and yet which have wounds he considers are unsuitable for operation.

Apart from these babies, Zachary operates on all other spina bifida babies requiring operation. He feels unable to predict which spina bifida babies are going to die and which will survive. He generally errs, therefore, in favour of treatment. When some kicking movements are observed after birth he advises urgent surgery in order to reduce handicap to a minimum and to preserve activity in the leg muscles. A dictum used by Zachary is that the fundamental purpose of operating is not to add years to the lives of these children, but to add life to their years. To reduce disability and to improve a person's capabilities are considered worthy ends of such surgery.

An alternative approach is that of Professor John Lorber who, in 1973, drew up a set of criteria for the treatment or non-treatment of newborn babies with open spina bifida. His criteria included the degree of paralysis present at birth, the presence or absence of hydrocephalus, the presence or absence of spinal deformity, and the existence of associated gross congenital anomalies. In other words, those babies likely to be paralysed, incontinent or mentally retarded are denied treatment.

The precise nature of these criteria is not my concern. What does interest me is the dependence some medical authorities place on technical criteria such as these. Robert Veatch has commented: 'We may become so infatuated with our technical abilities to accumulate data and tally scores that we run the risk of seriously misunderstanding the nature of the difficult decisions that must be made.' Veatch refers to this infatuation as the technical criteria fallacy.

At first glance this sounds a harsh judgment. After all, technical criteria are essential when making technical decisions. The alternative to the use of well-recognized and publicized criteria is dependence upon subjective assessments in which bias is hidden from view and from the scrutiny of medical colleagues, parents and society. The danger, however, is that a set of technical criteria can become so elevated that the end-result is to think that only these criteria matter. If this happens, religious, cultural and personal values are ignored. A child is thought to be of value simply because it conforms to certain biological norms; if it fails to conform there is no room for medical treatment. This is a serious predicament, because what has happened is that value choices have been medicalized, and the worth of life has been reduced to a rating on a scale of technical excellence.

An additional aspect to an undue reliance upon technical criteria is that the baby is being judged worthy or unworthy of treatment in terms of its medical prognosis. The quality of the child's future life is being made the basis of medical treatment in the present. However reliable this prognosis may be in strictly medical terms, and such prognoses are never infallible, the decision must include some evaluation of the meaning of that child's existence with varying degrees of impairment. This, by its very nature, is not solely a medical decision – it must depend in part on the beliefs, attitudes and value-systems of the parents, doctors and policy makers. Medical prognosis is only one factor in whatever decision is reached, the crucial decision-making lying in the hands of the family and its counsellors.

Lorber's criteria, whatever their merits technically, allow life to be dispensed with in too ready a fashion. Zachary's approach, with its more conservative overtones, attempts less and yet places greater value on the life that is possible. He does not elevate theoretical quality-of-life considerations, and does not compare the quality of life available to children with open spina bifida against that available to normal children. Nevertheless, the quality of life of *particular* children is improved when compared to what they would have experienced apart from surgical intervention.

In this regard it is interesting to note that the perceptions of physicians and parents often differ widely on the value of life for spina bifida children. A life defined as intolerable by physicians might come to be defined quite differently by parents, once they have experienced what it means to love that child. Surveys of the responses of parents to spina bifida children have repeatedly demonstrated that a birth, originally considered a tragedy, has later been recognized as a source of joy.

Doctors, by and large, do not share these feelings. A general bias in favour of perfect mental and physical health sees little value in a life that will never be able to attain such perfection. Counselling of women with spina bifida fetuses often emphasizes, therefore, the negative aspects of the condition, so that few couples decide against abortion.

What becomes of spina bifida babies, from whom treatment is withheld? These generally have head enlargement and open back lesions, presenting considerable nursing problems and frequently subject to a slow and painful death. In one report of 25 untreated children, three died in a few days, 18 within three months, and all 25 within nine months. All children received proper nursing care and appropriate food, but no further treatment and no antibiotics for infections. Non-treatment poses no legal problems, and yet it basically contravenes basic medical tenets of care, compassion and appropriate therapy.

A major difficulty confronting advocates of non-treatment is the uncertainty of life. A healthy baby can be injured 2–3 years later as a toddler, and then spend the remainder of its life paralysed or mentally retarded. What part does non-treatment then play in medical therapy? Children and parents also learn to live with disabilities, and many come to realize that physical and mental limitations are a part of the human condition. Life is more than simply a healthy body; it is aspirations, relationships, beliefs, self-esteem. It reflects our likeness to God, our creation in his image, and our dignity based on his love and concern for each of us, no matter how beautiful or ugly, how successful or fragmented we may appear to those around us.

In more general terms, genetic screening programs raise a host of pragmatic and theoretical considerations. On the practical front, these procedures should always be designed and conducted with the benefit or potential benefit of individuals and families in mind. The procedures should enable them to make responsible decisions about having or not having children and about proceeding or not proceeding with a pregnancy. No screening program should either impose constraints on childbearing by individuals with specific genetic constitutions, or stigmatize couples who, in spite of known genetic defects, still desire children of their own. Genetic constitution is not the only criterion to be taken account of in promulgating standards of biological normality. Further, since genetic defects cannot, in most cases, be treated, genetic screening programs should be conducted on a voluntary basis. Undoubtedly this has difficulties in practice, but so are the ethical choices that have to be made when abortion is presented as the only available 'treatment' of a fetal defect detected after screening.

The more theoretical issues concern our view of ourselves as unique persons. This is because human individuality is intimately dependent upon our biological, and in particular our genetic, make-up. We differ from each other genetically, and our sense of self derives from this. Our genetic uniqueness bestows upon each of us a different genetic destiny and it is this that, in part at least, makes us what we are.

But what if we know there is some genetic deficiency in our make-up? What if we know our biological identity is flawed? What repercussions may this have for our own sense of worth? In a similar way, how may our knowledge that another person or a fetus has a genetic deficiency affect our view of the worthwhileness of that person's life or the prospective value of that fetus's future existence?

Marc Lappé has commented: 'Genetic knowledge is a special kind of foreknowledge that can be used to label an individual as well as to predict some of his or her life prospects. The moment one acquires a "bit" of genetic information (for example, whether it is carrying a particular gene or chromosomal pattern), one has changed that fetus.' This is particularly true for a debilitating condition like Huntington's chorea, or a condition carrying a social stigma, such as the possession a few years ago of an XYY chromosome make-up. Even when more innocuous conditions are detected, or when some genetic defect in a child is uncovered, the result may be a change in self-image leading even to self-alienation.

Since we align our views of ourselves very closely with the quality of our genetic endowment, genetic data – once known – can have powerful psychological repercussions. The intimate relationship between selfhood and genetic constituency has, not surprisingly, many ramifications for genetic screening. The question to be faced is: what should be done with the genetic knowledge derived from screening? This will become an even more urgent question to answer, when it becomes feasible to detect a *propensity* for certain disease-states, especially in the absence of adequate preventative measures.

Screening for genetic diseases is just one example of the screening abilities of modern medicine. Our expertise at obtaining more and more 'bits' of information about the way in which people are functioning, or even will function in the future, is growing at a staggering rate. What is not growing at an equivalent rate is our ability to deal adequately with this information. Some forms of genetic screening may be providing us, therefore, with what can best be described as unusable information, and some of this unusable information may actually be detrimental to the welfare of patients.

It may not be too preposterous to suggest that some genetic information may itself constitute a far greater burden than some genetic diseases. Most disease processes, which can be currently identified by genetic analysis, cannot be meaningfully treated. Should the analyses, therefore, be carried out? What is the responsible path to follow? Information about which the medical profession can do little, and with which patients may be unable to cope, should perhaps be classed as irresponsible information. It cannot, by its very nature, be neutral, because it bestows upon the genetic scientist potential control over people's lives – how they should behave, whom they should marry, how long they may live. The ability to predict disease-states years ahead of the onset of symptoms will bestow upon the geneticists unheard-of powers.

In spite of these sentiments, detection of future disease-states by way of screening should not always be dismissed. When it is possible to use the information so obtained in a positive way, screening has an important part to play in medical therapy. For instance, certain individuals with a high risk of heart attacks (hypercholesterolaemia) or bowel cancer (familial polyposis) can be predicted in advance, and these diseases can be avoided by appropriate diet or regular check-ups respectively. The crucial point here is that detection of those at risk may lead to prevention of the appropriate condition. In other words, the screening is of benefit to the patient. It is not just providing data from which neither the medical profession nor the patient can learn something of therapeutic value.

Genetic screening needs to be assessed, therefore, from the perspective of its potential value to actual patients. It should not be used to create new categories of patient and disease. The emphasis will shift from patient to *potential* patient, and from disease to disease *propensity*. The danger of this shift is that it places upon genetic screening the aura of infallibility – and omniscience. After all, mistakes can be made, and genetic characteristics alone do not determine every aspect of our lives or health.

In the final analysis, we are actual people living in the present. It is *we* as individuals, not our genetic endowment, who contend with our circumstances. Our environments too help make us what we are. Important as our genetic make-up is, it is not us in our entirety. Genetic fatalism is out of place in human existence, since the future lies with us as whole people, not with our genes alone. It is we who set goals; they are not written inexorably in our genes.

Biological foreknowledge ushers in a new dimension of control. It is not just control over what has already happened, but control over what may happen in the future, or in some cases over what *will* happen in the future. This is indeed technology of a sophisticated order. On the other hand, even control of this order is incomplete; it has deficiencies because our knowledge is less than absolute. It is also subject to our whims, and these may be tainted by prejudice, class bias, racial superiority, or just selfishness and envy.

Increasing control over ourselves and others is an ability filled with ambivalence. We should approach it thankfully but also cautiously. Do we possess the maturity to handle it wisely, or is it more than we can usefully cope with ?

The prowess of modern biomedicine should always fill us with this tentativeness. Christians are aware of the awesome responsibility placed upon human beings by God. So, too, are they aware of human rebellion and moral carelessness, and of human arrogance and self-centredness. Power and the ability to control human inheritance are not to be shunned; and yet they are open to gross abuse, short-sighted misapplication and an inability to handle the resulting knowledge in personal terms. Herein lies the ambivalence from which we cannot escape and which we dare not underestimate.

## Improvement in quality

A central question in these realms is: how much health do people need? Fom this follows another: what sicknesses should be combated and, perhaps, what sicknesses should not be combated? These are notoriously difficult questions to answer. Some may even think they are sacrilegious questions, which should not be asked – let alone answered. They force us to look at ourselves; they bring us face to face with our fears, and they abruptly confront us with our expectations of the medical profession at the edges of life. In short, it is far from self-evident what quality of life we should be seeking.

Far too often we fail to make the distinction between 'needs' and 'desires', when deciding on our expectations of health. Daniel Callahan, director of the Hastings Center in New York, has defined 'need' as the minimal requirements for a satisfactory life, and 'desire' as those things we think necessary for an optimal life. Unfortunately, even this simple model breaks down in Western technological societies, because what people think they 'need' for a minimally satisfactory life is set at an extremely high level. What a poor society considers optimal, Western technological societies consider imperative. To make matters worse, technological societies are committed to economic growth, with the result that needs and desires become one. The satisfactory life and the optimal life cannot be separated because, as Callahan puts it, desire becomes king.

The significance of this for biomedical ethics is that quality control can be deceptive. Perfect health or complete social well-being is not, of necessity, a virtue, especially when viewed as a goal for society as a whole. Such a goal is probably unattainable; it would certainly be catastrophically expensive. What we should be considering then are the goals of medicine, assuming that what people desire from medicine is not necessarily what they need. There are limits to medicine's role in attaining human happiness and fulfilment.

From a Christian standpoint this conclusion is not an unexpected one. While conceding that biological solutions are incomparable in attacking essentially biological problems, they are ill-fitted for solving problems rooted in human nature. Progress in genetics, or any other branch of medicine, cannot dispense with the basic conflicts of human existence, simply because we are more than just biological beings: we have aesthetic, religious and personal aspects to us as well. To expect too much of medicine, therefore, is to underestimate the complexities of human existence. Fetuses or children with Down's syndrome are not simply biologically inferior specimens. They are human persons who, while suffering from a particular deficiency, also display the potential for meaningful, if limited, expressions of humanness. These children, no less than those we wish to call normal, have marks of God's image and are capable of at least some interpersonal relationships. To dismiss them as unworthy of existence, simply because of a low rating on a biological quality-scale, is to overlook these marks of humanness and to impose on medicine an aura of unwarranted optimism.

On the other hand, we cannot act as though quality-of-life assessments were irrelevant. They have to be taken into account. Such assessments, though, should always be made within a framework of an overall reverence and deep concern for human life.

Sometimes, particularly after very severe brain damage, we may have to distinguish between life as a state of human functioning and human well-being, and life as the existence simply of vital and metabolic processes with no human functioning. The challenge in this instance is to decide what constitutes humanness. This is no easy task, especially as any precise list of characteristics is unlikely to prove watertight in all circumstances. However, a start has to be made somewhere. My suggestion is that humanness includes potential or actual awareness of God, a potential capability or actual capability of, for example, conceptual thought, self-awareness, self-consciousness and creativity. Human beings also manifest capacities for love and concern, they relate to others and seek personal fulfilment. All these do not have to be present for humanness to be manifested and yet a potential for most of them is required. This follows from our creation in the likeness of a personal God, who has made us living beings capable (or potentially capable) of responding to him and to each other.

Christians contend that the person is always of incalculable value, even when marked by deficiencies and limitations. Nevertheless, a point is sometimes reached beyond which continuance of physical life no longer has human connotations and offers the person no benefit. To keep life going in these circumstances may amount to an assault upon that person's dignity and is the converse of an expression of human dignity.

It has been argued that any concession to quality-of-life concepts undermines the equality of all people. Richard McCormick has argued that not every life is of equal value, if life is taken to mean the continuation of vital processes in a persistent vegetative state. This view can legitimately stand alongside the contention that every *person* is of equal value. Decision-making within a quality-of-life framework must always be directed towards the benefit of the patient. When this perspective is maintained, there is no clash between quality-of-life assessments and a reverence for human life.

Extremely severe brain damage, for instance, may well prevent any present awareness of oneself or God, or even the future possibility of such awareness. By ensuring that no response will ever be forthcoming to one's circumstances or to God, such damage has removed all the marks of humanness. To keep physical existence intact beyond such a point is of no benefit to the patient, and may well demean the dignity of that person. In this extreme case, quality-of-life criteria cannot be ignored.

We need a balance between a profound sense of the dignity and worthwhileness of human life, and the realization that ambiguity attaches to some forms of human existence. These are immense dilemmas and medical technology, perhaps because of its brilliance, is a mixed blessing – for society and for some individuals. A Christian response is to temper the impersonality of runaway technology with human concerns, which are themselves an expression of God's concern.

Improvement in the quality of human life is sometimes regarded in a much more idealistic and futuristic way than I have just considered. In this, stress is laid upon human beings as on the verge of controlling life and hence of remaking themselves in virtually any image they wish. Implicit in such a hopeful vision is our ability to change the biological rules controlling our genetic inheritance.

A vision of producing ideal human beings is a grandiose one. It stems from the successes achieved over many years in the breeding of cattle, and from a dissatisfaction with human beings and human society as presently constituted. These are two totally different domains, the first being a matter of eugenic breeding and the second a profound questioning of the meaning of human existence.

A major difficulty with producing an ideal human product, whatever the 'ideal' may be, is that it invariably involves complex qualities, such as intelligence or moral attitudes. It is not a matter simply of producing a certain physique or certain hair colour. Intelligence and moral attitudes are central to what being human is all about, but they are determined by numerous sets of genes. What is more, the final product of genetic inheritance – the individual human being – is considerably influenced by his or her environment and by the diverse pressures of the environment. Even if it was ever possible to produce our ideal human being genetically, the resulting genetic-environmental product would be far from ideal.

These provisos are relevant no matter how sophisticated genetic engineering may become. There is a vast gulf between gene therapy, in which defective genes are replaced by normal ones for certain specific characteristics, and genetic manipulation, in which novel beings will be produced according to preselected specifications. In this context Leon Kass's perceptive comment is relevant: 'It is probably as indisputable as it is ignored that the world suffers more from the morally and spiritually defective than from the genetically defective.'

This is a perspective Christians should never overlook. An over-emphasis on the biological alone not only suggests that the biological is more important than the spiritual, but actually affirms this in practice. If our scientific and medical priorities are based on the pre-eminence of the biological, financial and human resources will be channelled in this direction to the detriment of environmental and preventative causes: hence the élitism of positive eugenics. This is not to argue that genetic defects are unimportant; rather they are to be viewed within the perspective of the individual as a whole person and not as a dismembered biological entity.

# 4
# New techniques and the beginning of life

## Fertilization and conception

Most of the debates in the biomedical areas I am exploring depend, in some measure, on when human life begins. Because of medicine's ability to interfere with the early stages of human development, investigative, experimental and therapeutic procedures are increasingly being undertaken on young embryos and fetuses. The question is repeatedly being asked, therefore, whether embryos just a few days after fertilization are human beings. If they are, ethical decisions will be required about what procedures can be employed on them. If they are not, ethical decisions will not be required; they can be used with impunity as experimental material.

The assumption we are making is that there is a clear-cut answer to the question whether a young embryo (or, for that matter, a 12 or 20 week fetus) is or is not human. This assumption depends upon yet another one, that conception is a well-defined point in time that can be readily recognized.

To most people it seems obvious that conception occurs when a sperm and ovum come together and that this takes place at some specified and, in theory at least, identifiable point in time. From that time onwards, human life exists. But is this as unequivocal, in biological terms, as we frequently like to think?

About one thing we can be sure: each new human life represents a continuation of human life in general. It is not the creation of life. Rather it is the bringing into existence of a new and unique embodiment of human life. To recognize this is not to denigrate the meaning or the value of each human life, especially in God's sight, but it does place it in perspective. We do not create life, either naturally or artificially; we have nothing like that sort of power. We simply act as agents, bringing a new generation of human beings into existence.

In this sense, human life does not begin at any specific stage of development, whether this be with the ovum, sperm, blastocyst, embryo, fetus or at birth. Neither does it begin with the first heartbeat, the first appearance of brain function, or at the time of viability. Human life is potentially, or actually, present at all these stages. Of course, for a new individual to appear, an ovum and sperm must come together and fertilize. Once fertilization has taken place, the nascent embryo represents the first expression of what may emerge much later on as a recognizable individual. But from what stage can the embryo be meaningfully referred to as an individual member of the human species?

The significance of fertilization is that, once it has occurred, the ovum becomes active and the genetic individuality of the embryo is established by the combination of genes from each of the parents. The resulting one-celled embryo, or zygote, is still capable of splitting to form two individuals. This twinning potential remains for as long as two weeks after fertilization. The first cell divisions of the fertilized ovum produce a cluster of equivalent cells, which are not at this stage integrated into a multicellular organism. This non-integrated state persists for a few days after fertilization. During this period it has been demonstrated in mouse embryos that cells can be removed without affecting the outcome of development – a complete mouse is born. A few more days of development pass before the cells which will give rise to the embryo proper can be distinguished from the cells which will form the placenta.

Conception is defined by developmental biologists in two main ways: it refers either to the processes concerned with the implantation of the fertilized ovum (blastocyst) in the wall of the uterus, or to the formation of a viable zygote (two-four celled fertilized ovum). Of these two possibilities, the first describes a later stage of development than does the second.

Implantation begins 6–7 days after fertilization and is completed by 13–14 days after fertilization. Prior to implantation, a woman is physiologically unaware of her pregnancy, the first signs of which occur towards the final phases of implantation. This definition of conception is the one adopted by, for instance, the American College of Obstetricians and Gynaecologists. The practical significance of this definition is that conception and fertilization are regarded as different processes. Whatever may be the validity of this distinction, this view of conception is a useful one for both the biologist and clinician.

When conception is equated with the formation of a viable zygote, it occurs prior to implantation. It takes place before a woman knows she is pregnant, and before pregnancy can be detected.

Both definitions I have considered are biologically plausible, although the equating of conception with implantation is a more useful one from a biological standpoint. Any implications of the definition adopted stem from the view that human life should be protected from the time of conception. If this view is espoused, definitions of conception may have repercussions on the allowability or otherwise of certain forms of contraception and of *in vitro* fertilization and embryo transfer. Nevertheless, biological definitions of conception should be analysed on their own merits, and not on whether they do or do not support an ethical viewpoint.

Although fertilization is a less ambiguous term than conception, it is even less amenable to detection in the routine clinical situation. If it is intended to use fertilization as the indication of the start of an individual human life, it poses considerable clinical difficulties.

Biology cannot be used to answer ethical questions of whether or not procedures such as *in vitro* fertilization or abortion are justified. This is because it is exceedingly difficult to use biological data alone to decide whether zygotes, blastocysts, embryos or fetuses possess 'human' characteristics. What characteristics make up 'humanness'? Different answers are given to this question, the differences undoubtedly stemming from a vast range of subjective and non-scientific impressions. If humanness depends on recognizable facial features, certain behaviour patterns, and an ability to evoke empathy, it emerges within the first six weeks of development. If it depends on the first signs of the nervous system functioning, its emergence is put at eight weeks after fertilization. More sophisticated nervous system activity, however, does not appear until about 12 weeks of development. It has even been suggested that a requisite IQ level is required for humanness, putting it at about one year of age!

It would be easy to deride these attempts at pin-pointing the essential elements of 'human' activity. They should not be too readily dismissed. Nevertheless their arbitrariness should make us wary of expecting too much help from biology, in deciding precisely when human life commences. It may even be that this is not the most helpful way of approaching the issue.

By definition, potential human life is present once a sperm and ovum have come together and cell division has taken place. But is this the crucial issue? I have doubts that it is. What is more important is the value we place on all human life, potential and actual, and that value is based upon moral and religious considerations. In these terms human material always deserves respect, even if it has developed only for a few days since fertilization. The significance of this principle will be worked out in the next chapter, when I discuss the ethical issues surrounding *in vitro* fertilization.

The way in which we approach this issue will reflect numerous basic presuppositions and will involve us deeply in Christian thinking. The present chapter on techniques is not the place to delve into such thinking. Nevertheless it is important, even at this early stage in our deliberations, that we distinguish between biological definitions and scientific techniques on the one hand, and ethical decision-making and Christian beliefs on the other.

The biological perspective I have just provided is a pragmatic one. Its emphasis is on the detectable beginnings of individual human life, because it is only the detectable and observable with which it can deal. In these terms, 1–2 weeks after fertilization is when an embryo begins to manifest its presence. Its chances of survival are also much greater from this time onwards, and that is another useful biological consideration.

Should considerations such as these be taken into account when determining what is or is not acceptable ethically? Are these issues relevant in discussions on *in vitro* fertilization or abortion? They are relevant if our views on these issues depend on beliefs about the 'moment of conception' or 'when human life begins'. Otherwise, they are not relevant.

## *In vitro* fertilization (IVF) and embryo transfer (ET)

It has been recognized for a number of years that the technique of *in vitro* fertilization is foundational to the whole area of genetic control. This is because it involves the fertilization of human eggs outside the body, in the laboratory and hence under human control. Once it became possible to interfere with the early stages of human development in this way, the remaining far more dramatic developments of ovum transfer, surrogate motherhood, frozen embryo banks, genetic therapy and human cloning would be accomplished given the time, money and determination.

It was fears of this order on the part of theologians, philosophers and biologists in the United States that led to a moratorium on *in vitro* fertilization investigations in that country in the mid-1970s. The lack of any comparable debate on the long-term ethical implications of these procedures in Britain and Australia allowed this work to continue in those countries. Although Robert Edwards, one of the pioneers of this work in Britain, has engaged in this debate, the debate there was neither sufficiently widespread nor vigorous in the 1970s to have political ramifications.

The amazement and rejoicing at the birth of Louise Brown in 1978 were the responses of a bemused public. Once again the medical profession had shown itself capable of indulging in the near-miraculous. Infertility had been overcome, and infertile couples by their thousands were queueing up for their own little miracle. Louise Brown was a perfect little baby, not a deformed monster. She was human; she was just like 'normal' babies. With her birth, it seemed as if all the grim forebodings and dire prognostications of the ethicists had been proved wrong. There was nothing to worry about; technology had emerged triumphant.

Similar reactions were evinced in Australia by the birth of Candice Reid in 1980. Her birth was followed in rapid succession by a number of others. Opposition to *in vitro* fertilization began to emerge, however, when it became public that superfluous embryos had been frozen for future use, and that other embryos had been used for experimental purposes. With these revelations, the public at large began to realize that the successes of *in vitro* fertilization were being bought at a cost, and that ethical issues could not be ignored. These issues were already being actively debated when America's first *in vitro* fertilized baby, Elizabeth Carr, was born at the end of 1981. Extensions to straightforward *in vitro* fertilization began to appear in 1983 with the first reported pregnancies using donated and also frozen embryos.

Over a period of three or four years, *in vitro* fertilization has become a household term. No longer is there any need to use the misleading equivalent 'test-tube babies'. The abbreviation, IVF, is now gaining rapid acceptance, as is ET to signify embryo transfer.

In 1966 Robert Edwards of Cambridge University demonstrated how eggs (ova) extracted from human ovaries could be cultured in the laboratory ('test-tube') with the development of ripe eggs. This was followed in 1969 by the fertilization of such eggs using human sperm, and the subsequent, apparently normal development of the fertilized eggs. Taking these techniques further Edwards reported that his group had been successful in taking some eggs as far as the blastocyst stage, by which time the fertilized egg had divided into as many as 60–100 cells. This is true IVF, and while the blastocyst represents a very early stage in development, it is sufficiently advanced for implantation into a woman's uterus and subsequent maturation. In 1976 it was reported that an embryo fertilized in the laboratory had developed for 13 weeks in a woman's uterus while, in July 1978, the first 'test-tube (IVF) baby' was born amid a flurry of excitement at Oldham, in England. Louise Brown was, in a real sense, the result of the combined work of Dr Robert Edwards and a gynaecologist, Mr Patrick Steptoe.

The success of IVF depends on two principal factors. These are knowing when to take an egg from the ovary, and obtaining the correct nutrient liquid in which the embryo will develop. In most IVF programs the woman is given hormones to stimulate egg production prior to carrying out IVF procedures. This is achieved by prescribing clomiphene tablets (fertility pills) or human pituitary gonadotrophins (fertility injections). In this way, egg production is controlled, and generally a few egg follicles mature in the ovary. Stimulation of the ovaries in this way enhances the success rate of egg collection; it also introduces a problem – that of having an excess number of eggs and, after fertilization, an excess number of embryos.

In order to obtain eggs from a woman's ovary, a laparoscope is used under general anaesthetic. This instrument is inserted through a small incision on the abdomen, and it enables the surgeon to see each ovary. The eggs, generally three but as many as six, are obtained with a needle and fine tube. Following 5–6 hours in an incubator, during which time the eggs mature, they are mixed with the husband's sperm in a nutrient liquid. Fertilization occurs in 3–4 hours, and can be detected microscopically 12–23 hours after insemination. The embryo is allowed to incubate for approximately 40 hours, by which time it consists of four cells. Some workers leave them for a further 20 hours, when they have reached the eight-cell stage. In one instance in the literature, an embryo was grown for nine days in the laboratory. These prolonged periods are not used, however, when embryo transfer will be carried out, since prolonged incubation of embryos causes degeneration. During normal development in the fallopian tubes, cell division does not occur beyond the 16–cell stage.

The embryos are examined under a microscope to determine whether or not they are healthy. Unfortunately, little is known about this; in practice, therefore, if the cells are dividing it is assumed the embryos are healthy. One or more of these embryos are transferred back to the mother's uterus, for the remainder of the developmental processes. Embryo transfer does not involve the use of an anaesthetic or surgery, the embryo being injected directly into the uterine cavity through the vagina and cervix.

One of the practical difficulties with IVF has been its low success rate – at present, about 20 per cent. This figure refers to the percentage of pregnancies per laparoscopy. A slightly higher figure is obtained per embryo transfer. Three treatments are generally allowed for each patient, and if these are carried out the chance of a pregnancy may be about 45 per cent.

A major reason for this low rate of achieving a continuing pregnancy in any one treatment cycle is that many of the embryos are abnormal or dead when viewed under the microscope. Even when this obstacle is overcome, many of the embryos are aborted at about four weeks. The rates of success vary from one program to another, and even at different times within a particular program.

Between 25 and 40 per cent of the fetuses arising from IVF die during gestation, mostly in the first trimester. Some of these appear to be due to genetic damage, although others may be a consequence of factors associated with the IVF procedures. These include damage to the wall of the uterus, and the introduction of infection, during embryo replacement.

The success rates of IVF and ET need to be viewed in perspective, to see what optimum rates can be expected. Due to the high loss of embryos in the early stages of pregnancy (about 65 per cent loss during the first 14 weeks) during the normal reproductive process, it has been estimated that following IVF and ET the highest level of successful births which can be expected will probably be of the order of 30–35 per cent.

Those embryos, which continue to develop in the uterus beyond four weeks, have a good chance of surviving to term. Of the first twelve IVF babies born, two were born prematurely at about 20 weeks, and one required corrective surgery. A new factor entering the picture is the high incidence of twins and even of triplets. This follows on from the implantation of two or three embryos into the mother. The use of three is preferred in some programs, since this number is associated with the highest incidence of pregnancies (40 per cent chance of a continuing pregnancy in one program, against 28 per cent with two embryos, and 12 per cent with one). Unfortunately, twins and triplets frequently lead to premature delivery and consequent difficulties for the babies.

In their early work Edwards and Steptoe in Britain required prospective mothers to undergo an amniocentesis at around 16 weeks' gestation. This is no longer a precondition of acceptance into that or other programs. Nevertheless abortion would be contemplated if there was suspicion of genetic damage. There has been some discussion about the comparative success rates of IVF and reconstructive surgery (microtuboplasty). In this latter procedure an attempt is made to overcome a wife's infertility by repairing her damaged or abnormal fallopian tubes. While success rates for the surgical procedure vary, depending on the cause of the damage to the tubes, a figure of 16 per cent has been quoted. The success rate for sterilization reversal may be in the region of 35–70 per cent.

The embryos not placed in the mother's uterus or preserved by freezing are discarded, or are used experimentally. Not surprisingly this is where controversy comes to the fore. These are the 'spare' embryos. Frozen embryos can be returned to the mother's uterus if another embryo has been aborted, in an attempt to ensure a subsequent pregnancy. Embryos stored in this way can be kept for decades, although a limit of 10 years has been imposed in some countries. Pregnancies have resulted following the transfer of embryos stored in liquid nitrogen at –200°C for periods of around four months.

Alternatively, spare embryos may be donated to another

woman, they may be discarded or used for research purposes. Experimental work which has been carried out has been aimed at determining how a normal embryo may be recognized. This entails detailed microscopic studies of the cells. If they have already stopped growing, sectioning presumably does not kill them – as they are already dead. If they are still growing, these procedures inevitably destroy them.

The work just described would, in general, come under the heading of *clinical IVF*. It refers to the use of IVF and ET in an attempt to initiate a pregnancy and produce a child. By contrast, *laboratory IVF* refers to the procedure when there is no intention of transferring any embryos to a woman's uterus for implantation, gestation and eventual birth.

Even this distinction, though, must not be interpreted too simplistically. The problem of spare embryos very quickly raises its head. Do investigations on them fall into the clinical or laboratory category? While they were produced in the first place with a clinical end in view, investigations are research-oriented, not patient-oriented. Then again, the whole IVF procedure is still experimental, and so the research element is prominent.

Up to the present the applications of IVF have concentrated on the alleviation of infertility brought about by a blockage in the woman's uterine tubes, due to disease, past infection, ectopic pregnancy or congenital abnormality. Even now, however, some couples in IVF programs have idiopathic infertility. In this instance husband and wife are clinically normal and yet fail to conceive. Other types of infertility which may be helped by IVF include those resulting from endometriosis in the woman, and instances where the husband has developed antibodies against his own sperm or where the husband has too few sperm (oligospermia) for normal conception. It is also interesting to note that sterilization and failed sterilization reversal have been regarded as acceptable indications for treatment in some programs.

The selection of couples for IVF programs varies between groups. In the Monash program in Australia, the requirements include: diagnosed infertility, an ability on the part of the couple to cope psychologically with the demands of the program, various medical criteria have to be met, and there must be an ability to meet the costs of the program. The couple may have other children, and the transfer should be part of treatment within an accepted family relationship.

The social significance of infertility stems from its widespread incidence. Approximately 7–10 per cent of couples are infertile, 30 per cent resulting from infertility in the male, 30 per cent in the female, 30 per cent in both, and 10 per cent being unexplained. When it is remembered that, in the United States alone, there are 1.4 million infertile women, the extent of the problem begins to manifest itself. Of these women, 40 per cent have abnormalities of the uterine tubes. Depending on the figures analysed, estimates of the number of couples who could potentially benefit from IVF in the United States are of the order of 450,000–600,000. It is probable that equivalent figures apply in other countries.

Infertility, however, is just one application of IVF. Others range from the use of human embryos for research purposes to the futuristic creation of human-animal hybrids. The dozen or so applications are best considered in two principal categories: those which are feasible at present and those which will require further technical developments before they become realistic possibilities.

The applications which fit into the first category are: the use of preimplantation embryos in research programs, ovum or embryo transfer (from the woman who provided the ovum into the uterus of another woman), the gestation of embryos and fetuses in surrogate mothers, the fertilization of ova and sperms from individuals not married to one another, and the establishment of human ovum and embryo banks. The more futuristic category includes various forms of genetic engineering prior to implantation such as the sex determination of embryos, the screening of embryos for genetic and/or chromosomal defects, and the repair of genetic defects. Even more futuristic vistas include ectogenesis (the maintenance of embryos *in vitro* beyond the implantation stage, and perhaps ultimately throughout the whole gestation period), the use of ectogenesis as a source of embryo parts for transplantation into children and adults, cloning, and the creation of human-animal hybrids.

Laboratory IVF research also has applications. These are

very basic research issues, which are the subject of considerable research at present. The difference, however, is that, whereas current research uses animal tissues, future research could well employ living human material. The areas include: mechanisms of fertilization, the growth and differentiation of cells, the investigation of chromosomes and genes, and the effects of radiation, freezing and chemicals on fertilization and early development.

## Artificial insemination

This procedure brings us into the realm of current practice, the extent of which is difficult to determine. Nevertheless, there can be little doubt that it is a very widely used technique. A few years ago it was estimated that well over 10,000 artificial inseminations a year are carried out in the United Kingdom. It has also been estimated that this technique has been successfully used in the United States about 300,000 times.

The two forms of artificial insemination are by sperm from the husband (AIH) and by sperm from a donor (AID). Of these, the latter is increasingly becoming an accepted means of circumventing the prospect of a childless future for many infertile couples, especially as adoption becomes increasingly difficult. The two are often viewed as part of the same program. If AIH is unsuccessful on perhaps three occasions, AID is seen as the logical next step. Where IVF is also available, the failure of AID may be followed by IVF. This progression depends, of course, on the nature of the infertility; it may well be recommended where the cause of the infertility is not obvious.

Sperm can be stored in liquid nitrogen at very low temperatures, thereby maintaining indefinitely their viability. Consequently sperm from numerous donors can, in this way, be maintained with the building-up of sperm banks. These banks mean that sperm can be not only kept, but also coded according to donor characteristics. As a result, an extensive choice of donor sperm is made available enabling the closest possible match in physical and mental characteristics between the husband and donor.

Each donor is carefully screened to ensure that there are no mental or physical conditions to render him unsuitable as a donor. Not surprisingly, therefore, AID births have a lower-than-expected number of abnormalities.

An immediate problem is to decide who is entitled to receive AID. The whole-hearted consent of both husband and wife is generally required, and as far as possible should be insisted upon. An equally pressing problem is the selection of donors. It is relatively easy to choose medical students, as has frequently been done, and while careful screening is carried out this cannot be exhaustive. Assuming that eugenic ideals are discarded, the most that can be expected of donors is that they are responsible citizens with acceptable IQs.

The legal issue in this debate revolves around the question of whether AID constitutes adultery. Although there has been some doubt in English law on this latter point, it appears that AID, even apart from the husband's consent, does not amount to adultery by the wife. However, as English law now stands, the child undoubtedly is illegitimate, although this is not so in some American states.

An issue I should like to consider further is that of the donation of sperm. AID has been described by George J. Annas as 'a cottage industry on the verge of mass marketing'. This stems from the scale of the operation. For instance, he refers to two commercial sperm banks in the United States, each of which fills over 100 orders a month, and which are on the verge of marketing sperm directly to consumers. A major obstacle, however, in discussions of AID has been the secrecy surrounding it, and consequently an inability on the part of observers to assess the extent of AID, let alone the standards of its practitioners and the guide-lines being employed by them.

A study published in 1979 by M. Curie-Cohen and co-workers in the United States analysed 379 practitioners of AID and approximately 3,500 resulting births. Among the results of this study were: payment of up to $35 per ejaculate to most 'donors', the predominant use of medical students and hospital residents as donors, the fact that 37 per cent of physicians kept records of children born after AID and only 30 per cent on donors, and the multiple use of some donors.

The emphasis of many AID procedures is to protect the interests of donors and physicians, rather than recipients and children. The lack of permanent records on donors means that AID children can never determine the identity of the genetic father. In view of the desire of many adopted children to learn the identity of their biological parents, a similar desire may one day characterize the majority of AID children – once they learn how they were conceived. The lack of records on donors also means that if a donor is responsible for any genetic defects in future children, there is no way of detecting the responsible donor. Registration of all AID children could overcome some of these pitfalls, with appropriate safeguards for all parties concerned.

Although AID has the potential for eugenic practices, it is not generally carried out with eugenic goals in view. Even the prevention of genetic disease cannot be adequately accomplished on present procedures. The randomness of these procedures has usually been regarded as a strong argument in their favour, and yet the genetic ignorance implicit in them raises serious long-term questions.

While this is the normal situation, an occasional eugenic proposal makes headlines. One such example is the Repository for Germinal Choice in San Marcos, California. In this, donors of germinal material consist of Nobel Laureates in science and other high achievers, who are free of known impairments. The aim of this venture is to increase the number of offspring of the most creative scientists of our time.

The recipients, in their turn, are genetically selected; they are young women of superior health and intellect, under 35 years of age, and with a sterile husband who agrees to the process of insemination. Recipients may choose, from written descriptions of two or more donors, the one whose characteristics they would most like to have in the father of their child. The end result is that couples are being offered the opportunity to choose the specific father of their child or children, and to do so from among some of the most creative people of this generation.

While complete anonymity is maintained, semen donations are categorized by all known heritable characteristics. Hence this is the closest approach yet to the adoption in practice of eugenic principles. Geneticist Hermann J. Muller, who was an inspiration for this venture, described it as 'the most significant contribution of my life' – even ahead of the accomplishments for which he was awarded the Nobel Prize. Since we do not know the outcome of this attempt at eugenics, and will not do so for many years to come, the debate at the technical level cannot be taken any further at present. In many ways, however, it is a reversion to the interests and ideas of a former era.

## Cloning

This is asexual reproduction, with the result that the new individual or individuals are derived from a single parent and are genetically identical to that parent; hence the exact copies. No longer are egg and sperm required, as in normal *sexual reproduction*, with each contributing its half complement of the necessary number of chromosomes to chart a new life. Cloning is based on the knowledge that any ordinary body cell, such as a cell in the skin or lining of the mouth, contains every bit of information needed to recreate the body in its entirety. Every cell in the body, except the sex cells, is equipped with a full complement of chromosomes necessary to make a new person just like the existing person. Under normal circumstances this does not happen, because the genetic apparatus of each cell is largely switched off, allowing any one cell to produce only certain kinds of new cells. For example, skin cells produce only new skin cells, muscle cells give rise to muscle cells, and cells of the nervous system to further cells of the nervous system.

Over the years, however, research workers have made many attempts to overcome this restriction. These have generally been aimed at finding ways of reproducing an animal through the development and growth of an unfertilized cell. Reproduction without the intervention of sperm is referred to as *parthenogenesis*. The term comes from the Greek word *parthenos*, a young girl or virgin. It may be likened to virgin birth, and is a process that occurs naturally in plants and some insects.

As long ago as 1896 a German embryologist, Oskar Hertwig, found that sea urchin eggs could be fertilized simply by adding strychnine or chloroform to the sea water. Sperm could thus be eliminated from the fertilization process. In the 1930s and 1940s various workers devised ways of obtaining parthenogenetic frogs and rabbits, using various kinds of physical shock and chemical methods to replace sperm. This is not cloning, but it has proved a forerunner of the actual thing.

Cloning is generally brought about by the removal of the nucleus from a mature but unfertilized egg and its replacement by the nucleus of a specialized body cell from an adult organism. A whole adult cell, albeit an undifferentiated one, may also be employed. The aim is that the total replicative machinery of the body cell nucleus will be switched on, and will subsequently proceed to divide and differentiate, thereby recreating the individual from whom the body cell had been taken. The resulting individual will, quite literally, be 'a chip off the old block'.

Cloning was first accomplished in animals in the 1960s by Dr John Gurdon in Oxford. Working with the South African clawed toad, he started with an unfertilized egg cell and destroyed its nucleus by radiating it with ultraviolet light. He then replaced the destroyed nucleus with one taken from an intestinal cell of a tadpole of the same species. The egg cell with its new nucleus began to grow as if it had been normally fertilized. As with all cloning, the resultant adult organism was genetically identical to the organism serving as the source of the transferred nucleus. In this way it is possible to produce an unlimited number or clone of identical creatures.

Cloning in humans would amount to much the same as this. The egg would be taken from a woman and its nucleus would be replaced with the nucleus from the body cell of another person, say Mr A. The egg with this new nucleus would then be replaced in the woman's womb for maturation through a normal pregnancy, and finally birth. The cloned baby would be genetically identical to Mr A, from whom the body cell nucleus had come.

This is all very well, but how likely is it that cloning will be accomplished in humans? Two major difficulties have generally been foreseen. The first concerns the very small size of human eggs compared with frog eggs. This is a problem microsurgery will have to overcome, although significant steps in this direction have been taken with the initial reports of mammalian cloning. The second difficulty concerns implanting the egg with its new nucleus into a woman's uterus for subsequent routine development. This has already been overcome in the guise of *in vitro* fertilization in humans. In 1968, American biologist, Robert L. Sinsheimer, predicted that it would be possible to clone a human being in ten years. As far as we are aware, the ten years have passed and a human clone has not been born – assuming that David M. Rorvick's 1978 book, *In His Image*, was a hoax (see chapter 6). The technical difficulties, however, are not insurmountable and we must accept that, in the technical realm, it is a feasible procedure.

Of the many reasons given in favour of human cloning, a number stand out as the major ones. First, cloning would open the way to the copying of the finest genetic combinations in the human species, whether these be individuals of great intelligence, business acumen, artistic creativity or beauty. Just as we now read the writings of great writers or listen to the music of great musicians, no matter when they lived, cloning would make possible the existence in a different generation or even a different age of further individuals with the same hereditary endowments as those possessed by the original artists, scientists, or business people. This is undoubtedly the most idealistic reason in favour of cloning, because implicit within it is the hope that the human race can be bettered in this way.

Indirectly related to this reason is the second, that cloning would make possible scientific experiments with human beings on a vast scale. The availability of sets of genetically identical humans would open the way to diverse types of genetic engineering studies, without the disadvantages associated with having to wait generations for the results. It would almost be as easy to use humans as it now is to use bacteria or frogs. Again, the rationale here is the improvement of humans, although the experimental aspects of cloning are now becoming more evident, and the role of control is coming to the fore.

Third, cloning would ensure that an individual could have a child with a hereditary endowment of his or her own choosing. A man, for instance, could have a son genetically identical to himself or a woman a daughter genetically identical to herself. Alternatively, it would be possible for an individual or couple to have a child with a genotype of someone famous or of a dead relation, or a friend, or a spouse. Reasons for such cloning may stem from an individual's desire to perpetuate his or her own genetic stock, an infertile couple's desire to have a child, or an individual's longing to have a child with the genetic characteristics of his or her hero.

In medical terms, cloning may provide a means of bypassing the risk of genetic disease. A couple, in which one partner had a genetic defect, could avoid the risk of passing on this defect to their children by having cloned children of the healthy partner. Another supposedly medical reason is that clonal reproduction would ensure that clonal offspring had interchangeable parts, because all members of a clonal colony would be identical and thus able freely to exchange organ transplants. Tissue rejection would then become a phenomenon of the past, at least as far as clones were concerned.

Further reasons urged in favour of cloning have a more futuristic tenor. For instance, it is sometimes argued that cloning would lend itself to the production of teams of people for specialized work in which togetherness is a premium. Into this category would fall astronauts, deep-sea divers and perhaps surgical teams. Even more far-fetched is the suggestion that cloning, combined with deep-freezing an individual's embryonic replica until required some time in the future, would enable people – in the guise of their various cloned selves – to live in more than one historical era.

## Recombinant DNA technology

Over recent years the revolutionary aspects of genetic engineering have become apparent with the emergence of a technique for manipulating genes from living organisms. This is the sphere of recombinant DNA technology, the benefits and hazards of which lie in the power it will afford human beings to design and create combinations of genes quite different from those resulting from the slow re-shuffling found in nature.

This has been made possible by the discovery of restriction enzymes, a class of enzymes used by bacteria to recognize and subsequently destroy foreign DNA. As such, they constitute a protective mechanism. However, now that they are amenable to human manipulation, they can be employed to rearrange genetic material in combinations unlikely to occur under natural circumstances. This is genetic manipulation.

Laboratories world-wide are now devoted to taking genes from one organism and planting them in another. In this way it has already become possible to produce facsimiles of human interferon, human growth hormone and human insulin. Other substances currently being produced by gene splicing are beta endorphin, the hormone thymosin alpha-1, and the enzyme urokinase which is used to dissolve blood clots. Of these, the insulin is closest to commercial production.

These nascent techniques have spawned nascent companies. Chief among them is Genentech Inc., Cetus Corporation, Biogen S. A. and Genex Corporation. The oldest of these, Genentech, was founded in 1976, currently employs a staff of 200 and has signed research agreements with such pharmaceutical companies as Hoffman-La Roche and Eli Lilly. Genentech is using gene-splicing procedures to produce interferon, one variety of which is undergoing clinical trials. It is also working on the mass production of human insulin.

These companies represent consortia of businessmen and scientists. Some biochemists and molecular biologists have become millionaires overnight, as the distinction between industry and academia has become blurred. This was accentuated by the United States Supreme Court's decision in 1980 that man-made organisms may be patented. Nevertheless, potential conflict of interest between pure science and commercial enterprises has led to ambivalence and hesitation among some universities in the United States. There is little doubt, however, that a number of marriages of convenience between universities and industry will be consummated in the next few years, following Stanford University's early lead in this direction.

What is significant about the current debate on genetic engineering is that attention is being focused on the positive medical applications of these techniques. This is in stark contrast to the discussions of the mid-1970s, when the emphasis was on the potential hazards of recombinant DNA technology. Indeed, such was the concern that it led to a temporary self-imposed moratorium by many of the scientists most intimately involved in the pioneering investigations. At the end of 1974 the Ashby Report was published in the United Kingdom, and in 1975 further guide-lines to forestall possible dangers were issued in the United States. Subsequently other countries followed suit.

In recombinant technology, DNA is spliced from one cell type to another. Bacteria or viruses are broken open with detergent, and plasmids (small rings of genetic material, DNA) are extracted. A fragment of this DNA can be removed using restriction enzymes, which cut the DNA chemically at specific points along its length. This fragment, or gene, can then be inserted into the DNA of *Escherichia coli*, a bacterium that normally flourishes harmlessly in the intestinal tract. As a result of this exchange, the *E. coli* has a DNA segment, that is, a gene, from another cell and each time that bacterial cell divides it will pass on the new gene to the next generation. Because bacterial cells divide rapidly, it takes only a few hours before there are thousands of bacteria containing the hybrid DNA. This bacterial colony is a genetic clone, which will produce the protein determined by the inserted gene.

The pioneering work along these lines was carried out in 1973, and what was done then was to insert into the *E. coli* bacterium a gene making it resistant to the antibiotic streptomycin. As one would expect, the genetically manipulated *E. coli* were indeed resistant to streptomycin. It was perhaps unfortunate that this model was used as the first demonstration of the recombinant technology, because it led to a great deal of fear about what would happen should such drug-resistant bacteria escape from the laboratory; hence the moratorium and safety guide-lines.

It is this technique which will enable human insulin to be produced by genetic means. The first step in this direction was taken in 1978, when it became possible to make chemically some fragments of the gene for insulin. Since then, synthetic genes for the amino acid chains of insulin have been inserted into *E. coli* DNA. The *E. coli* have responded by producing insulin chains. When this becomes feasible on a large scale, it will mean that human insulin, made by bacteria, will be available, and insulin manufactured in this way should prove both safer and cheaper than the insulin presently obtained from cattle and pigs.

Other frontiers for recombinant DNA technology include the production of a large range of human hormones and vaccines against, for instance, hepatitis and malaria. More dramatically, it could lead to the mapping of the 100,000 or so human genes and this, in turn, might make possible the replacement or repair of individual defective genes. This capability may open the way to the prevention – by gene therapy – of genetic conditions such as haemophilia and sickle-cell anaemia. In agriculture one may be able to look forward to self-fertilizing food crops, low calorie sugar, and perhaps bacteria capable of collecting scarce metals by leaching them directly out of the earth. Even more futuristically, some suggest this would open the way to the production of human beings with whatever genetic constitution is desired.

# 5
# New beginnings for human life

## IVF as technology

IVF does not cure infertility, since it is not directed at the woman's uterine tubes. It is a way around infertility, by focusing on the embryo rather than the mother. As such, it is an illustration of half-way technology, in that the medical condition giving rise to the infertility remains unrelieved. This is not a condemnation of IVF. It is simply a reminder that, since IVF focuses on the embryo rather than the mother, the medical condition giving rise to the infertility remains unrelieved. The technological expertise solves the problem in a technological manner, so that each child produced by this technique – now and in the future – will have to be produced technologically. The solution to the human dilemma of infertility is being obtained by non-human, technological means.

IVF illustrates our dependence upon technology. While this does not pose any major problems on a small scale, a totally different situation may arise if 5–10% of the population have expectations of IVF. The financial and resource repercussions would be major, and perhaps debilitating. The costs of setting up adequate laboratory and clinical establishments would entail a shift away from other medical priorities. While the community may readily accept this re-allocation of resources, it is a movement in the direction of increased dependence upon technology and away from humanizing influences. In the long term, this may have considerable repercussions for our view of our own humanness and human relationships. The financial costs of IVF, therefore, need to be balanced against other pressing areas demanding scarce financial resources. Wider human interests must also be taken account of at the level of society, as well as at the individual and family levels.

Quite apart from these future vistas, the costs of current IVF programs are worth considering. The program in Melbourne, Australia cost $1 million to develop, with $3,000 being the estimated cost per month on the program (including hospital and doctors' fees). In the United States, the cost per treatment is put at $4,000 (excluding doctors' fees). These costs, of course, are not the cost per live baby produced, which would be vastly higher depending on the success of the program. These are still early days, and undue emphasis should not be placed on the costs. They are regarded as high or low, depending on one's perspective. Nevertheless they cannot be ignored.

IVF is a tool of technology, and is therefore capable of being employed in a wide variety of ways. The applications of IVF illustrate this (chapter 4). Most people in the community, including Christians, may readily accept some of the applications, and yet hesitate at others. What needs to be realized is that IVF, as a tool, allows all these applications. It does not discriminate in favour of some, at the expense of others. The alleviation of infertility is no more important than the manipulation of the embryo in ways most societies would consider repugnant. Society decides how it is, or is not, to be used. Each application, therefore, has to be examined on its merits. To agree with IVF in the alleviation of infertility must not be taken as agreement with all its other possible applications.

Like all technological tools, IVF is sometimes a failure. Not every couple, who might be expected to benefit from it, does so. At present the majority of women on IVF programs either fail to become pregnant or abort early in the pregnancy. The successes of IVF, therefore, have to be balanced against the failures, those who are disappointed and frustrated having their last hope of a child dashed. This is as much the human face of IVF, as is the loss of self-esteem and depression caused by the infertility.

A major drawback with much media publicity is that little, if any, attention is paid to the couples for whom IVF programs are a failure. It is not unusual to hear of women who have had as many as 3–6 unsuccessful attempts at pregnancy, who have given up jobs to spend days in bed following each attempt, and who may spend hundreds of dollars each month on laboratory procedures and drugs. For these couples the emotional strain may prove intolerable, and their faith in technology may prove of little avail.

For many, IVF is a medical technique and is to be judged by its ability to help an infertile couple. It has to be seen, therefore, within a therapeutic framework, and it has been compared to the treatment of genetic disorders or to the use of insulin in the treatment of diabetes. If this argument is accepted, however, the rate of success of IVF as a medical technique has to be compared with that of the surgical repair of the fallopian tubes (microtuboplasty). IVF has to be assessed against other medical possibilities, and also in terms of relative financial and ethical considerations.

Paul Ramsey, the American ethicist, contends that the treatment of infertility should be only by direct surgical therapy, and never by IVF. For him, IVF is not a medical procedure, because it is being used to treat what he regards as human desires and not human illness. I believe this is an unduly rigid distinction, which ignores the psychological and marital consequences of a couple's infertility. Nevertheless, a couple's desires for a child can become excessive and may even take on pathological overtones. It must also be admitted that IVF is an illustration of the use of a medical technique as a social tool.

Ramsey's emphasis on the individual as the goal of medical treatment is a welcome one, although his limitation of medical concern to the patient alone and to actual illness alone raises profound questions about the nature of personhood. Medicine frequently takes account of non-biological questions and of the future welfare of future human beings. While it is true that both these aspects of medical practice can be misused and, if allowed, may open the door to the sociological manipulation of medicine, it is hard to see how medicine can be concerned with the welfare of the whole person and yet ignore the contributions of these areas.

## The humanizing possibilities of IVF

The element of human control in IVF has elicited two quite different responses to the procedure. The amalgam of human intervention and a laboratory environment has led some to condemn IVF as dehumanizing, on the ground that baby-making and love-making have been separated. Others, however, have seen the IVF planning as being supremely human, especially since an obstacle to marital (and human) fulfilment has been overcome.

These responses may well reflect radically different theological perspectives. The first views human beings as creatures in God's universe, who should not tamper unduly with the God-created natural order. This perspective does not limit us completely, but it does provide a framework within which we are to work. The second perspective recognizes that human beings are to share with God in his continuing work of creation. We are co-workers with him in maintaining and improving the patterns and processes in nature. We may even have the task of altering the procreation in previously unforeseen ways.

It is not my purpose to assess these different theological perspectives. Nevertheless it is important to realize that IVF converts what is intimate and personal into an impersonal process.

Leon Kass has argued that the laboratory production of human beings is no longer human procreation, because making babies in laboratories is a degradation of parenthood. He writes: 'Human procreation is begetting. It is a more complete human activity precisely because it engages us bodily and spiritually, as well as rationally.' From this basis he has drawn the following conclusion: 'What is new is nothing more radical than the divorce of the generation of new life from human sexuality and ultimately from the confines of the human body, a separation which began with artificial insemination and which will finish with ectogenesis, the full laboratory growth of a baby from sperm to term.'

To move away from the physical and sexual is to deprive procreation of its human connotations, because it no longer involves the diversity of factors constituting human love. This may have implications for the family as a biological unit, because the wholesale transfer of procreation to the laboratory would undoubtedly undermine the justification and support which biological parenthood gives to the monogamous marriage. It is in the family that we learn to become persons, experiencing the basic form of human love and caring, and learning to take possession of our capacity to relate in love. To undermine the family, therefore, would be to compromise the ordinary conditions of our growth as persons.

These, I believe, are strong arguments against the *indiscriminate* use of IVF. However, those children who have been conceived by IVF have undoubtedly been the products of marital love. What has happened, though, is that the meaning of marital love has changed. The failure of the physical side of this love has deprived it of its full human connotations. Nevertheless it is still love, and the birth of a baby via IVF is giving it a physical side it could not otherwise have.

Clinical IVF is an extension of the sort of interference found in delivery by Caesarean section, hormonal induction of labour, and artificial insemination by the husband (AIH). Each of these has a legitimate place in reproductive technology, as long as there are strong therapeutic grounds for their use. Each of them can also be used unwisely. Clinical IVF should not, therefore, be regarded as a routine procedure, even when it becomes far more widespread than at present. In precisely the same way, delivery by Caesarean section should not be carried out as a routine procedure. What is called for, however, is moral caution rather than moral prohibition.

A related distinction is that sometimes drawn between the *natural* and the *artificial*, since it has been argued by some that the natural means of conception is the only acceptable one, although the use of artificial means of helping a child later in the reproductive process may be legitimate.

This distinction is a particularly treacherous one. The concept of the 'natural' is highly relative. If it is argued that it is not natural to have a baby by IVF, it is equally unnatural to wear spectacles or clothes made of artificial fibres. Is it unnatural to travel by car along motorways or by jumbo jet in the air? The answer must in all these instances be 'yes', and yet this does not make these activities unethical.

For me, there is no inherent objection, on these grounds, to IVF and ET where conception by natural intercourse is impossible. This view takes account of the whole procreative process and also the overall situation of the husband and wife. The potential of IVF lies in its ability to rectify a missing element in the union of husband and wife, so that it may become a legitimate means of healing in certain situations. Nevertheless this does not justify its use as a way of bypassing the normal means of human procreation in the absence of a therapeutic rationale. A technical form of reproduction is inferior to one involving the bodies and personalities of two individuals, and should be resorted to only when the other fails. There is no likelihood that either IVF or its technical off-shoots will become a panacea for human ills, because these technological innovations are as fraught with dilemmas as are other aspects of the human predicament.

## Fetal harm and fetal consent

IVF makes possible the alleviation of infertility by intervening in procreation outside the body, as opposed to within the body via hormonal or surgical measures. As such, the manner of the technological intervention has been altered, because it is the fetus which is now the subject of the intervention, rather than the mother. Ramsey considers that experiments on fetuses are unethical, because fetuses are unable to consent to the procedures. Basic to this attitude is the possibility of harm to the fetuses and, coupled with this, the objection that a hypothetical or unborn child is being submitted to a dangerous procedure. Closely connected with the issue of fetal harm is that of fetal consent. A fetus cannot consent to the procedures of IVF, which furthermore are not therapeutic for the fetus. Ramsey has expressed this issue in various forms: the possibility of damage to the IVF baby cannot be completely excluded, and the discarding of mishaps is virtually obligatory. Furthermore, such hazards are being imposed non-therapeutically on the child-to-be without its consent. Since this fetus has been artificially conceived, the risks to which it is exposed are man-made and, therefore, need not have arisen in the first place.

Even the plight of an infertile couple does not, according to Ramsey, justify IVF, as 'it is not a proper goal of medicine to enable women to have children . . . by any means – means which may bring hazard from the procedure, any additional hazard, upon the child not yet conceived'. For Ramsey, the child-to-be cannot volunteer, and therefore should not be exposed to any risks inherent in IVF. The solution for the parents is to forgo having children.

Ramsey's argument from mishaps has another aspect to it, and this is that the risks in IVF must, under no circumstances, exceed the risks of the natural procreative process. This is the crux of the debate from his angle, because for him artificial fertilization and gestation must not be placed on a parity with the natural processes of human procreation. To do so is to advocate that human reproduction is replaced by manufacturing, making the overriding criterion one of the quality of the product.

The risks to the fetus are difficult to evaluate. They are considerable, but so are risks of normal internal fertilization. It is generally accepted that, for internal fertilization, of 100 human eggs: 84 are fertilized, 69 are implanted, 42 are alive one week later, 37 at the sixth week of gestation, and 31 at birth. Of the newborn, a small per cent will have a range of developmental abnormalities. There is no reason to believe that external fertilization (IVF) will experience less risks.

Although the risks to the fetus are probably no greater, or at least not much greater, in IVF, there is an important difference between normal internal fertilization and IVF. In the former, the risks are to potential rather than actual entities, and are inherent in normal conception and development. In IVF, these risks have been brought to actuality by direct human interference, and what was potential – and perhaps by the nature of the situation always potential – has been made actual. Risks have, therefore, been created, and these are risks which would not otherwise have existed.

Closely connected with the issue of fetal harm is that of fetal consent. A fetus cannot consent to the procedures of IVF, which furthermore are not therapeutic for the fetus. Prior to the application of IVF, the fetus is still potential – it is a 'hypothetical child'. Kass argues: 'One cannot ethically choose for him the unknown hazards he must face and simultaneously choose to give him life in which to face them.'

On this view, a being should not be brought into existence, if there is any possibility of damage from the procedure. In assessing this objection to IVF, it is difficult to know whether a demonstration that IVF does no more harm to the fetus than does normal internal fertilization would be sufficient to overcome it in the eyes of its proponents. It is even possible that IVF may cause less damage to the fetus. It is certainly true, of course, that any risks associated with IVF procedures are 'man-made' in a way in which risks associated with natural fertilization are not 'man-made'. For myself, I find this objection unconvincing, as long as the risks are negligible.

The objection to IVF on the grounds of a lack of fetal consent is equally difficult to uphold. Embryos and fetuses can never consent in advance to their conception, whether this be by natural or artificial means, and whether or not there is any likelihood of fetal abnormality. To link too closely the issues of fetal consent and fetal harm will lead to the unenviable position of advocating that only 'perfect' fetuses should be conceived.

There are numerous instances in which a procedure or a medical condition or even the age of the mother may increase the incidence of fetal damage. For example, a sleeping pill, amniocentesis or Caesarean section can all affect a fetus, without its consent. Although these may be established procedures, the incidence of fetal damage is far from negligible even now and was much higher when the procedures were first introduced. And yet they are widely used. The major difference between these procedures and IVF does not lie in the relative degrees of possible damage to the fetus. Rather it lies in another consideration. The possible dangers of such procedures are balanced against the likely benefits, the benefits and the dangers being divided between the mother and fetus. In IVF, though, the distribution of benefits and dangers is unevenly distributed, with the benefits being for the mother and the dangers confined to the fetus. This is an important consideration, which we should not overlook.

Another instance in which fetal harm may ensue is when an embryo has a 25% risk of suffering from a severe congenital abnormality. Such a fetus has not consented to its existence and yet a couple giving rise to such an embryo are not prohibited from doing so.

The welfare of an individual-to-be cannot be considered in the same way as can that of already existing individuals. Frequently the welfare of a prospective child is beyond many facets of detailed planning, quite irrespective of the method of conception. This is a part of the unknown into which we, as humans, are moving, and it simply illustrates one dimension of our finiteness.

I do not find the consent issue a convincing one. Is it meaningful to talk about the right of a potential child not to be born? Do non-existent children have a right not to exist? I doubt whether we can expect useful answers to these questions. On the other hand it is important to consider what responsibility adults may have for bringing unwanted suffering into the life of a human being whose existence rests on our decision to procreate it.

This is an issue well-known to genetic counsellors. It has to be faced by couples with histories of certain genetic conditions. IVF differs from these other instances only in the people making the decision. In the case of IVF, these are reproductive technologists; in the case of genetic diseases, it is a couple themselves, against a background of advice. The responsibility is of the same magnitude in both instances.

## Spare embryos

The question of spare embryos has become a crucial one in the debate on the ethics of IVF and ET. It is no exaggeration to say that it has proved the catalyst to widespread opposition to these procedures.

The fertilization of two or more eggs from a woman at any one time brings into head-on conflict pragmatic and ethical considerations. The pragmatic consideration that the simultaneous transfer of two embryos increases the possibility of successful implantation has to be balanced against the startlingly novel ethical question of our obligations regarding those embryos which are not transferred back to the woman from whom the eggs were taken.

Clifford Grobstein has summed up the ethical dilemma in this way: 'If it is moral to remove a human egg from a woman and fertilize it . . ., is it any less moral to do anything more to the subsequent early embryo other than to reinsert it into the uterus of its donor?'

A whole range of responses can be given to this seemingly straightforward question. We may contend that it is moral to carry out IVF and ET, but that it is not moral to do anything with the resulting embryos other than reinsert them into the donor. If we adopt this position, all eggs removed from a woman and successfully fertilized will be reinserted. This is the procedure used, for instance, in the Norfolk Clinic in Virginia.

On the other hand, it may be contended that spare embryos do not warrant any particular protection, since they do not possess rights, or because society has few obligations with regard to them. Under these circumstances the spare embryos may be frozen and inserted in a later cycle into the donor, or they may be offered to another woman or to a surrogate mother, or they may be used as research tools.

Regardless of the use to which these embryos are put, the debate revolves around the issue of the status of pre-implantation embryos outside the maternal body. This, in turn, raises issues such as whether the pre-implantation embryo is a human being, a potential human being or potential person, an entity with limited rights since it manifests pre-individuality, or an entity with no rights at all.

These possibilities are a clear indication of the conflicting values of society in this area. What is all too clear, however, is that these are far from theoretical questions. Whatever answers we give to these questions will determine what manipulations we are prepared to accept, and even encourage, on pre-implantation embryos. The dire urgency of these issues is highlighted by the use that is already being made of them for research purposes.

## IVF and research

Robert Edwards eloquently defends the use of spare embryos in the furtherance of scientific objectives. These objectives include an improved understanding of human growth *in vitro*, with the aim of improving the alleviation of infertility and inherited disorders.

This, however, is just the tip of the iceberg. The development of current IVF technology has involved the study of pre-implantation human embryos *in vitro*, sometimes without any expectation that these embryos will be returned to the uterus for continued development. If this technology is to be improved, there is a continuing need for research of this nature. A by-product of this research is that it may well contribute to a better understanding of genetic and developmental abnormalities in natural reproduction by internal fertilization. It may also contribute to an understanding of normal and abnormal growth, teratogenesis and aspects of cancer.

This technology as we know it, and as it is being fostered by its major proponents, is intimately dependent for its present status and its future efficacy and safety on research emanating from pre-implantation human embryos. Whether or not this has to be the case is another matter. What it raises, however, is the very fundamental issue of our perception of the status of the pre-implantation embryo.

This, however, is only the beginning. There is no reason to believe that useful scientific data will be obtained only from pre-implantation embryos. An inevitable extension of current studies will include the use of post-implantation stages of human development. Such studies would allow analyses of many aspects of organ, tissue and cell maturation, and would allow the culture of individual types of embryonic tissue – such as nervous tissue. Such cultures would prove of immense value in helping unravel the intricacies of tissue and cell differentiation. These, in turn, may have important clinical applications, dependent on the use of cultured fetal organs and tissue as replacements for defective organs and tissues in children and adults.

The potential applications of such studies are enormous. Edwards has written: 'The enormous research potential for science and medicine and consequent benefits for ameliorating mental and physical suffering, is for me decisive in debates on the ethical dilemma. The question of children conceived *in vitro* involves one set of ethical issues; the rights or otherwise of embryos *in vitro* raises quite different arguments about the value of research in relation to ethics.' Another writer has argued that the potential benefits of this type of research are so great that responsibly unfettered research should be whole-heartedly welcomed.

The question we have to face is whether this is the direction in which we wish to go. It is quite a new direction because it entails the use of human material. While there will be differences of opinion on precisely what is the best way of describing human embryonic tissue, most would accept that a human embryo is different from a rat embryo or a mouse embryo. It is true that Peter Singer refuses to concede this distinction classing it as an example of 'speciesism' – a prejudice in favour of members of one's own species. For him, the newly created embryo is not entitled to a special moral status which makes it wrong to destroy it. In spite of this plea, for most people, including myself, human life is different from non-human life, and this has ethical implications from which we cannot escape.

In case it is thought that this discussion has little contact with reality, it is worth noting that a number of statements were issued in 1982 and 1983 about laboratory experimentation using human embryos. Some of the most provocative emanate from various British medical bodies. In November 1982 the Medical Research Council's guide-lines contended that such research is ethically acceptable on condition that any resulting embryo is not returned to the uterus, and that the research is directly relevant to clinical problems such as contraception and the treatment of infertility and inherited diseases. The guide-lines also allow the deliberate fertilizing of human ova *in vitro*, as well as the use of fertilized ova no longer required for therapeutic purposes, provided that the informed consent of both donors is obtained. The MRC proposals specify that human embryos should not be cultured *in vitro* beyond the implantation stage, which is generally taken as 13–14 days after fertilization. Neither should they be stored for unspecified research use. One of the most far-reaching issues is the support given for studies on interspecies fertilization, because of their value in providing information on the penetration capacity and chromosome complement of sperm from subfertile males. In this case, embryos should not be allowed to develop beyond the early cleavage stage.

Liberal as these guide-lines may be, those advocated by the Royal Society and the Royal College of Obstetricians and Gynaecologists (RCOG) go even further in some respects. Both argue that the implantation stage is too soon in human development to be taken as an end-point for research. The RCOG specifies 17 days after conception, corresponding to the early development of the nervous system. The Royal Society allows a degree of flexibility, leaving the decision to local ethics committees. Underlying this flexibility is the premise that the value of the information potentially obtainable from this research is to be the primary consideration in how long the embryos are maintained. The Royal Society guide-lines allow for a range of research possibilities, including the investigation of the teratogenic effects of drugs and viruses, studies of metabolism and gene expression in early development, and the genetic manipulation of embryos.

The British Medical Association's (BMA) ethical guide-lines for IVF and ET approve observations of spare embryos, although these should normally be completed within 5–10 days of fertilization and always within 14 days. The BMA's recommendations do not use the word 'experiment', and insist that embryos which have been manipulated in some way should not be replaced in a woman's uterus. It has been suggested that these guide-lines would allow observations aimed at quality control of embryos, but not those involved in the testing of hypotheses.

Other recommendations of these organizations and of the National Health and Medical Research Council (NH&MRC) in Australia include, in general, the legitimacy of the donation of ova or sperm by a third party and the approval of embryo freezing, but opposition to surrogate motherhood and the limitation of IVF and related procedures to those within 'an accepted family relationship' ('a stably cohabiting hetero-sexual couple').

Guide-lines such as these, particularly those relating to experimental studies on pre-implantation embryos, raise a plethora of contentious issues. They bring into the open the intense conflict between the demands for greater scientific knowledge and respect for human embryos. This, in turn, brings to the fore the status of the early human embryo.

According to an editorial in the British journal *Nature* (28 April 1983), the Royal Society's guide-lines are based 'on the proposition that an early embryo is not a living thing, in the sense of being potentially autonomously self-replicating, but rather a kind of passing parasite, dependent on a uterus for full development'. For those with this point of view there is no problem, except to decide when during embryonic development this state of affairs changes. And this is a problem which has received practically no attention up to the present time.

The question remains: what is the status, moral and biological, of the early human embryo? Can an answer be based solely on scientific criteria, as the writer in *Nature* attempted to do, or must it have reference to specific ethical and moral viewpoints?

The desire to find a strictly scientific answer is a strong one, especially for those with no religious position. Another illustration of a scientific answer is provided by Grobstein, who suggests that the pre-implantation embryo does not function as a multicellular organism. From this it follows, according to him, that the pre-implantation period is a period of pre-individuality in a developmental sense.

Viewpoints such as these ignore the *potential* of human embryos, no matter how early in development they may be. Each of them has the potential to become a human being in the fullest, most mature sense. To isolate any embryo from this future dimension, and to treat it as though it was an end in itself *as an embryo*, is to fragment the history of an individual human being. Such fragmentation reflects an ethical stance, and is not an inherently scientific approach.

I am not suggesting that human embryos must be treated as if they were fully-developed human beings. This they are not. Nevertheless they should not be treated simply as a *means to an end*, that end being the pursuit of scientific and medical information.

Ethical issues concerning laboratory IVF research bring into focus one's view of the early embryo. If it is not regarded as human, laboratory IVF research may actually pose few problems, since concern about damage to the embryo and of what will be done to the embryo does not arise. In contrast to this, Bernard Häring expresses his opposition to laboratory IVF in these terms: 'The very probability that we may be faced with a human person in the full sense constitutes, in my opinion, an absolute veto against this type of experimentation.'

Leon Kass, in his extensive treatment of laboratory IVF, starts from this same point. According to him, the human blastocyst is human in origin and is *potentially* a mature human being. It deserves our respect for what it is now and prospectively. This is not the same as saying that a blastocyst deserves the same respect as a fully-developed human being. On the other hand, perhaps the early embryo should be treated as a previable fetus with, in Kass's words, 'constraint imposed on early embryo research at least as great as those on fetal research'.

When considering IVF research, a distinction should be made between (a) living fetuses facing abortion, (b) living aborted fetuses used in research, and (c) embryos produced for the express purpose of experimentation. The fetuses in (a) are unwanted, regardless of the reason for this. In (b) the research is conducted on the available products of abortions, which were not undertaken for the sake of research. The procedure outlined in (c), however, has as its aim the deliberate creation, and ultimately deliberate destruction, of embryonic material. This would appear to place this type of laboratory IVF in a class of its own.

A more ambiguous case is that of the spare embryos of clinical IVF. These have not been produced for the express purpose of experimentation, and so do not fall into category (c). Their situation is akin to that of (b), except that they have been deliberately produced in a laboratory, whereas the aborted fetuses in that category have not. The problem here is whether it is better to allow these spare embryos to die, or to use them with the aim of increasing knowledge about fertilization and early embryonic development.

If this research is on dead embryos, there would seem to be no problem. This is the same as any research carried out on dead fetal or adult human material. A more difficult situation arises if the embryo is alive, and still developing.

Experiments on living embryos can be carried out only by denying their possible viability and their potential significance as human beings. Once this is done, however innocently by most researchers, the way has been opened to all the possible applications of IVF. The fundamental issue is whether or not respect should be shown to human embryos, in view of their potential for full humanness.

It is difficult to see how respect for potentially human embryos can be maintained if they are regarded as nothing more than experimental material. Once they are viewed in this way, no logically-consistent limits can be placed on the whole gamut of IVF applications. A moratorium on laboratory IVF research would undoubtedly limit the expansion of our knowledge of reproductive principles and the causes of abnormal embryonic development. This, I believe, is a sacrifice we shall have to make, if we are to retain any guidelines on human experimentation. It should also be borne in mind that animal experiments will still be possible.

It is essential to realize that the way in which information is obtained is more important than the information itself. If information is obtained unethically, it will in all probability be applied unethically. If human embryos, no matter how early in development they may be, are produced with the express purpose of simply providing scientific information, that information has already taken precedence over the significance of human existence.

## An assessment of IVF

There is an ambivalence about IVF from which we cannot escape. One would like to give a simple answer on the legitimacy, or otherwise, of IVF. But this is not possible.

IVF and embryo transfer, as a means of treating infertility, are compatible with a respect for embryonic and potential human life. The death of spare embryos parallels the death of numerous embryos during normal internal fertilization. Since embryonic wastage is the price that has to be paid for the birth of a normally conceived child, it is hardly surprising that it also has to be paid in IVF.

Risks are taken in nature; so must they be in the laboratory. If the risks of the laboratory procedure are no greater than those usually found, they do not constitute grounds against IVF. Kass writes: 'To insist on more rigorous standards, especially when we permit known carriers of genetic disease to reproduce, would seem a denial of equal treatment to infertile couples contemplating in vitro assistance.'

Harm to fetuses and children does not come only from IVF. It comes from pregnant women smoking cigarettes and drinking alcohol, from a lack of parental affection for a child, from poor nutrition before and after birth, and from family break-up. IVF, therefore, must be viewed in the broad context of human relationships and aspirations.

The possible applications of IVF, however, far outrun that

of infertility, and extend well beyond the alleviation of infertility in married couples. Precise guide-lines are required, and yet these will mirror divergent community attitudes rather than specific Christian ones.

From a Christian perspective, IVF should be limited to married couples, because only in this way will it enhance human relationships rather than diminish them. It should be used to support family ties and strengthen natural biological roots within a family.

IVF is legitimate if it helps a married couple have a child of their own; a child derived from their own bodies, an outcome of their marriage. In this way it serves a therapeutic purpose. This is an acceptable goal, but it must be seen within the context of family love and the marital bond. If it is used to allow anyone to have a child regardless of family ties and obligations, it becomes a threat to family life. For those with a high view of family life, ovum transfer into the uterus of a woman from whom it did not come, the fertilization of eggs and sperm from other than married couples, surrogate motherhood, cloning, and human-animal hybrids are not acceptable.

For society in general, however, the limitation of IVF in this way may equally not be acceptable. Although surrogate motherhood, cloning and human-animal hybrids may not be generally acceptable at present, ovum transfer and the fertilization of eggs and sperm from unmarried partners (even though they may constitute a stable relationship) will be acceptable to many. This is evidenced by the guide-lines already referred to, and also by the widespread acceptance of AID. It should not be too readily assumed, however, that ovum transfer will become a routine procedure. The Ethics Advisory Board of the Department of Health, Education and Welfare in the United States, in its 1979 report on IVF research, stated that embryo transfer should occur only between lawfully married couples. In Australia the government of the state of Victoria issued a report in 1982, which ruled out the donation of eggs. The significance of this stipulation is that the major IVF programs in Australia are carried out in Victoria.

A more general reason for limiting IVF and ET to married

couples stems from the scarcity of resources. While this may not be a factor as long as IVF and ET are carried out on a fairly small scale, it will undoubtedly become significant when these procedures are routine and widely available. The financial side of IVF and ET programs will then be of major concern to society, so that the use of these programs to enable *anyone* to have a child, regardless of any obligation to society, will become an issue in its own right.

To argue that IVF may be legitimate in certain circumstances does not mean it should always be used in those circumstances. Its widespread use must still be balanced against attempts at curing fertility by direct treatment of blocked uterine tubes. It can be dehumanizing or humanizing, depending on the way it is used. Since it does not involve the physical union of two people, it is less human than normal fertilization. It lacks much that is deeply intimate and fulfilling. However, when used on therapeutic grounds, it represents a creative human means of circumventing a biological deficiency. A technological approach like this, however useful under certain circumstances, is always a second-best.

By far the most difficult issues arise from the freezing of spare embryos, and from the use of these and other embryos for research purposes. Once embryos are frozen, a decision regarding their future will have to be taken at some stage. By far the simplest course of action from an ethical angle is to desist from using hormone stimulation of the woman's ovaries. There are then no spare embryos and hence no frozen embryos. The choice in this instance is between clinical efficiency and ethical acceptability.

Once clinical efficiency is the course of choice, spare embryos will be available as research material or they may be discarded. In practice, however, once the pragmatic course of producing spare embryos has been embarked upon, the most likely next step will also be a pragmatic one, namely, the use of the spare material as a source of scientific information. To discard this material would, in the eyes of those involved in such programs, be a waste of valuable material.

I find it difficult to resist this argument, even though it can also be argued that the death of spare embryos is the most ethical course of action. It is most akin to what would happen naturally. However, human intervention has been so prominent in the production and maintenance of spare embryos, that to allow them to 'die' is out of character with all that has gone on before.

Once spare embryos are produced, and as long as they are superfluous to the therapeutic needs of the donor, they will probably be used for research. Nevertheless I have grave doubts about experimentation on living human embryos, even when the embryos are over and above those required in a clinical IVF program. To class such embryos as 'pre-embryos' does not get around the problem of their potential for humanness. While it is true that early human embryos do not possess internal conscious awareness, they do possess the potential for this awareness. However understandable the reasons behind the legitimization of this research, the borderline between this research and laboratory IVF is a very fine one. The only sure way around this dilemma is to refrain from producing spare embryos.

At this point it is important to draw a distinction between fertilized ova (embryos) and unfertilized eggs. I agree with those who argue that eggs, which are not to be implanted, do not have any special status beyond that normally ascribed to human cells or tissues. Grobstein's succinct phrase is instructive: 'The capability of producing a person under appropriate circumstances should not be confused with realization of the capability.' The embryo, unlike the unfertilized egg, is in the early stages of realizing this capability.

Underlying much debate over these matters is the assumption that the moral status of the embryo changes at the point of implantation. This is quite unsubstantiated, and appears to be principally based on the subjective feeling that something which is small and very immature has less worth than something which is larger and more mature. Kass comments: 'The blastocyst . . . deserves our respect not because it has rights or claims or sentience . . . , but because of what it is, now and prospectively.'

As we have already stated, there is an ambivalence about IVF from which we cannot escape. It is not a question of whether it is wholly good or wholly evil. Some aspects of IVF programs have far-reaching ethical implications and IVF itself has consequences for societies' attitudes towards issues such as abortion and adoption. We dare not ignore the agony of infertility; but neither dare we ignore the multitude of ramifications which the manipulation of embryos may have for our view of the significance of the whole human endeavour.

Throughout this discussion I have made few references to obviously biblical principles. This is because the major need at the moment is to assess what issues are raised by IVF, and then to analyse those issues. The main points to have emerged are that IVF is a product of technology, and hence must be viewed in terms of the benefits and shortcomings of technology (chapter 2). Clinical IVF is closely associated with therapeutic abortion, so that one's views on therapeutic abortion and on the theological and biological status of the embryo (chapter 7) are highly relevant to some aspects of the IVF debate. At a more theoretical level, IVF confronts us with the perplexing twin problems of fertilization and conception (chapter 4), problems that sit astride the theological and biological areas.

These are difficult issues which, by their nature, are also ambiguous ones. They take us beyond clear-cut biblical guide-lines. Nevertheless biblical guide-lines on respect for human (and potential human) life, the importance of human relationships, accepting responsibility for our actions, and the finiteness of human wisdom, are relevant. It is these which form the basis of a Christian approach to the technological manipulation of human reproduction.

## Legal and social issues in IVF

Hovering in the background of most discussions about IVF is the poignant question of embryonic rights and parental consent. Do human embryos have no rights at all? If they do have rights, at what stage do they acquire them – at conception, at implantation or at some later stage of development? Whose consent is required to carry out research on embryos? To whom do the embryos belong? It is frequently asserted that the consent of the parents is required to carry out therapeutic treatment on an embryo. Does this also apply when the embryo is used for research? Can an embryo be the material possession of the donors, when they do not intend to become its parents?

These are the type of questions which are increasingly being asked, and yet to which there are few answers at present. Legal issues tend to focus on whether an embryo is a person or property. Unfortunately, legal rules about personhood or property were developed without considering the possibility of an independent embryo. In current legal terms, therefore, the destruction of an embryo amounts to one of the criminal offences of murder, child destruction or abortion.

Each of these descriptions appears inappropriate. Murder, in legal terms, applies to a human being which must have an independent existence. Destruction of an embryo does not, therefore, amount to murder. Child destruction refers to the wilful death of a child, that is capable of being born alive, but before it has an existence independent of its mother. An embryo, however, has never been dependent on its mother. Abortion describes the procurement of a miscarriage. This, again, is inappropriate in the case of the destruction of an embryo, which has never been carried by the mother.

These are legal indications against describing the fetus as a person. They are supported by the traditional legal view that a fetus is not regarded as distinct from its mother. Further, for an unborn child to be entitled to an inheritance or to compensation for prenatal injury, that child must be born alive. An embryo is even further from being born than a fetus, and hence in legal circles it is not generally considered to be a person.

Legal issues requiring an answer in IVF include: 'In what circumstances should destruction of embryos be legally permitted?' and 'Who should have legal authority to make decisions about the lawful treatment and use of embryos?'

Difficult as these issues are, they are compounded when ovum transfer and surrogate motherhood are considered. Colin Thomson, an Australian lawyer, has set out some of the possibilities in this way: 'Mrs A's ovum is fertilized by

Mr B's sperm and carried to term by Mrs B; Mrs A's ovum is fertilized with her husband's sperm, carried to term by Miss C and the child returned to Mr and Mrs A. Questions of parenthood and legitimacy arise where the biological mother (who provides the ovum) is not the same person as the bearing or surrogate mother (who carries the fetus and gives birth).'

These are issues to which there are, at present, no clear answers. The law has assumed motherhood to be biological, so that the woman supplying the ovum is regarded as the mother even though the remainder of the fetus' development takes place in another woman. It is difficult to believe that this definition will remain unchallenged if surrogate motherhood becomes commonplace. The identity of the mother is crucial to questions of the child's legitimacy, and to questions of its inheritance, maintenance and custody.

Even now the idea of drawing up a contract between the parties in surrogate motherhood is gaining currency. Such contracts may include remuneration to the surrogate mother in return for her bearing the child and then giving it back to the intended parents. However, in an area as emotive as this, contracts of this nature may prove both unenforceable and unacceptable to society.

An IVF child born with an abnormality may be able to seek compensation from the doctors involved in an IVF program. In some legal systems prenatal damage is compensatable. It is a short step to regarding preconception damage in the same way. While it may be difficult to prove liability, the situation will probably arise.

In social terms, IVF cannot be completely isolated from societies' attitudes towards abortion and adoption. In countries where abortion for social reasons is readily obtained, adoption has become socially unacceptable and adopted babies have become very difficult to obtain. In Australia, for instance, couples waiting for an adopted baby have a 10 per cent chance of obtaining one. In cities where IVF programs are in operation, many such couples transfer from the adoption waiting-list to the waiting-list of the IVF program – where the chance of success is not greatly in excess of 10 per cent. If they are not accepted into the IVF program, or if the wife does not succeed in becoming pregnant, they may transfer back to the adoption queue.

The agony of infertility may be compounded by the agony of failure on the IVF program and perhaps even further by the agony of failing to obtain an adopted child. Counselling and support are imperative for these couples, and yet some IVF programs are conspicuous by their failure to help couples cope with further disappointment. It has to be asked whether IVF programs are not linked too closely with undue optimism, and hence are not preparing couples adequately for disappointment. This is a pertinent consideration when it is realized that there are at least 50 failures for every successful pregnancy.

The consequences of infertility were met at one time by adoption. The scarcity of children for adoption is a direct result of abortion-on-demand policies. IVF is being viewed by some as an answer to this predicament, and yet in the final analysis it can only amount to a limited technological response to the predicament. Its limitation stems from the fact that IVF can help less than 50 per cent of infertile couples; it is also expensive. A salutary reminder of the way in which human problems may be compounded by human ineptitude is provided by the realization that if 1 per cent of the pregnancies currently terminated were allowed to continue to term and the babies made available for adoption, there would be no waiting-lists for adopted children. This figure applies in Australia and is probably typical of the situation in most Western societies. Perhaps a community education program is required to persuade at least some pregnant women, who do not wish to keep their babies, to make them available for adoption.

## Artificial insemination

There is much in common between the basic ethical issues underlying artificial insemination and those just discussed in connection with IVF. It may seem as though I am dealing with these issues in the wrong order, since artificial insemination is a simple and well-tried procedure, whereas IVF is still on the verge of the experimental. And yet, surprising as it may seem, IVF has been debated far more profoundly and vigorously than has artificial insemination.

As we saw in chapter 4, the two major forms of artificial insemination are distinguished by the source of the sperm – the husband in one instance, and a third party or donor in the other. These forms of artificial insemination are homologous insemination (AIH) and heterologous insemination (AID) respectively. AID should be further subdivided into insemination for reasons of a husband's infertility and insemination for eugenic reasons.

The simplest form of artificial insemination from a Christian angle would appear to be AIH. When the cause of a couple's childlessness is the husband's low fertility or an inability to have normal sexual intercourse, the artificial introduction of the husband's semen into his wife's uterus may be a means of bringing fulfilment and wholeness to the marriage. If a longing for children on the part of either husband or wife, or both of them, can be satisfied by AIH, there would appear to be nothing intrinsically wrong with the procedure. On the contrary, it seems to be a commendable procedure.

When AIH is employed in this manner, its use is a therapeutic one and its justification stems from its therapeutic role. It is being used to overcome a physical or psychological impairment in the husband-wife relationship. Children are desired, but their conception has been made impossible by this impairment.

There is no difficulty here, but what about a relationship where sexual intercourse is not desired – for whatever reasons – but a child is? It may even be that the couple hopes to change the unsatisfactory nature of their relationship by having a child. This is a more difficult ethical situation, although one that probably cannot be used as an argument against AIH.

Another interesting extension of straightforward AIH is provided by the impregnation of a wife with her husband's semen, either after his death or when he is working and living in another country. These illustrations of what we may call 'posthumous AIH' or 'long-distance AIH' may seem far-fetched, and yet they are eminently feasible. Underlying both types of AIH is the previous provision for all these eventualities, by storage of the husband's semen. This may be done because the husband has an incurable disease, or because his working conditions are hazardous. It may even be done simply because of the normal hazards of routine daily existence.

AIH, under these circumstances, may seem to be nothing more than a sensible, loving response on the part of a husband and wife facing separation, and consequent childlessness. It may be that this is a legitimate response under some circumstances. Nevertheless great care needs to be taken here, because all too easily what emerges as of supreme importance is the production of a child, isolated from the human and sexual relationships so essential to the oneness of husband and wife. Even AIH can assume impersonal overtones if the child is seen in isolation from the overall psychological and physical unit of husband and wife.

Rules and legislation are inappropriate in determining whether AIH is being used ethically or unethically in instances of this kind. Neither is it sufficient to object to AIH because it is unnatural or artificial. Artificial intervention in conception is not, as I have argued earlier in this chapter, questionable. The crux of the issue is, as Helmut Thielicke, the German pastor-theologian, has pointed out, the range and the limits of artificial intervention. In most instances in which AIH is contemplated, the acceptable limits from a Christian standpoint are not transgressed because it serves to enhance marital love and its expression in child bearing. Even with AIH, though, care has to be taken that it is employed with these limits in mind. If child producing is separated too widely from love making, for inadequate reasons, the impersonal and artificial side of AIH can overshadow its potential for enlarging human vistas and deepening human values.

AIH is a move in the direction of the artificial control of human reproduction. From a purely technical standpoint AID is on a par with AIH. It is simply the next step in a therapeutic progression. The failure of AIH to result in a pregnancy, on account of the quantity or quality of the husband's semen, is the indication for proceeding with AID.

The simplicity of the technology, however, should not overshadow the complexity of the ethical status of AID. This stems from the involvement of a third party. Although this third party is involved only via his sperm, it means that AID introduces into the marriage relationship a foreign element – at least as far as the reproductive process is concerned.

The major concern about AID in Christian circles is whether the introduction of sperm from a third party by artificial means constitutes adultery. If adultery consists solely of the physical insemination of a woman with the sperm of one who is not her husband, then AID is adultery. Alternatively, if the essence of adultery is a breach of faith leading to the sexual union of a married woman with someone other than her husband, AID does not amount to adultery.

In the New Testament (Matthew 5:27–28; 19:5; Luke 1:34; 1 Corinthians 6:15–17) the words used to describe the physical union of a man and a woman indicate, first, that the two are 'joined' or 'cemented' together and second, that they 'know' each other in a very profound sense. Together they point to the deep emotional and spiritual relationship between the two, the physical side of which is signified by sexual intercourse. As a result, Professor Gordon Stirrat concludes, 'that relationship does not depend on the procreative aspect of sexual intercourse and, therefore, AID of itself does not infringe such a relationship between a man and his wife or produce it between a woman and the donor'.

It appears, therefore, that a breach of faith is essential to a definition of adultery. Consequently, when AID is carried out with the consent of the husband and wife, and the semen is obtained from an unknown (to them) third party, no adulterous relationship is involved. However, the elimination of the adulterous aspect of AID has been brought about by reducing it to a purely biological procedure. Thielicke argues that by biologizing the reproductive process in this manner, the personal character of the marriage is safeguarded. This, in itself, is a radical departure from traditional views of Christian marriage and, for some, may constitute sufficient grounds on which to oppose AID.

There is, however, a divergence of opinion within Christian thinking on the acceptability or otherwise of AID for Christians. Some argue that there is no biblical basis for condemning AID as unethical. Further, some see in the Old Testament a close equivalent to AID. In Deuteronomy 25:5, there is an example of natural insemination, according to which it was a kinsman redeemer's responsibility to impregnate the wife of his deceased brother. This is not, of course, AID and there is no suggestion that it is followed today, especially in view of the involvement of sexual intercourse and the possible involvement of polygamy. AID appears to have definite advantages over this Old Testament example.

Whatever we make of this Old Testament command to produce offspring for a deceased brother, it is not AID and is not likely to be emulated today. If its rationale lay in preventing a widow being left childless and heirless, we have to ask why this was so important in that culture. We also have to ask what relevance this has for AID which, in conventional terms, is employed to provide a child for a husband and wife.

For some Christians AID by mutual consent of married couples is not regarded as a moral evil. It may even be viewed as a great good in some instances. Norman Geisler adopts this position, and he justifies AID whenever it is used 'to promote and preserve complete and whole human personhood'. The question then becomes how we determine when AID has this result. For others, the question is whether it can ever have this result.

Arguments adduced in favour of AID regard the source of the reproductive cell as of far less importance than the love, care and nurture of children. In these terms, children constitute an essential element of marriage, so that the means by which they were conceived becomes largely irrelevant.

Accepting that there is no explicit biblical teaching against AID (by its very nature, we should not expect explicit biblical teaching on this subject), and that it is not equivalent to adultery, does this make AID an acceptable alternative for Christians? On what grounds is it rejected by some Christians?

The first question we need to consider is whether the desire for a child is sufficient reason to have one – no matter what methods are employed. This question has implications extending far beyond AID. It is relevant to the IVF debate and also, in different guise, to cloning. Most people would argue that *anyone* is not justified in acquiring a child by biological means, as *anyone may* include single people and homosexual couples. But is a married couple, in which one or both partners are infertile, justified in acquiring a child by any biological means? Is the unremitting desire for a child a longing for personal fulfilment and marital wholeness, or is it an example of an inordinate desire?

Opinions differ. A report of an Anglican Commission, *Artificial Human Insemination*, published in the late 1940s, asked: 'On what rational ground is it urged that while sexual desires ought not to be indulged at will, parental desires may be? . . . If we persuade ourselves that because we want a thing so much it must be right for us to have it, do we not thereby reject in principle . . . the very idea of limitation, acceptance, of a given natural order and social frame . . . the creatureliness of man?'

Against this argument may be placed one based on a couple's *right* to bear children. This, however, is not a strong case, since the right to bear children is the right to be allowed to bear children. And that right is not an issue when infertility is the obstacle to having children.

Longing for a child is understandable, and yet if carried to excess may well amount to an inordinate desire. Such a desire may lead to the breaking of the family unit, and may amount to an envious longing for something unattainable. Sympathetic as we should be to those in this position, it is far from unique. We have only to think of the longings for a marriage partner, a fulfilling sexual relationship, professional success or financial security, to realize the universality of these desires and their strident religious overtones. AID as a tool of technology may bring satisfaction at one level, but we have to ask whether it touches the religious longings or heals what may be rebellious desires?

Another major psychological argument against AID centres on the reactions of the husband; he may reject the child who is a constant reminder of his own weakness. This issue is a purely pragmatic one, which either may or may not occur in practice. In some instances this may amount, in hindsight, to an argument against AID; in other instances it would not.

This, however, is a superficial response to AID. More profoundly, AID may be a manifestation of a couple's unwillingness to share a common fate, that of being unable to bear a child due to the biological inadequacy of the husband. Sharing in this instance would amount to forgoing having a child or, alternatively, having a child by adoption. Either of these options would circumvent the possibility of a broken marital relationship, and may amount to the truest expression of love for one's neighbour.

The thrust of this objection to AID is not so much that it is patently wrong, but that it is a superficial answer based on the view that a couple's relationship is essentially a sexual and biological one, and that sexual intercourse is nothing more than a purely biological process. If this is all that sexual intercourse amounts to, the artificial, anonymous and impersonal aspects of AID are perfectly acceptable. It is a technological means of overcoming a problem rooted in a failure of biological or sexual functioning. Conversely, if sexual intercourse is regarded as more than a purely physical and psychological relationship, the artificial, anonymous and impersonal aspects of AID will amount to a threat to human relationships.

Enormous care must be exercised before approving AID. Its simplicity and innocuous appearance are deceptive. We should not accept the view that human beings can do anything they wish, and can solve all problems confronting them. Perhaps one of the supreme virtues is the ability, on occasions, to accept loss, inadequacy and suffering.

It is well known that marriages can be very successful even in the absence of children, although most would regard such marriages as deficient in a desirable element. The essential ingredients of a stable marriage, namely faithfulness between husband and wife and their love for each other, are nevertheless present. A child can be introduced into a family from outside by adoption, and by integration into the family become a part of it. This is a movement away from the biological family unit and yet is free of ethical objections and is very often psychologically and socially successful.

By contrast, AID introduces into the family unit only half an outsider, namely a child carrying the wife's genes but not the husband's. In this regard, the child is more a part of the family than is the adopted child. However, in order to accomplish this, a biological bond between the husband and wife has been severed. AID involves a radical separation between the sexual and reproductive functions of the marriage relationship, between marriage and parenthood.

The danger of this separation is that once human beings, and in particular procreation, are subdivided into a biological aspect that can be technologically manipulated, and a personal aspect that is above such manipulation, the integrity of human parenthood has been lost.

AID, even when accompanied by the best of motives, illustrates this cleavage in an extreme form. It highlights the reproductive function to such an extent that, in order to fulfil it in the case of one of the partners, the sperm of someone from outside the marriage relationship is used. It is at this point that AID is so different from AIH. It is difficult to avoid the conclusion, therefore, that AID is an example of man putting asunder what God has joined together. This is because conception and the subsequent stages of fetal development constitute a unity, just as the sexual and reproductive aspects of marriage form a unity. For Christians, these are unities built into the marriage relationship, and to disrupt them is to fragment the marriage bond. The sexual aspects of marriage find their fullest expression within marriage and hence, in Christian terms, are confined to it. In similar fashion, if the conception of children is a manifestation of the mutual love of husband and wife – and this is the biblical position – it can find expression only within the marriage framework.

The unity of the love-making and life-giving facets of marriage constitute the heart of the Christian conception of marriage. Technological inroads into reproductive control pose a threat to this unity, in that they make separation of them a feasibility. This does not, however, justify wholesale rejection of such control. Artificial contraception is the obvious example of a technological inroad with possibilities for good and evil. If applied with the goal of preventing the birth of any children in a marriage, it severs the unity of love-making and life-giving, unless there are strong medical reasons against pregnancy and childbirth. On the other hand, when used judiciously to space the birth of children and prevent the birth of an excessive number of children (from the point of view of the welfare of the whole family), contraception may augment the unity of marriage and parenthood in societies where most of the children born survive to adulthood. In the case of AID, however, the introduction of an extra-marital element means that the technological inroads themselves have ethical implications, and these, on balance, appear to me to be foreign to a Christian view of the marriage bond.

When AID is employed on eugenic grounds, as in the Repository for Germinal Choice program, far more extensive considerations come into play. The elevated status accorded to scientists, especially Nobel Prize winners, is symptomatic of the arbitrary élitism of the whole endeavour. Creative scientists and their genes are being worshipped, rather than the God who brought both into existence. Quite apart from the major question-mark alongside the genetic value of the whole enterprise, we are confronted with its quasi-religious pomposity.

Underlying these endeavours is the postulate that biological solutions are the only acceptable ones for mankind's future. All questions are reduced to biological parameters, with human beings viewed as motley amalgams of the biological and nothing else. This *reductio ad absurdum* is all too common today, and here we have an example of it in all its starkness. Human beings are regarded as nothing without the right combination of genes, and the family unit is a hindrance if it obstructs the coming together of the appropriate genes. No longer is there any place in society for the weak and disadvantaged, or for the ill and retarded. All that matters is biological perfection.

Of course, there is no such state as biological perfection; there is not even any assurance that these procedures will produce their desired goal. Repository for Germinal Choice is, almost without doubt, the aberrant fancy of misguided individuals. Nevertheless, it reflects far more numerous and many more subtle examples of biological reductionism spread throughout contemporary society.

And then there is the promise that exceptionally gifted individuals, if they are born by these proposals, will change mankind for the good. They may affect mankind, but it may be for evil. The idealism of these proposals needs to be tempered by the realism of the biblical view of mankind, with its reminder of the fallenness of the human race. This is not to argue that genetic constitution is irrelevant, only that it needs to be assessed in the context of real people living in a real world. People are not just an assembly of genes. Everyone is important; everyone has a dignity because of who they are in the sight of God. All are loved and cared for by God, whether their fathers were Nobel laureates or coal miners, university professors or factory workers.

Those of greatest benefit to the human race may or may not be characterized by great intelligence or brilliant creativity. The use of abilities for good ends, self-sacrifice and determination are frequently of as much value as a massive intellect. Love of one's neighbour, and supremely love of God, are more significant than a fortuitous (or even partially directed) combination of genes.

# 6
# Tampering with heredity

## The mass production of humans

In 1932 Aldous Huxley, in *Brave New World*, wrote:

> One egg, one embryo, one adult – normality. But a bokanovskified egg will bud, will proliferate, will divide. From eight to ninety-six buds, and every bud will grow into a perfectly formed embryo, and every embryo into a full-sized adult. Making ninety-six human beings grow where only one grew before. Progress.
>
> Standard men and women; in uniform batches. The whole of a small factory staffed with the products of a single bokanovskified egg. 'Ninety-six identical twins working ninety-six identical machines!'

Like so much science fiction, Huxley's vision of a factory mass-producing identical babies has far more truth to it than we may wish to admit. While such a process is not present reality, it has a basis in plant and animal experiments and is seriously debated by scientists, philosophers and theologians.

The mass-production of identical offspring is known as *cloning*, a term that comes from the Greek word, *klōn*, meaning 'twig', 'slip' or 'cutting'. The process of cloning results in the production of a number of individuals, all identical to the original individual from which they were derived. It is frequently pictured as a means of xeroxing human beings. Using a different metaphor, it is human propagation by cuttings. However cloning is described, it could amount to a means of obtaining 1, 20, 100 or 1,000 copies of a human person, all genetically the same as the person from whom they were produced. If this process were continued from one generation to the next, it may become equivalent in the long run to conferring immortality of a sort upon the original person.

Cloning is the technique that will allegedly enable us to produce an endless stream of exact copies of Mozart or Einstein, of Hitler or Mao Tse-Tung, of our next-door neighbours and even of us. Our great men, petty tyrants, folk heroes, sportsmen and ordinary citizens, could all be candidates for cloning. Fathers would be able to generate unlimited 'sons' genetically identical to themselves, and similarly, mothers and their 'daughters'. Strictly speaking, clones would be neither sons nor daughters, being replicas of the fathers and mothers themselves. Cloning would, so we are sometimes jubilantly told, lead to the manufacture of thousands of identical soldiers, all appropriately selected for certain conditions of battle. Alternatively, we could mass-produce robotic-like people for carrying out tedious mass-production, assembly-line tasks, or a Hitler could achieve his dream of acquiring a whole race of super-Aryans. On the other hand, one biologist tells of a recurrent nightmare of his: seeing eight Albert Einsteins in Grand Central Station in New York buying eight copies of the *New York Times*.

Cloning is, unquestionably, one of the most provocative and forbidding of the genetic engineering techniques under discussion today. It is unfortunate that probably more alarming nonsense has been written about this technique than any other in the genetic arena. Nevertheless it is worth discussing, because it dramatizes in an extreme form many of the ethical problems which are rapidly becoming evident in relation to other genetic techniques, such as IVF and AID, discussed in the previous chapter. It pushes the ethical discussion much further than do those techniques, and hence raises in a dramatic way the most fundamental of all issues – what are human beings for?

In 1978 David Rorvick, a science journalist, wrote a book, *In His Image*, claiming to be an account of the events leading up to the first birth by cloning of a human being. According to this account, an American millionaire in his sixties wanted to leave posterity a clone – an identical replica – of himself. In order to do this he enlisted David Rorvick to find a biologist willing to work on the project in complete secrecy and with unlimited finances. Despite a chasm of unknowns, the work from the start utilized humans. Conveniently, the laboratory was situated in some undisclosed, idyllic-sounding paradise where there appears to have been little difficulty in obtaining women 'volunteers'. Unfortunately, these 'volunteers' were not informed of the nature of the experiments and, during their dubious hospital stay, eggs were obtained from them. A few of the women acted as surrogate mothers to carry eggs cloned with cells from the donor millionaire. Eventually one of them carried a clone to term, and was apparently living with the millionaire and his one-year old clone son towards the end of 1977.

Probably every authority on genetics denounced this book as a fraud, and in 1982 one of the scientists mentioned in the book won a legal suit against Rorvick and the publishers on the grounds that he had never engaged in or advocated the cloning of a human being. The publishers conceded that they believed the story to be untrue. Unsavoury as this whole incident is, it provides some idea of the intense interest in the subject.

## Conformity or creativity?

Reasons advanced in favour of cloning were outlined in chapter 4. From that account of the process it should have become evident that the major aim of cloning is to minimize differences between human beings. Instead of diversity, it aims at conformity. Rather than live with the unknown, its goal is to restrict the unknown and to limit us to the confines of the known. In this, it is at odds with normal sexual reproduction, the purpose of which is to mix genes from two partners and produce a genetically novel individual. This is why we are all, with the exception of identical twins, genetically unique persons. We are the first of our kind and we shall also be the last. This has been of enormous significance biologically, and we should think very carefully before contravening such a basic biological principle. Clones are genetic dead-ends.

Cloning would condemn us to plan the future solely on the basis of the past. Creativity would be limited to the confines of what had already been achieved, leaving little room for new insights, daringly original experiments or new vistas of faith and hope. We would be prisoners of the known, the prison warders being the genotypes of past generations. This is conservatism of the most reactionary kind, expressed for the first time in biological as opposed to political terms.

Such conservatism is inevitable because of our inability to anticipate the future. This makes it impossible to gauge the fitness of a chosen genotype for a future generation, when it will have ripened into its phenotype (outward expression). What sort of human beings will be required in the future? What type of people will respond best to the demands of the future? We have no idea; and it may well be that the successes of the past will not be the successes of the future. Cloning, therefore, is not an automatic solution to all our ills, precisely because it limits us to the known and is not the creative force required by biological, let alone social, systems.

This consideration, by itself, should prove sufficient to convince Christians that cloning is unacceptable. Creativity and change are important facets of human existence, since they reflect our likeness to God who is himself creative and innovative. The writers of the Bible repeatedly testify to the manner in which God initiates change and also responds to change in the lives of his people. He does not sit back and allow events to work themselves out to some inexorable end. He intervenes and guides his people, finding creative new directions for them. He is always on the move, enabling his people to adapt to new situations and to find appropriate solutions to novel challenges.

This may seem a long way from cloning, and yet it highlights the contrast between staid conformity and exciting creativity. Cloning is a particular biological and social answer to some aspects of the human predicament. A more appropriate answer from a Christian angle is provided by the 'new way' opened up by God in Jesus Christ, since this enables individuals and communities to respond to the challenges confronting them by utilizing their abilities and talents, whatever these may be.

A related question raised by cloning is this: are we, by conscious choice, capable of improving on the natural method of producing great leaders, thinkers and creative giants? The natural method is haphazard sexual reproduction; cloning is relatively non-haphazard because it is asexual. We are so accustomed to 'improving on nature', that to question this procedure is sometimes regarded as tantamount to heresy. And yet, this has been a recurrent theme in eugenics from Victorian times up to the present. Having agreed to select for ideal types, whether by appropriate mating, AID or cloning, the dilemma is: select for what?

In the case of cloning, a choice can be made only on the basis of external (phenotypic) characteristics, such as intellectual ability, creative talents or altruism. For a particular individual, these characteristics would have arisen under the environmental conditions and social pressures prevalent during the years when he or she was growing up and maturing. A question we cannot answer is whether the abilities and talents displayed by this individual would be as useful under different circumstances. Quite apart from that unknown is the even more fundamental one, of whether we emphasize intellectual ability, competitiveness, co-operativeness, high achievement, empathy, artistic ability, or anything else.

How do we decide which of these, or many other, characteristics are so valuable that they should be preserved? Undoubtedly, different criteria would be employed by different individuals and societies. Nevertheless, whatever the answers given to this question, they will all depend on a whole array of social, political, philosophical and theological presuppositions. There are no self-evident answers, and there are certainly no biological answers. Cloning cannot be viewed, therefore, in a biological vacuum, since it demands of us answers based on our view of the human endeavour.

This illustrates a point repeatedly encountered when discussing our response to scientific advance. The more we take over from nature, the more choices we are forced to make and the greater the responsibility we must shoulder for our future welfare. While we cannot turn our backs on the role of decision-makers, the consequences of this trend require urgent consideration. We are being ushered into a domain demanding a rigorous grasp of ethical thinking, the sort of grasp most decision-makers do not possess. It may be demanding of us a level of thinking we are not even capable of undertaking.

Sometimes it may be preferable for 'nature to take its course'. What needs to be decided is when this is the path to follow rather than that of human control. I believe this is the type of decision-making we should be seriously contemplating in some areas. The issue then becomes whether research on human cloning should be allowed to proceed, or whether there should be a moratorium on this research.

The conclusion I have reached is that human cloning is an inherently unworthy procedure, and that it should not be allowed to develop. Part and parcel of human responsibility is the willingness on occasions to say 'no' to a future development, if its disadvantages and drawbacks appear to outweigh its potential benefits. A related consideration is the strong likelihood that society will not be equipped to tackle the ethical issues cloning will ultimately raise if it is implemented in the human community.

The advantage of taking a definite stand at this early stage is that it can, at present, be discussed in a relatively unemotional way. This will not continue to be the case, when it is a feasible proposition. Once a technological procedure is available, there will be pressure from sections within society to use it. The availability of IVF and ET in some countries is an excellent example of this. It is then too late to discuss the most fundamental of ethical issues surrounding the procedure, because it has become far too closely intertwined with emotive and personal considerations.

If we do not want a technique to be used in society, by far the best time to stop it is before research has advanced too far, when the technique is still some way from implementation. This is the stage which human cloning has presently reached, so that it is still feasible to advocate the halting of any human research in this area.

## Drawbacks of human cloning

Cloning has come under intense criticism on strictly scientific grounds. The finished product we call an adult human being is a result of environmental factors and not just genetic ones. Although identical twins frequently have an amazing amount in common, they also demonstrate considerable differences when raised in different homes, let alone different cultures. What would a twentieth-century Leonardo da Vinci be like, living in San Francisco and teaching at Berkeley? Would his multi-faceted genius manifest itself in the same ways as that of the Leonardo history knows? To this there is no answer, although it is unlikely that a cloned Leonardo would bear much resemblance to the original Leonardo.

The environments provided by the womb, early childhood, education, family, society and culture all contribute to that unduplicatable 'experience in history', which is the real individual person and which complements genetic endowment. One writer, with respect to Mozart, has written: 'To produce another Mozart, we would need not only Wolfgang's genome but mother Mozart's uterus, father Mozart's music lessons, their friends and his, the state of music in eighteenth-century Austria, Haydn's patronage, and on and on, in ever-widening circles.' There can be no question that without Mozart's set of genes there would have been no Mozart. But, on the other hand, we have no right to assume the converse, that his genotype cultivated in another world at another time would have produced an equally creative musical genius. Cloning provides only part of a human being, and that quite drastically limits its alleged effectiveness.

Most of the reasons in favour of cloning are readily

dispensed with. Genetic disease, while a major consideration at present, is being tackled by genetic counselling and will probably in future be alleviated to a large extent by the results of presently-occurring recombinant DNA research. Rejection of organ transplants will, almost definitely, be overcome by advances in immunology.

The central issue to be tackled is whether the postulated advantages of cloning outweigh its disadvantages. I do not think they do. Cloning, in order to achieve its goals, necessitates altering the whole of the human person and not just aspects of that person such as tissues or organs. The human person becomes less important than, for instance, rejection problems in organ transplantation or the whims of couples to have a child with specified characteristics. But what is more important: the life and potential of a *new* human being or the hopes and aspirations of a human being whose opportunities are *past*? It is tempting for those of us alive now to think that we are of greater significance than those of the next generation. It is all too easy to dismiss the younger generation as being feckless and superficial, simply on the grounds that those of the younger generation are different from us. Such differences are important – biologically, socially and spiritually – and we should accept that we cannot relive our lives in the experience of a human being of the next generation.

Although cloned individuals would have much in common, in genetic terms, with identical twins, there would be radical differences. Of these, the paramount one would undoubtedly be that the members of a clone had been produced in order to resemble the characteristics of someone else. Their value in the eyes of their progenitors would lie in the extent to which they replicated a previous person, and thus manifested once again certain features of that person. They would not be brought into the world in order to develop as unique individuals and to *be* themselves, but to perform specified functions and develop specified traits. Clones would be in the unenviable position of knowing that they had been brought into the world as biological replicas, with a preordained future mirrored, as far as possible, in someone else.

Would this matter? Is it of any significance to a person why he or she has been conceived? Are parents' motives of lesser or greater importance than the raw materials with which a human being commences life? Answers to these questions depend on a number of considerations, including whether the motives for bringing a child into existence will lead to restrictions on that child's freedom to develop as an individual, and on whether the raw materials provided by the 'mother's' or 'father's' genetic constitution will be better than what sexual reproduction would have provided.

There are no simple responses to these considerations. However, the extreme nature of cloning may well have major psychological repercussions for clones. From a Christian standpoint, it is also relevant to stress that human beings are important for *what they are*, and not for what they might be or because they mirror the virtues of someone else. Acceptance of people in their own terms, with the opportunity of developing themselves, reflects the attitudes of Jesus Christ, who loved people for what they were – in their humanity and in their brokenness.

The goal of those who follow Christ is to become whole people and truly human individuals. To be redeemed is to live more authentically human lives, to experience more deeply human concerns and to enter more fully into the experiences and suffering of our fellow humans. Christ makes all this possible because he experienced all we could ever experience and he understood all we could ever want to understand. He perfectly identified himself with us, opening the way to a life of self-giving and genuine commitment to others.

Cloning, however, leads in the opposite direction. Its aim is to limit the opportunity for self-fulfilment and the challenge to find oneself; its consequences would be the stunting of human growth. The example to be followed is no longer that of Christ, the perfect human; it is now that of another human, the progenitor of the clone. In making this transition from Christ to a human being, God as a reference-point has been replaced by a human model. The freedom to find oneself and true freedom in God and his

Son, Jesus Christ, may well be vanquished by a constraining tyranny, to be a reflection of someone else.

Of course, cloning may not inevitably have this result. Clones may be left to develop their own potential, in ways quite different from those of their progenitors. This is quite possible. But it begs the question: why produce clones? What sort of people are going to want to produce clones, and for what purposes? The beneficial purposes are, as I have already shown, trivial; they do not stand up to examination in strictly medical terms. What stands out, therefore, are the selfish ends. If this is the case, cloning becomes an untenable procedure.

Cloning confronts us with our expectations of human beings. What are people for? Are they simply to satisfy the longings and desires of a select autocracy? Are they to be chattels of the State, mindlessly serving it and all its demands? Are they to be the playthings and virtual slaves of their parents? Or are they of intrinsic worth; with a dignity inherent in their existence as human beings, and not in their functional value to a particular social or political system or even to their parents and family? Christians have no doubt about the answer to these questions. Human beings are to be respected simply because they are human beings created in the image and after the likeness of God himself. Individual people are ends in themselves and are of significance for what they are and represent – the handiwork of God.

Human life is precious to God, as revealed by his creation and redemption of mankind. To undervalue human life and to create life irresponsibly is to fail to take seriously the work of God. In particular, it negates the incarnation and Christ's commitment to humanity in becoming one with God's creation; it adopts values quite different from those of Christ for whom human life was worthy of his own life.

The dignity of human beings is essentially a dignity bestowed by God in creation and revealed supremely in redemption. This dignity rests not upon what human beings can accomplish in material or social terms, but upon the fact of God's love. This, in turn, can be seen in Christ's death for mankind, with its reminder that all of us live under the protection of God's eternal goodness and loving concern.

Human dignity, therefore, is based upon what individuals are in the sight of God and never upon what they can do for society, for mankind, or even for God. The implication of this is that those who have no functional value in society, the genetically disadvantaged and the mentally retarded, still have an 'alien dignity', an importance in the sight and purposes of God. For Helmut Thielicke, only in this alien dignity is there any security in a world where manipulation, biomedical and otherwise, is a factor within society.

This is not to argue that we should not attempt to eliminate genetic disadvantage or mental retardation. Rather, individuals with such conditions deserve protection and support. They are human beings, for whom Christ died. Their dignity depends upon this, not upon their genetic status. It also depends on their capacity for using their abilities and for relating to their fellow beings and to their Creator. To interfere with this capacity and its manifestations is to damage the dignity of an individual. It is in these terms that cloning, used for self-centred and evil ends, becomes an 'undignified' procedure.

Human beings are not experimental playthings, to be modified and re-created at the behest of an army of latter-day biologists. They are of value in and of themselves, with a personhood to be nurtured because of what they are. This is a principle of enormous relevance to contemporary discussions about the quality of human life. Unfortunately, much of the cloning debate regards human beings as paltry. The creation and discarding of human beings are discussed as though they were nothing more than experimental trivia. It is not our prerogative to bring people into the world simply to serve as production-line fodder. We bring into the world human beings in all their beguiling diversity and with all their potential for goodness or evil, brilliance or mediocrity.

Cloning, were it ever to become a commonplace procedure, may be a step towards a technocratic version of the celestial city. But in that city human beings would readily lose any sense of the meaning of humanness, and drab conformity would easily replace the often erratic but truly brilliant dimensions of human life as we know it.

### Why not clowns instead?

Clones have a fascination for many people, encompassing our love for technology and our longing to exert ever-increasing control over our environment and our progeny. With what, then, should we contrast clones in order to highlight the direction in which they are leading? I believe that a useful, if unlikely, comparison is with clowns.

The first point to note about clowns is their dress and antics, which reinforce our view of them as lowly, insignificant figures, surrounded by forces beyond their control but never beyond their ability to provoke laughter. Their inconsequential bumblings are caricatures of our own folly; they reveal what we seek to hide, and yet these revelations are manifestations of one aspect of the human condition. They help us laugh at our failings, and in laughing to realize that humans are sometimes stupid and often frail. It is not surprising, therefore, that clowns are melancholy beings, underlining the irrational and uncontrolled in human existence.

Unlikely as it may sound, the clown enshrines one of the most fundamental of human attributes. This is the ability to ponder and meditate, and to indulge in activities that have no immediate goal. Humans are capable of play long after childhood has passed. One facet of this is the potential for self-criticism, and for laughing at oneself. To be human includes the ability to indulge in inconsequential humour and wit.

Clowning allows people to act in an eccentric way and, in so doing, to demonstrate to others the value of eccentricity. It is nothing less than an exploration of one's humanity. To deny a place for humour in life is to deny to people the potential to assess themselves, at least in some regards, as human beings.

Humour ensures that we, as humans, see ourselves in perspective. It shields us from making idols of ourselves or others, enabling us to acknowledge the limitations and discrepancies of human life. But humour in the incongruities of human existence is made possible only against the backdrop of a belief in the congruity and orderliness of human existence. In this, it is at odds with sarcasm and cynicism, which question the meaning and value of human life.

It is significant that much of science fiction is grim, especially where humans have assumed responsibility for controlling other humans. No longer can there be any room for clowning; life has become a harsh routine in which an élite controls and directs a subjugated populace. Inconsequential wit has no part to play in a world of robotic slaves. It is superfluous and is not readily computerized; hence it can be dispensed with. In these futuristic visions the concept of human dignity has been lost. In contrast, where there is a high regard for the dignity of individuals value is placed on what they *are*, regardless of their value to society. This is an essentially Christian stance, based on the reliability and steadfastness of the world, and of the intrinsic value of human beings. It is only when individuals are valued for themselves that their eccentricities, oddities and incongruities can be accepted. Their potential for clowning and for expressing some of the absurdity and joy of human existence is allowable only when they are accepted as people whose value stems from what they are as ordinary beings.

'To be oneself' is a fundamental prerequisite for human life. This may involve being different from others, going one's own way, refusing to conform to society's *mores*. While certain strictures are essential in any society, there must also be a requisite degree of freedom for at least a modicum of self-expression. When this is not permitted, living transcends both comedy and tragedy; but once these are lost, so too is hope. And when hope is lost, only absurdity remains.

Clowns and clones respectively epitomize individuality and lack of individuality, diversity and conformity, creativity and compliance. Clowning allows for eccentricity and humour; it is in many respects a comic possibility; it acknowledges us to be what we are, no matter how grotesque; it gives us names, so that we can live out our individuality. Cloning, by contrast, demands predictability;

it is pretentious, and sees us as little more than computerized numbers; it allows us to be only what we have been designed to be. The contrast between the two is similar to that between a cathedral with its gargoyles and many delightful nuances and a down-town skyscraper with its sterile functionality.

We should value clowns with their ability to make us assess ourselves and our goals, with their talent for forcing us to laugh at our pretensions and arrogance, and with their childlike guile that helps us see ourselves in perspective. We are not such impeccable geniuses that we have earned the right to manufacture future generations in our own image, whether by cloning or some extreme forms of genetic engineering. There is no justification for abrogating to ourselves the position of God, and for bringing into being creatures in our own likeness.

Should we even take seriously these grand designs or should we laugh at their arrogance? After all, biological cloning, even when a practical proposition in humans, will fail in its main intent; it will not produce individuals identical to the original people. Why bother? Why take our grand visions so seriously, knowing their tragic outcome? Why not sit back and question the purpose of such futility? Why not ponder a while and laugh at the incongruity of our efforts?

The way of the clown is not an easy one in a world dominated by scientific gadgetry and impersonal expertise. Nevertheless, it is a way we cannot afford to ignore, because it places human values above human technology so that human beings remain in control of the tools at their disposal. It is a means of ensuring that human beings are the measure of things, rather than man-made things determining the lines along which humans are themselves structured.

This is a challenge faced by all of us. Ours is a world of many forms of engineering, all of which are modifying human existence in quite dramatic ways. These trends are demanding decisions about how we use these powers, and these decisions depend upon fundamental attitudes and beliefs. Whether we want a race of clones is up to us, and whether we acquire such a race will depend upon whether we still believe in the virtues of clowning.

## Dehumanization

It is unfortunate that dehumanization is such an emotive term. It has sometimes been so glibly used in connection with biomedical techniques that the impression is given that all those techniques are dehumanizing. This is grossly misleading. Nevertheless the possibilities for dehumanization should not be overlooked. While its relevance is not confined to cloning, it can be usefully discussed in this context.

The fascination of cloning stems from its suggestion of eminently visible control, with its production of mass-produced, identical beings. What more could a controller desire? Here we have a vision of a human creator, creating other humans in a foreordained image. The fact that this is only limited control and that it is not true creation is irrelevant. The illusion is a powerfully seductive one.

Cloning opens the door to dehumanization, the treatment of fellow humans as objects rather than as beings like oneself. To dehumanize is to deny others the opportunities to become *whole* people and to exercise *freedom* as individuals. On both counts, cloning is indictable by over-emphasizing a single dimension of human life and by restricting the freedom to develop as individuals with intrinsic value.

Dehumanization may also occur when the origin of a child is removed, for no good therapeutic reasons, from the sphere of marital love. Alternatively, it may occur when the principal criterion for human survival becomes biological quality, thereby ignoring the non-biological traits of human existence and hence the wholeness of the human condition. Dehumanization is an ever-present possibility: routinely conceiving apart from sexual intercourse, isolating child-bearing from the family unit, and transferring pregnancy to the laboratory as a routine procedure. Each of these, when performed out of choice and for no overbearing medical reasons, reduces a human activity to an inhuman, impersonal technique. The intimate cohesion of body, mind and personality is lost, and human existence is demoted to a robot-like mechanism. When employed in this context, these techniques contravene the basic biblical constraints of the significance of individuals, the unity of marriage and parenthood, and the cohesion of parenthood and child-bearing.

The over-emphasis of a single dimension of human life is a move away from wholeness, as is the neglect of any particular dimension. Genetic treatment, for instance, has an important role to play in the attainment of wholeness, although dangers are present if a single dimension of human existence is isolated and magnified to the detriment of the person in all his or her relationships. It is because of considerations like these that children with Down's syndrome, for instance, may bring out essentially human characteristics in those closest to them in spite of their relative lack of biological quality. Conversely, the attainment of biological quality by aborting an afflicted fetus may, in some situations, be at the expense of compassion, love and sacrificial self-giving.

The integrity of the family is central to a Christian perspective, since it is essential for the attainment of biological, social and spiritual wholeness. And yet the reductionism of modern biomedicine leaves little room for the family. Biomedicine in its starkest form is not especially concerned about any effects its procedures may have on the family, and yet in Christian terms family relationships cannot be ignored. These relationships are particularly at stake in the genetic area, with AID as the procedure of immediate concern. Extravagant use of IVF and routine use of cloning could easily do the same in the future. Further, any form of brain manipulation, and the use of mood-affecting drugs, while having their immediate consequences on an individual, have indirect effects on all members of the family.

If we take the family unit and its relationships seriously, therefore, the integrity of the family has to be fought for in a society dominated by biomedical techniques. It has to be put forward as an underlying principle, which must not be transgressed. Otherwise we shall find that we have been overtaken by a society paying little regard to family ties and responsibilities.

## Human engineering

Recombinant DNA technology is an illustration of truly high technology. At present it is in the developmental stage, when it is expensive and creatively highly demanding. It is exciting, and now that it is making exceedingly rapid progress, the scientific data are proving more interesting than the pseudo claims about producing ideal human beings. As with other examples of high technology in medicine (see chapter 2), recombinant DNA technology is surrounded by surprisingly few ethical difficulties. Perhaps the major one is whether or not vast financial resources should be committed to this research. Even here, however, the potential dilemma has been largely dissipated by the involvement of industrial concerns in the development of products important for future medical therapy.

The priorities of this research, therefore, need to be assessed in terms of its potential benefit to mankind. The production of a more satisfactory form of insulin is surely to be welcomed. In much the same way, the elimination of some genetic deficiency diseases would be immensely beneficial. Cures would be provided for myopics, diabetics, haemophiliacs and many others. Such applications of genetic manipulation lie, of course, well in the future; and yet they would simply be highly efficient genetic extensions of so much that we take for granted in contemporary medicine. As such, they are illustrations of the function of science as a way of investigating the natural world, exerting control over it and living out this exercise of authority in a responsible manner. Alongside this must be placed the possibility that recombinant DNA research probably is dangerous territory; but it cannot be regarded as forbidden territory unless we abrogate our responsibility as human beings.

Where has this left us? The reasons for genetic research are paramount. The goal of producing a master race has no place in a human perspective. Neither, however, should we oppose genetic research for no better reason than fear of the unknown. The prospective benefits of recombinant DNA research are immense; they must be taken seriously as they may well offer immense benefits for mankind. This is medicine of the future at its most sophisticated.

This new tool will, of course, have to be employed wisely. It will have to be seen constantly as a means of expanding medicine's healing powers, not as a way of manipulating people for social reasons. Genetic therapy will have to be genuine therapy, its goal being the alleviation of suffering (actual and potential) and the expansion of human horizons. In these terms, it should be welcomed by Christians.

# 7 The ethics of therapeutic abortion

## Genetic abortion

An issue from which there can be no escape in the contemporary world of biological quality control is that of abortion. Much genetic counselling revolves around it; hopes and expectations for healthy babies are more and more frequently coming to centre on it. When used as a means of genetic control, induced abortion highlights the sometimes conflicting interests of biological quality and human concern, aspirations after ideal human traits and valiant struggles against appalling deficits.

Abortion places upon the medical profession the mantle of both biological and social control, and this in turn presents many ordinary people with one of the most pressing and pervasive of human dilemmas. The planned destruction of human life brings us face to face with the meaning and finiteness of human existence. It forces us to examine the control we exert over future human lives and the reasons for bringing yet-to-be-born beings into existence.

Genetic concerns now constitute perhaps the major ground for therapeutic abortion—abortion for medical reasons. They include genetic and chromosomal abnormalities such as those of Down's syndrome, haemophilia, Tay-Sachs disease, disorders following maternal German measles and many other mental and physical defects. Not surprisingly, ethical difficulties abound in this realm, and the perplexities here are far greater than when considering therapeutic abortion on other grounds, such as maternal illness. There are a number of reasons for this.

The most obvious is that, while other medical grounds for therapeutic abortion are becoming less frequent, genetic grounds are rapidly gaining in importance. An increasing number of genetic diseases can be diagnosed before birth but, for as long as they cannot be cured before birth (if at all), abortion is the option of choice for many people. When used in this manner, abortion is regarded as a curious form of 'cure'. This view, coupled with pressures to alleviate maternal and family anxieties at the thought of a deformed or retarded child, constitute powerful, if ambivalent, grounds for genetic abortion.

Even more difficult is the frequent lack of certainty that a fetus to be aborted will actually be physically or genetically deformed. The risk of a defect is a statistical one. This may be as high as 50 per cent in conditions such as haemophilia, although lower for other disorders such as fetal deformities resulting from maternal German measles. When aborting for a statistical risk, more healthy fetuses will be killed than deformed ones.

This equation introduces a conflict: the destruction of normal fetuses against allowing into the world defective ones. In practice, of course, this choice does not arise, because the outcome of the pregnancy is generally unknown. If an abortion is not carried out, either a healthy or a defective baby will be born. If it is carried out, the life of a healthy or a defective baby will have been destroyed.

In such instances, if abortion is contemplated, a responsible decision will take into account the fetus, and also the parents and siblings. However, any decision to deprive a fetus of its potential for life is a weighty one, depending as it does on the conclusion that the detrimental effects of the birth will outweigh the benefits such a life may bring. At its highest such a decision will take account of the severity of the genetic disorder and the quality of life the afflicted child would probably have had; the physical, emotional and economic impact on the family and society; the reliability of diagnosis; and the increase in the load of detrimental genes in the population if the afflicted individual later has children of his or her own.

This is not to justify such a course of action, but it does give some idea of the framework within which this matter should be approached. Whether or not abortion is ever contemplated on therapeutic grounds, the decision that is taken will have consequences for other people and for society. From consequences of one sort or another, there can be no escape.

The issues are much more complex than is generally imagined. Discussions on therapeutic abortion for non-genetic reasons are sufficiently difficult, revolving as they do around the issue of whether a fetus is aborted for the sake of the mother or for the sake of society. The factors to be considered are relatively clear, and underlying these is the assumption that genuine benefit will result to one of the parties.

Unfortunately this is not the case when abortion is contemplated on the ground of fetal deformity. This is because account must now be taken of additional considerations. Is it possible to abort a fetus for its own sake? Is it right to inflict upon a fetus the consequences of a particular disability, whether it be Down's syndrome or Tay-Sachs disease? In this instance it has to be decided whether abortion will benefit the fetus, the parents, society, or none of them.

Some genetic disorders are so severe that it is sometimes argued that abortion is for the good of the *fetus*. In other words, non-existence will benefit the fetus by preventing intolerable suffering, severe retardation or gross malformation. The choices may be limited: non-existence or a less-than-optimal existence; non-existence or what may appear to be a travesty of an existence; non-existence or intolerable suffering. The underlying tension is the same: our *inability* to provide the fetus with a future existence approaching normality is pitted against our *ability* to give that fetus nothingness or non-existence.

Included within this nothingness is the absence of suffering, not an unreasonable achievement if the prospective suffering would have been very considerable. And yet, elimination of future suffering in this manner introduces a new dimension into medical practice. In contrast to the usual attempts of the medical profession to alleviate suffering in existing beings by the attainment of an optimally healthy *existence,* the goal of genetic abortion is to overcome abnormality and suffering by means of *non-existence*. A disease is 'cured', not by making the patient better, but by bringing that patient's existence to an end. Instead of eliminating suffering and so enhancing a person's continued existence, the basis of genetic abortion is that the eradication of suffering and continued existence are incompatible. Hence the idea that a fetus may actually benefit by its own non-existence. But is it possible to have benefits without a beneficiary?

A choice is being made, not for ourselves, but for someone who is unable to make a choice for himself or herself. But is the choice *for* or *against* the fetus? Is it in the fetus's best interests or is it in opposition to these? In a sense, it is probably neither. It cannot be in the long-term interests of the fetus, unless non-existence is always preferable to existence. However, the extent to which it is against the fetus is an imponderable without the benefit of hindsight.

The dilemma is twofold. The weight placed on the status of the fetus will depend on numerous factors, which in turn will reflect a myriad biological, ethical and theological concerns. In the second place, we do not possess the ability to eliminate all the genetic abnormalities we should like to eliminate. We have to live with our own limitations, and hence the need to recognize the limits of our responsibility. Malformed fetuses are not generally the result of irresponsible actions on our part, and as we are far from being totally competent at eliminating or rectifying genetic abnormalities, we must resist the temptation of undue activism. Less than godlike abilities should be accompanied by less than godlike responsibility.

Very easily the good of the fetus becomes the good of the *parents,* and this is the second possible response to the question of whose good is involved. This justification for genetic abortion seeks to take account of the welfare of those who will be most involved in the care of a retarded or malformed child. Unfortunately it is a notoriously difficult concept to define. Its vagueness and ambiguity mean that, in practice, it can be made to mean whatever society wants it to mean.

Moreover, it may be difficult, or even impossible, to decide in advance whether experience with suffering will strengthen or disable a particular family. The care of a severely defective child can be an overwhelming financial and emotional burden on parents. It may well be that some families will be unable to cope, although it is extremely difficult to predict the outcome in any specific instance. For other families in similar circumstances it may prove a difficult, but humanizing, experience. The concept of parental good, therefore, is highly relative and subjective, and certainly cannot be used as a rigid guide-line in favour of therapeutic abortion in all instances of fetal malformation.

The abortion of a malformed fetus may be regarded as the sacrifice of an unhealthy fetus in the hope of subsequently conceiving a healthy replacement one. Understandable as this attitude is, it is a step on the road to making human persons interchangeable. This sounds a harsh judgment on an all-too-human response to deformity and illness. Nevertheless a distinction needs to be made between the following: the desire for a healthy, normal child; the desire that a particular child should be healthy and normal; and the desire for health and normality in *a* child. In the first two desires, the respective focus of concern is on a not-yet-existing individual and on an existing individual. By contrast, in the third case the focus is on a *state* of healthiness, rather than on the health of a specific individual. What has become all-important is a state of health, as opposed to the significance of a particular fetus.

Beyond the good of the fetus and the good of the parents is the good of *society*. When contemplating genetic abortion, this is a reason continually lurking in the background. Cost-benefit analyses have been made on a number of genetic conditions, and the results invariably show that the medical expenditure on genetically abnormal children and adults far exceeds that of prenatal detection and subsequent abortion. The underlying assumption is that normality is preferable to abnormality and should, whenever possible, replace abnormality. This assumption, if taken to extremes, questions the political, let alone biological, equality of human beings, and places the good of society above that of individuals.

Attractive as financial arguments undoubtedly are, issues of social importance cannot be readily reduced to the sole criterion of cost, without an accompanying loss in human terms. If financial criteria alone were considered, most medical services would disappear. There are no simple means of quantifying social justice, nor of maintaining individual freedom within society, nor of attaining acceptable standards of health throughout society. Decisions relating costs to the goals of a society must always be made, and these are intrinsically relative decisions based on ethical standards and value-judgments. They depend upon beliefs about what constitutes normality, about individual freedom of choice, the dignity of human life and the status of the fetus.

In spite of these considerations, economic analyses cannot be discarded. The more sophisticated health technology becomes, the more expensive it becomes; the more dependent we become upon technology, the more we have to use it. The resulting dilemma is a fundamental one; we cannot afford the technology, but neither can we do without it (chapter 2). Perhaps, some would argue, the only escape from this inexorable spiral is the non-existence of the abnormal and retarded. Should societies conclude that this is the case, however, they will be allowing health technology to operate in an uncharted ethical wasteland.

Each of these reasons for genetic abortion raises issues beyond the narrowly biological. Purely genetic considerations are inadequate in reaching a decision; after all, a human life is at stake, not merely a set of chromosomes and genes. A closer look at some of the issues raised by genetic abortion, therefore, necessitates a consideration of the value we place upon the fetus.

### Status of the fetus

Fetuses are human beings; they are genetically part of the species, *Homo sapiens*. But is a fetus at a particular stage of development a *person,* in the sense that it has as strong a claim to life as a normal adult human being? If it is a person in this sense, it also has the claim not to be killed.

A framework within which this debate is frequently carried out is to consider the options provided by prominent embryological landmarks. The question asked in this instance is: '*When* does the fetus *become* a person?' The possibilities opened up by this appraoch are: (a) conception; (b) implantation at 6 to 10 days; (c) the transition from embryo to fetus at 8 weeks; (d) quickening at approximately 20 weeks; (e) viability at around 26 weeks; (f) birth; (g) a year or so after birth.

Whichever of these options is adopted, the fetus is regarded as a non-person prior to a particular stage of development and as fully personal following it. A line is drawn at some stage during development, this stage serving as a transition between two quite different preceding and subsequent states. This transitional stage, wherever it is drawn and for whatever reasons, has enormous repercussions for ethical concepts as well as for legal and social attitudes. Taken together, these options constitute the *critical stage* approach to an assessment of fetal status.

Prior to the critical stage, the fetus has no claim to life. With its onset, however, it acquires a claim to life virtually as strong as that of an adult human. Regardless of which critical stage is adopted, therefore, considerable moral weight is placed on it.

An alternative approach is to regard the fetus as a potential person. According to this *potentiality principle,* a potential person is an existing being which, while not yet a person, will become an actual person during the normal course of its development. A human fetus is such a potential person. This principle takes seriously the continuum of biological development, and refuses to draw an arbitrary line to denote the acquisition of personhood. At all stages of development the fetus is on its way to personhood and, if everything proceeds normally, it will one day attain full personhood in its own right. It is part of a continuing process, the end-result of which is the emergence of an individual human being characterized by full human personhood.

Inherent in a potential person is a high probability of future personhood. With this goes a claim to life and respect, a claim that in very general terms may be proportional to its stage of fetal development. The claim is always present but, just as the probability of an older fetus becoming an actual person is much greater than that of a very early embryo becoming a person, it becomes stronger with development until, at birth, the potential person is so similar to an actual person that the consequences of killing it are the same as killing a young person.

The potentiality principle requires serious consideration. While it does not ascribe absolute protection to the fetus, it does place a high value on fetal life at all stages of gestation. Furthermore, it treats with considerable seriousness the developmental continuum of which the fetus is a part, and it recognizes an essential link between prenatal and postnatal life.

It would be wrong to conclude that this principle denies that the fetus is a 'person'. It never does this, although it is prepared to assess fetal capabilities in terms of the extent of its biological development. It accepts that, while fetal material is always genetically human, the very rudimentary stages of its development manifest few qualities of established personhood. This *never* provides grounds for lightly disposing of the fetus, but it is an important consideration if the future welfare, and perhaps existence, of the fetus has to be considered for any reason.

The potentiality principle is prepared to concede that, although the fetus is a member of *Homo sapiens,* a 6-day-old embryo differs in profound respects from a 6-month-old fetus. Once again, this does not justify doing whatever one likes with the 6-day-old embryo; it is human material to be treated with care, dignity and respect. Nevertheless, the young embryo is much further from manifesting the qualities of full human personhood than is the 6-month-old fetus, and its chances of doing so are much less than are those of the older fetus. Perhaps one way in which we demonstrate this difference is by our own quite different reactions to the accidental loss of a young embryo and the loss of a potentially viable baby. Such differences are acknowledged by the potentiality principle, which in no way demeans the status of the fetus. Neither does it condone irresponsible actions on our part.

Before going further we need to look at the biblical references to the unborn, asking how far the biblical writers take us. The principle references I have in mind are Psalm 139:13–16; Isaiah 49:1; Jeremiah 1:5; and Luke 1:41–44. In light of these, as well as related passages, we can make a number of general statements.

1. The biblical writers include the fetus within the human community. The unborn are expressions of the promises of God, and play an essential part in many of the purposes of God. The beginnings of adult human life are to be found in the unborn.

2. Conception is repeatedly recognized as a gift of God (Genesis 4:1; 16:2; 29:31–32; 30:22–23; Ruth 4:13). It is an action of creation in which both humans and God have their essential parts to play. In the Old Testament God is frequently seen as opening or closing the womb, within the context of faith and of his own purposes.

3. The knowledge and care of God extend to the fetus. This is brought out as God's servants look back at his concern for them throughout their own fetal life, as in David's awareness of God's care of him before his birth, and also by the way in which God's sovereign purposes for Jeremiah were enacted before his birth. However, God's purposes did not commence at conception; they commenced in eternity. God 'saw' David long before he was formed in the womb; God chose Jeremiah and consecrated him as a prophet long before Jeremiah's body took on the form of a human being. In a similar vein, Paul argues that the followers of Christ were chosen by God, not at conception or at birth, but before the creation of the world (Ephesians 1:4).

4. The importance of the fetus in the unfolding of the life of an individual is supremely brought out by the incarnation of Jesus, who commenced his human existence as a fetus. Even the life of the Son of God was, for nine months, enshrined in the life of a fetus.

5. The fetus is regarded as an integral part in the continuum which constitutes the prenatal and postnatal aspects of human life. For instance, the struggles of Esau and Jacob in the womb of Rebekah prefigured their struggles in later life (Genesis 25:23). Samson's mother was told to abstain from alcoholic drinks during her pregnancy (Judges 13:7). This was relevant to his life as an adult, since he was to be a Nazirite and therefore would be forbidden to drink wine.

These principles provide insights into God's purposes in the lives of those who emerged as, and were ordained to be, significant in God's kingdom. God protected them in the womb as well as in life, and we are told about this in a spirit of praise and worship. The context in which we read about God's concern for the unborn is always one in which there is a living relationship between God and one of his people. Job, in his perplexity, exclaimed,

> Your hands shaped me and made me. Will you now turn and destroy me? Remember that you moulded me like clay. Will you now turn me to dust again? Did you not pour me out like milk and curdle me like cheese, clothe me with skin and flesh and knit me together with bones and sinews? You gave me life and showed me kindness, and in your providence watched over my spirit. (Job 10:8–12)

These biblical passages touching on fetal life are confessions about God and his purposes. They do not impart information about the precise status of fetal life, although by implication they provide helpful pointers to the attitudes we should adopt towards fetal life. In Ecclesiastes we even get an admission of agnosticism about embryological events: 'As you do not know the path of the wind, or how your body is formed in a mother's womb, so you cannot understand the work of God, the Maker of all things' (11:5).

The passages I have looked at do not provide a complete guide to God's providential dealings with prenatal humanity. There is much that is left unsaid. They tell us nothing about those numerous embryos and fetuses which have been spontaneously lost during the early stages of prenatal development. They fail to tell us when human life begins, or whether a very early embryo has the rights of a person. They provide no data about the individuality of the unborn, nor about the significance of the unborn relative to that of adult human life. They do not provide guidance in assessing the relative merits of a 5-day-old embryo, a 5-month-old fetus or a 5-year-old child.

These are major silences which we would do well to ponder before proceeding any further. We have to ask ourselves very seriously whether specific references such as the ones I have quoted lead to concepts like 'the sanctity of human life' or 'the inviolability of fetal life'.

The next level of analysis is that provided by the biblical teaching on human life, especially on the nature and value of human life. This has been dealt with in chapter 1. The main themes to emerge there were (1) human beings have been created by God in his image and likeness; (2) both the creation and redemption of mankind demonstrate that human life is precious to God, from which it follows that a dignity has been bestowed upon all human beings by God; and (3) the actions and motives of humans have been polluted with the result that conflict and alienation characterize so much of our existence.

The dominant themes of these principles can be narrowed down to the role of human responsibility in decision-making, and to the significance of the individual. Both these themes are of crucial importance in an analysis of fetal life and its relationship to human life in general. However, these themes have to be worked out in the context of conflict. Whatever views on the fetus we may emerge with will have to be broad enough to cope with the tensions and uncertainties of a fallen world.

Since fetuses are human beings, they are one of us—or, perhaps more accurately, they are the earliest versions of ourselves. Each one of us was once an embryo, and then a fetus. There is a continuity between the fetus and ourselves that we dare not deny. Fetuses, therefore, have an intrinsic value, just as we have intrinsic value. They achieve significance because they are one with us within the circle of humanity. The fetus throughout its development is important; it is an entity of significance and dignity. There is, therefore, a gap of profound dimensions between an unborn human and an appendix. An unborn human has the potential to become a fully developed, mature human being, whereas an appendix has not. Once a fetus has been conceived, that fetus must be regarded with seriousness and concern. A new human life has commenced, and under all normal circumstances that life is to be nurtured and protected.

One aspect of our responsibility as human beings is to protect other humans, especially the weak and disadvantaged. Such protection should extend to the fetus which, in Paul Ramsey's words, is 'live enough not to be dead, not yet mature enough to be an infant, yet a human being enough to deserve protection.'

The question we are now left with is whether this protection should be absolute from day 1 of gestation onwards. Do the embryo and fetus, no matter what their stage of development, have *exactly the same status* as postnatal human life? Are there any differences between what we were as fetuses and what we are now as adult humans?

Obviously there are differences between fetal human life and postnatal human life. Fetuses manifest few of the characteristics of human persons; their intellectual and rational abilities are limited or non-existent. They may be one of us, but they have yet to manifest the characteristics we expect of personhood and of beings made in the image and likeness of God.

In reflecting upon considerations such as these, Christians provide one of three responses: early fetuses are persons (from day 1 of gestation); early fetuses (and in the opinion of some, later fetuses) are non-persons; fetuses are potential persons from day 1 of gestation (the potentiality principle described on pages 156f.).

Whatever stance we adopt has to take serious account of the biblical and biological data. In my view these data can best be interpreted in terms of the potentiality principle. This is not a simple matter, and a great deal of serious discussion is still required on this issue. The position I am adopting is a personal viewpoint, and I realize that many Christians will wish to interpret the data in other ways. Nevertheless, I believe the potentiality principle is an option for Christians. Its high view of the status of the fetus means that, in practical terms, the fetus will be resolutely protected under all normal circumstances.

The perspective I wish to develop, therefore, is that each fetus is a human life, representing a potential for personhood from very early in its development. From this early stage it is a potential person, and from about eight weeks onwards has a recognizable individuality as manifested by its circulation and brain activity. It is well on the road to full personhood, and for most practical purposes may be considered to be a person. Nevertheless, I do not wish to draw a line between when a fetus *is not a person* and when a fetus *is a person*. Throughout the whole of its development the fetus is potentially an actual person, and deserves the respect and treatment due to a being with this sort of potential.

Discussion of the status of the fetus should not, however, be limited to the period of gestation. A fetus is part of a more extensive continuum, the end-result of which is the emergence of an individual human being manifesting, under normal circumstances, the myriad facets that go to make up full personhood. The processes of this continuum, however, do not begin at conception; neither do they end at birth.

They commence prior to conception in the relationship of two people. Not only this, but in a very real if profoundly mysterious sense these processes commenced in eternity, at least for God's servants and when considered in hindsight. It was the Lord himself who said to Jeremiah: 'Before I formed you in the womb I knew you, before you were born I set you apart; I appointed you as a prophet to the nations' (Jeremiah 1:4–5). The sovereign purposes of God cannot be overlooked, although the interaction of these purposes and human responsibility is beyond our comprehension. From a human angle, we are to exercise responsibility in our decision-making and under no circumstances are we to procreate or destroy life irresponsibly or selfishly, for that is to pour scorn on one of God's most precious gifts to mankind.

The other end of the continuum is also somewhat nebulous. A new-born baby is a very incomplete human person, with an enormous amount of biological development, range of environmental influences and wealth of educational experiences still required for normal maturity and growth. These constitute some of the relationships so necessary for the developmental continuum to be brought to fruition. Birth may signify the end of fetal life, but in terms of the overall development of a human being it fades into comparative insignificance. Neither a fetus nor a child is merely a biological organism; each has before it the goal of wholeness as a member of the human community, but for this to be achieved nurture and protection, care and guidance, love and discipline—both human and divine—are needed.

To contemplate a fetus, therefore, as if it had attained mature personhood, in the sense in which older children and adults have, is misleading. The fetus is on its way to becoming an actual person and, by the later stages of fetal development, will have most of the characteristics of actual personhood. As we consider the personhood of a fetus, we rely heavily on its potential and on what it *will* become. As development proceeds, less weight is placed on future potential and more on actual status, and this continues until adulthood is reached. The fetus, therefore, is an integral part of the human endeavour, and yet we must beware placing greater value on it than on human life after birth.

A corollary of the continuum-potentiality argument is that there is no developmental point at which a line can be drawn between expendable and non-expendable fetuses, that is, between non-personal and personal fetuses. It may be preferable to carry out abortions earlier rather than later during gestation, but that is a biomedical and not an ethical decision. Under all normal circumstances, a fetus has a right to full personhood.

Having stated this, however, it is necessary to concede that we do not place an absolute value on human life as, according to most moral codes including the biblical one, there are circumstances in which life may be taken or at least may not be unduly sustained. If this is the case, it is difficult to argue that the fetus has an *unqualified* right to protection. The fetus is an integral participant in the human endeavour, and must be viewed in the context of all the relationships of which it is a potential part.

We are left with a twofold perspective: our view of the

fetus should be a high one, but it should not be an absolute one. The fetus, being weak and defenceless, should receive very considerable protection, but that is not the same as guaranteeing absolute protection. Furthermore, even when absolute protection is guaranteed in theory, it cannot always be sustained in practice.

## Perspectives on abortion

Although the purpose of this chapter is to consider therapeutic abortion on the grounds of fetal abnormality, this section and the following two will examine abortion in more general terms. This will, it is hoped, provide essential groundwork for the more specific instances of abortion that are relevant to the topics in this book.

In discussing the status of the fetus, I referred to critical stage approaches (p. 156). The two most frequently held critical stages are conception and birth. Dissimilar as are these two critical stages, both entail absolutes. The view that the fetus has the status of full personhood from the moment of conception implies *absolute protection* for the embryo and fetus at every stage of development. By contrast, when birth is equated with the attainment of personhood, the fetus is regarded as an integral part of the mother—entirely dependent upon her in status as well as function. On this view the mother is given an *absolute right* to decide whether or not she wants the pregnancy to continue; the fetus has no rights or claims of its own and is to be disposed of entirely as the mother pleases. The emphases placed upon conception and birth correspond, respectively, to the Roman Catholic and abortion-on-demand positions, perhaps the most influential viewpoints on abortion in developed societies.

Abortion-on-demand follows from bestowing upon the fetus a non-person status. Birth, or even some time after birth, marks the onset of personhood; hence, abortion-on-demand is the logical practical outcome. There need be no therapeutic rationale for abortion, which may be carried out solely at the mother's behest.

While conceding that a human fetus is of the species *Homo sapiens,* Joseph Fletcher contends that the fetus is not a person 'since it lacks freedom, self determination, rationality, the ability to choose either means or ends, and knowledge of its circumstances'. Fletcher adopts this position because, in his eyes, the essence of a person is reason, so that a minimum of intelligence is required to class a human as a person. Since a fetus cannot meet this test, it is not a person.

The practical consequences of adopting a non-personal view of the fetus are far-reaching. Fletcher writes: 'The ethical principle is that pregnancy when wanted is a healthy process, *pregnancy when not wanted is a disease*—in fact, a venereal disease. The truly ethical question is not whether we can justify abortion, but whether we can justify compulsory pregnancy.'

Somewhat similar arguments are used by Fletcher when discussing infanticide. Both abortion and infanticide can be justified if and when the good outweighs the evil. What becomes all-important is the *quality* of human life, rather than the state of merely being alive.

Fletcher's absolute position blinds him to any appreciation of a fetus's potential for personhood. Since a potential person is not an actual person, it is, according to him, a non-person. Hence there is nothing in between a being with rights and a being without rights. For Fletcher, the only test of personhood is rationality; failure to meet up to this test indicates absence of personhood and, one imagines, the forfeiture of a claim to existence.

At no point does Fletcher seek to incorporate within his approach a supernatural dimension. The purposes God may have for a fetus or adult are regarded as irrelevant to his humanistic objectives. His deliberate effort to humanize decision-making is offset by a relative disregard for fetal life, and he fails to justify his fundamental postulate that the essence of a person is reason. This one-dimensional view of human existence falls far short of the multi-dimensional perspective of humans in the image and likeness of God.

Beyond this, it contravenes the essential Christian principles of the dignity and worth of *all* individuals and potential individuals, because it makes no attempt to balance the claims of different individuals and conflicting interests. It pays no regard to the need to work out what it means to *be* human in this situation, accepting that whatever the mother desires is automatically granted. Implicit in this response is a denial of the concept of wholeness in the mother's life, and a disregard for the integrity of the family unit and the reciprocity of its members. In claiming to free the mother to be herself, it shackles her to a self-centred existence, in which she herself and her own interests become all-important to the exclusion of the legitimate interests of those around her and of the demands of God.

The Roman Catholic position on the inviolability of fetal life began to take definite doctrinal shape in the seventeenth century. Ideas prior to this time are important, however, as many of the most influential ideas in Christian circles originated with the Church Fathers, whose concern was with the origin of the soul and its time of union with the body.

Four major ideas stem from the Church Fathers. According to *Traducianism* (*generationism*), which is attributed to Tertullian, the soul comes into existence with the body as a biological transmission from Adam via the parents. This fitted in well with the doctrine of inherited original sin. *Creationism* stemmed from Clement of Alexandria, who held that the soul was immediately and directly created by God in each fetus. A third alternative was that no soul is present in the fetus until the moment of quickening, and among the proponents of this view was Augustine of Hippo. A fourth possibility was put forward in an incidental manner by Gregory of Nyssa, who used the distinction between 'fully' and 'potentially' human; for him, the unformed embryo is a potential human being. A similar position was espoused in the fifth century by a set of writings known as the Irish Penitentials. These graded the severity of their penances as follows: 'The penance for the destruction of the embryo of a child in the mother's womb, three years on bread and water. The penance for the destruction of flesh and spirit (i.e. the animated fetus) in the womb, to do penance for fourteen years on bread and water.'

This distinction between *fetus animatus* and *fetus inanimatus* persisted unbroken in the Roman Catholic tradition until the late nineteenth century. For instance, in the Middle

Ages Thomas Aquinas proposed that the soul is created some time after conception. This was the predominant medieval view, which leaned heavily on the Aristotelian tradition of delayed animation. According to this view, animation occurs around the fortieth day of gestation in the case of a male fetus and the eightieth day in a female. For Thomas Aquinas, it is at these times that the soul is 'infused', respectively, into male and female fetuses.

Except for three years between 1588 and 1591, no major shift towards absolute protection for every stage of fetal development occurred in Roman Catholic thinking until 1679. In that year a decree by Pope Innocent XI condemned what he regarded as certain erroneous views on abortion, and in this we may have the seeds of an absolute protection position. However, it was only with decrees of 1884, 1889 and 1902 that absolute prohibitions against the destruction of fetal life under *any* circumstances were issued by the Roman Catholic hierarchy.

More recently, Pope Pius XI in a 1930 encyclical emphasized the inviolability of fetal life on the grounds that it is equally sacred with the life of the mother. Canon 747 is even more explicit: 'every aborted fetus shall be baptized without any condition, if it is known with certainty that it is alive, no matter at what period of gestation it is aborted. . . . The obligation imposed extends to even the smallest fetus, even though it be aborted immediately after conception.'

For Roman Catholic moral theologians, to abort a fetus with full knowledge and free consent is to commit murder. This is consistent with the Roman Catholic view that an unborn child is a human person with all the rights of a human person, and this status applies from the moment of conception.

Nevertheless the Roman Catholic position is not always absolute. The inevitable practical dilemmas associated with abortion are accommodated by distinguishing between *direct* and *indirect* abortion. Of these, it is the direct variety that is prohibited, namely, any action having as its primary aim a deliberate attempt to kill the fetus. On the other hand, indirect abortion may sometimes be allowed. This occurs when an action has the secondary effect of expelling or destroying a fetus, and is justified under the principle of double effect. If, therefore, an action has two effects, one of which is good and intended, and the other evil and unintended, it is justified. The result of this principle is that if an action has, as its primary effect, the saving of a mother's life, it may be justified even though the death of the fetus occurs as the secondary effect. This does not mean that all abortions to save the mother's life are justified; some of the major examples quoted are the removal of a cancerous uterus with fetus inside and the termination of an ectopic pregnancy.

The major attraction of the Roman Catholic position for Christians is its high view of human life. It has the strengths of all absolute positions and it places the unborn directly in God's will. In practice, however, issues are often not so simple, and while we may wish to believe that abortion is always morally wrong, dilemmas abound. These are inevitable and are brought starkly into focus by genetic issues.

The purported rigidity of Roman Catholic reproductive ethics is based on natural law. A fetus, once conceived, has the right to develop; this is an expression of natural forces and is a duty allotted to the mother by nature. Taken to its logical conclusion, this leaves no room for human responsibility. Instead, the erratic and impersonal forces of the natural environment are allowed sway. I do not consider this accords with the biblical emphasis on the responsibility God has bestowed upon mankind to control our environment. Since certain facets of future human life have been given over to human control, genetic counselling, IVF, cloning and genetic engineering all have to be faced.

A Protestant advocate of the inviolability of fetal life is Paul Ramsey. An underlying principle for Ramsey appears to be that it is relatively unimportant to establish at what point during gestation a fetus becomes human. God values all humans, no matter at what stage of development they are.

This leads to the inevitable conclusion that, when two lives are in conflict, both are of equal sanctity. Under most circumstances, therefore, Ramsey is driven to adopt the distinction between direct and indirect abortion, only indirect abortion being permissible. The only exception is when both fetal and maternal lives are in danger. In this instance, he allows for the killing of the fetus. Even here, however, he reiterates that the motives towards both fetal and maternal lives should be identical. This being so, it is not clear what ethical principles he is using to decide in favour of saving the mother's life. Apparently, it is the fetus's aggression against the mother, and direct abortion is the only available means of saving this life. This argument does not circumvent the difficulty that the fetus is innocent and an innocent life is being taken.

Ramsey contends that at the blastocyst stage (60-100 cells) fetal life should be given protection and accorded the sanctity and dignity of a human person. This stage, he argues, is the point at which the first origins of *individual* human life can be established. This is the earliest point after conception when, in Ramsey's opinion, an individual human life begins to be inviolate. Before the blastocyst stage it is uncertain whether there will be twinning, while by the late embryonic stage the major functioning organ systems are established.

In taking this stance, Ramsey has much in common with the genetic school, although in practice he refuses to accept conception as the starting-point of individual human life. In some respects he gives the impression that the precise point is not important. What is important is that the particular point represents the beginning of human life and hence the beginning of the dignity and sanctity of that life with its moral claim to respect and protectability. Ramsey's concern is with the intimate connection between human life and equal worth—the onset of the one inevitably entailing the onset of the other as well.

In spite of this, Ramsey places considerable store by the significance of the blastocyst stage as the origin of human life. This enables him to class as legitimate contraceptives intrauterine devices and any 'morning after' pills that may be developed. In no sense are they abortifacients since the pre-blastocyst stages are 'prehuman organic matter'; they represent potential individual human life, thereby for Ramsey removing them from the realm of ethical dilemma.

Ramsey's aim is to define the outer limits of the human community. Having done this, his intent is to see that all members of that community are treated with equal justice; human beings must not be competitively evaluated. All are equal from the blastocyst stage throughout fetal and postnatal life and then through to old age. Against the background of this guiding principle he deprecates the developmental school, which assigns degrees of value to the fetus at different stages of development. For Ramsey there is no gradation of values; there is equal value or none at all.

Ramsey espouses a form of genetic determinism. The genetic composition of a fetus is, according to his view, definitive of that life, rather than preconditional for that life. Once a blastocyst is in existence, all considerations other than the survival of that life become irrelevant—with the one exception previously mentioned. That life must continue, because it is equal to all other human lives.

Ramsey's approach provides little guidance in dealing with the human and social conflicts that sometimes arise when considering whether or not a pregnancy should continue, especially when those conflicts are genetic in nature. The existence of a blastocyst virtually precludes an abortion, regardless of the factors involved. An intransigent emphasis on genetic existence, regardless of its quality, may in some instances overrule profoundly human considerations. Ramsey's major contribution in this realm has been in considering how far doctors should go in prolonging the lives of deformed children.

Like Ramsey, Helmut Thielicke starts from the premise of the inviolability of fetal life. Once conception has occurred, the man and woman have *become* parents. This emphasis stems from a biological foundation, the fetus throughout its development having its own 'autonomous' life. Thielicke argues that it is the possession of a circulatory system and brain that establishes the fetus as a human being.

When confronted by the borderline situation of conflict between the lives of mother and fetus, Thielicke resorts to the notion that conflict between one life and another can occur only in a fallen world; it could not have occurred in the original order of creation. What this means is that it is illegitimate to use principles based on the original created order to resolve issues of conflict. What we see in the world as disorder does not reflect God's creatorhood or will, and so we must expect a conflict of values.

The order of creation would, according to Thielicke, demand that nature take its course, and maternal and/or fetal life be lost. This, however, is inappropriate in a fallen world and a responsible choice has to be made. For Thielicke, theological ethics do not provide a right-wrong answer in such a borderline situation. There is no slick solution, and whatever course of action is taken—sacrifice of her own life on the mother's part or abortion—will incur guilt. We must live in the light of God's forgiveness and we must exercise our freedom.

In the end, therefore, Thielicke allows for abortion in borderline situations, admitting that, within his basic affirmation of the sacrosanctity of fetal life, quantitative differentiations have to be made between conflicting lives. Decisions have to be taken; responsible choices must be made. He realizes the dangers inherent within such decision-making, and yet contends that, where conflict exists, onerous choices are obligatory. From this we can infer that, in the case of abortion on genetic grounds, decisions have to be made on the basis of all the relevant evidence available. Overall, however, one gains the impression that Thielicke would not regard genetic considerations as constituting a strong enough case for abortion.

## Biblical guide-lines

From a Christian point of view, it is imperative to ask whether these approaches are consonant with biblical principles. It is perhaps unfortunate that biblical data directly relevant to abortion are scant. This is hardly surprising, although it should impress upon us the need for caution in this difficult realm.

No biblical passage speaks of humans possessing personhood before birth; nor does any passage condemn abortion as murder. The one passage usually quoted, both in favour of abortion and against it, is Exodus 21:22–25. This reads: 'If men who are fighting hit a pregnant woman and she gives birth prematurely [she has a miscarriage] but there is no serious injury, the offender must be fined whatever the woman's husband demands and the court allows. But if there is serious injury, you are to take life for life, eye for eye, tooth for tooth, hand for hand, foot for foot, burn for burn, wound for wound, bruise for bruise.'

According to some commentators, this passage distinguishes the killing of a fetus from murder, on the ground that the fetus is not equivalent to an adult human life. The destruction of the fetus is not a capital offence, whereas the death of a woman is regarded as such. In contrast to the mother, the fetus is not regarded as a soul (*nephesh*), and greater worth is placed on the mother as fully personal than on the fetus she carries. Loss of a fetus merited a fine, whereas the killing of a baby, child or adult, led to the death of the murderer (Exodus 21:12).

An alternative interpretation of this passage is that verse 22 is a demand for damages for causing the woman to go into premature labour. The following verses exact further compensation if either mother or child suffers physically. The mother and fetus are considered to be equally human.

Some commentators argue that a better translation for these verses might be along the following lines: 'If men strive and hurt a woman with child, so that her children come out of her, and yet no mischief follows, he shall be surely punished. . . .' Consequently, the passage is then regarded as teaching that fetus and mother were regarded as equal. The support of theologians, such as John Calvin, for this interpretation is frequently mentioned.

It is unfortunate that this latter interpretation is, on occasion, used as justification for placing the origin of the human person at the moment of conception. Such a viewpoint is not, by its very nature, a strict theological interpretation of this, or any other, biblical statement. Enormous care has to be employed, therefore, in moving from any particular interpretation of the Exodus passage to a particular stance on abortion. Under no circumstances must this passage be interpreted as undervaluing fetal life. Further, it is dealing with unintentional abortion, not with deliberate abortion.

Arguments against abortion sometimes use, not biblical evidence *per se,* but the opinions of Jewish writers such as

Philo and Josephus or of early Christian writers as found in the Didache, the Epistle of Barnabas, and the Apocalypse of Peter. While there can be no doubt that these writers as well as later ones in the fourth and fifth centuries forthrightly condemned deliberately induced abortions, it would be unwise to treat these views as biblical or to move directly from them to the current debate on therapeutic abortion.

It may also be relevant to observe that no biblical text forbids procuring an abortion. This is in striking contrast to Assyrian law which, between 1450 BC and 1250 BC, prescribed death by torture in cases of induced abortion. The silence of the Old Testament is notable, particularly since the Mosaic Code is normally more extensive and severe in sexual matters than are other codes. Never in the Old Testament is a fetus exacted for a fetus, in contrast to the Assyrian Code. This was probably a means of protecting a fetus.

The Old Testament silence on abortion has proved a difficulty for present-day commentators. It may be interpreted as suggesting that God does not invariably prohibit abortion. Alternatively it may be taken to mean that abortion was considered so vile that no need was seen to proscribe it. Either way, little stress can be placed on an argument from silence.

The Old Testament cannot be used to bolster any specific position on abortion. Nevertheless, as we have already seen, it does place great value upon the fetus. For instance, conception is recognized as a gift of God, and is an act of creation involving both humans and God—as in Psalm 139:13–18. The fetus is also recognized as an essential part in the continuum which makes up the prenatal and postnatal facets of a human life.

God's concern for his servants extended to a concern for them before, as well as after, birth. This is exemplified by David's awareness of God's care of him prior to his birth (Psalm 139:13–16). A New Testament illustration of the same principle is provided by the account in the first chapter of Luke's Gospel, in which John the Baptist as a six-month fetus in his mother's womb 'leaped for joy' (Luke 1:41–44). I am not inclined to follow those who argue that John the Baptist, as a fetus, was filled with the Holy Spirit, nor that

John's joy was prompted by the two-week-old zygote of Jesus. The more important point to emerge from Luke's account is that God was at work in John the Baptist's life, even prior to his birth.

We can conclude from these biblical examples that God always places considerable importance on fetal life, and that his purposes encompass antenatal as well as postnatal life. Nevertheless, very important as these principles are, they should not be used to suggest that the fetus is to be equated with a living person; it does not have all the responsibilities and possibilities of a living person. Rather, the fetus is being built into the image and likeness of God, and the Bible never treats it as more than this. On the other hand, the fetus is never merely an expendable tissue of the body; God is at work fashioning it into a being with Godlike characteristics.

The difficulty for Christians is to decide what precise conclusions to draw from these principles. My own conclusion is that the fetus is to be treated with dignity and respect, so that under no circumstances will abortion ever be lightly undertaken by Christian couples. It should be contemplated by Christian couples only under the most extreme circumstances, the nature of which will be discussed later in this chapter.

Other Christians will disagree with this conclusion, arguing instead that abortion should not be contemplated by Christian couples under any circumstances whatsoever. In arguing thus, emphasis will be placed on concepts such as the sanctity of human life, and the commencement of human life and personhood at conception. I have very considerable sympathy with this viewpoint, although I do not believe that concepts such as these follow of necessity from the biblical data. Neither do I believe that an absolute prohibition on abortion within Christian circles is a feasible position in practice. There are exceptions, which even ardent anti-abortionists have to concede, as I shall shortly contend.

In practical terms the position I am advocating probably differs little, in practice, from a strong anti-abortionist stance. The principal difference is that I am prepared to admit there may be circumstances where, very regretfully, even Christians may have to contemplate an abortion. The compromise nature of all such decisions reflects our fallenness and alienation from the highest purposes of God.

Abortion presents us with a dilemma. On the one hand, we do not have a biblical warrant to class it automatically as murder; and yet, alongside this, we must cling to the seriousness of abortion. Induced abortion is a man-initiated process by which a potential human life is destroyed. A developing person is prevented from developing further and from becoming a human being in the fullest sense of that term.

And yet there is no way out of this dilemma. It is basic to personhood and to the responsibilities God has bestowed upon human beings. The dilemma is further compounded by the fallenness of the human condition. Our highest ideals are frequently shattered by self-centredness, pride, arrogance, deception and lust, and the consequences for fetuses and children may be tragic.

The question of abortion confronts us with the grandeur and tragedy of the human situation. To expect trite answers in this realm is to demean the magnificence of God's creation and the vast ramifications of human rebellion against God. Any approach to abortion that takes seriously the meaning of human existence must rely on human reason, compassion and understanding, and on everything else that constitutes what we are as persons capable of making morally sensitive, discriminating and finite judgments. The possibility of abortion confronts us with the fact of our creatureliness and the dilemma of limited alternatives.

## Possible grounds for therapeutic abortion

Although my interest in the present context is on abortion for genetic reasons, I shall refer briefly to abortion-on-demand and to abortion based on danger to the physical health of the mother and as a consequence of rape and incest. This is not intended as an exhaustive study of abortion; it is merely an indication of my own position.

Under *all* normal circumstances, the attitude of a Christian couple is to regard the fetus and all that it represents as a gift of God; they do not have the option of wondering whether the gift is to be accepted or rejected, even if the conception was unplanned. They have, as C. S. Lewis expressed it, already entered the incalculably momentous role of being parents and ancestors. Before rejecting a fetus, they must ask themselves whether the decision is one that can be taken before God and in responsibility to him.

The fact that a mother does not want the fetus, for no better reason than that she does not want it, is a totally unacceptable ethical ground for abortion. The question is whether or not the fetus was *willed,* in the sense of whether or not sexual intercourse was freely undertaken. If it was, then as human beings we must accept the consequences of our actions. This is what human responsibility is all about. If, therefore, intercourse was freely undertaken by consenting parties, a fetus resulting from this intercourse has the right to live. To abort on the grounds of convenience is a morally abhorrent abrogation of the responsibility bestowed on human beings by God.

Gordon Scorer has argued very persuasively that to destroy life for reasons of convenience is to devalue it. Once it is decided that life is no longer uniquely precious, relationships in society become less important and may ultimately become meaningless. Scorer writes: '. . . life has no existence and meaning apart from relationship with other lives. When we debate the rights and wrongs of induced abortion, we are debating a problem of human relationships much broader and more significant than that of a woman with an unwanted fetus. We are concerned with society's attitude to human life.'

These are ample grounds, I believe, for arguing without compromise against abortion-on-demand, or against using abortion as a form of contraceptive. Nevertheless, we have to ask as morally responsible people whether any circumstances whatever may obtain (quite apart from fetal abnormality) in which abortion is permissible.

Whatever grounds for abortion there may be, however, they are always to be regarded as exceptions to the general rule of fetal protection. Only the most extreme circumstances can provide grounds for abortion, which should be undertaken only in response to otherwise unresolvable dilemmas. There may be situations in which abortion, tragically, is the least evil of the possible options.

For instance, the *physical health of the mother* may be placed in jeopardy by the continuance of a pregnancy, although this is a relatively rare reason for termination today. It is, however, sometimes a legitimate reason because, according to most commentators, an actual person is of greater intrinsic value than that of the fetus she is carrying. In other words, the mother's actual humanity is of more value than the unborn's potential for it.

Abortion in this instance is allowed by practically all ethicists, thereby converting all absolute stances into relative ones. This is the one generally recognized exception to the rule of fetal inviolability. An absolute anti-abortion stance cannot cope with direct conflict between maternal and fetal lives.

*Rape* raises the question of whether a woman should be forced to be a mother against her will, and this immediately raises the further issue of whether a woman should be allowed to be treated as anything other than a fully human person. In this instance, the confrontation is between the conflicting demands of the personhood of the woman and the right to be born of a child conceived in evil.

If conception has occurred without the consent of the woman, it would appear to follow that abortion is allowable if, and only if, the woman is under extreme stress as a result and she requests it. This is because a woman is more than just her body; she is a person created in the image of God. Rape, therefore, is a denial of her personhood and of what she *is* in the eyes of God.

A life generated by rape only serves to underline the manner in which the mother's rights to health and self-determination have been infringed. As such, the rights of an actual person, the mother, take precedence over the rights of a potential person, the fetus. As Norman Geisler has expressed it: 'A potentially human person is not granted a birthright by violation of a fully human person unless her consent is subsequently given.'

Similar arguments apply to incest, where both rape and eugenic considerations are relevant. To quote Geisler again:

'Allowing an end to blossom in the name of a potential good (the embryo) seems to be a poor way of handling evil, especially when the potential good (the embryo) may itself turn out to be another form of evil. It is better to prevent the evil from coming to fruition than to perpetuate it.'

## Abortion for genetic reasons

I now turn to my major concern in this chapter—abortion for genetic reasons, when there is fetal abnormality.

A frequently quoted ground for abortion is the mental health of the mother. In the present discussion I am concerned with this as a possible reason for abortion when *the fetus is known to be seriously deformed.* My contention is that there may be extreme instances where this should be seriously considered, although such instances will always be exceptions to the general rule of fetal protection. By their very nature they are compromises, because what is being done is far from ideal. And yet there may sometimes be family situations in which a whole host of adverse social conditions taken together may lead to an inability to cope with the birth of a severely deformed or retarded child. An abortion may, under such dire circumstances, be regarded as the least tragic of a number of tragic options.

I argue in this way because, in Christian terms, we have to be concerned with life after birth as well as life before birth. The choice in this instance is between the good of the fetus and the good of the mother and family, the assumption being that whatever course of action is adopted, the good of one party will be denied. Both the fetus and the family are flawed, and it is this combination that constitutes the conflict. If one or other of the parties is not flawed in a major way, abortion would not be an acceptable course of action.

I am not, therefore, advocating easy abortion and certainly not abortion-on-demand. My argument is based on the premise that the decision to abort is made on profoundly serious grounds and not for overtly self-centred reasons, and I would *always* prefer an alternative course of action. The question which arises, therefore, is whether there are alternatives to an abortion on the grounds of an inability to cope with the demands of a retarded or abnormal child?

Undoubtedly there are alternatives and, from a Christian point of view, alternatives aimed at preserving fetal life would be preferable to fetal destruction. One alternative would be to continue with the pregnancy and make the child available for adoption. If the child is mentally retarded or physically deformed, however, there may be a plethora of difficulties, including guilt on the mother's part in relinquishing the child and the adverse effects on the child's development of an institutional environment if it is not adopted. Another alternative would be for the mother (and family) to keep the child, and to be supported subsequently by a caring community. This is the ideal situation, and yet how often does it eventuate in practice?

These are not easy issues, and I do not believe there are easy answers to them. Fetal preservation is always the course of choice in Christian terms, and yet the welfare of the subsequent handicapped child and of the surrounding family also needs to be taken into account. This, too, is a part of Christian holism.

The good of the parents is difficult to justify in straightforward terms. It is an elusive concept, and has always to be balanced against what is being inflicted on the fetus. The welfare of the parents has to be taken into account, as does that of the prospective child. The question is: how can this be done? Generally speaking, far too little information is available in specific instances, and our ability at predicting future outcomes for both parents and child is abysmal.

No matter what our inclination, we need to return to a basic principle, and this is that genetically defective individuals are human beings who, in many instances, have unmistakable marks of personhood. Even very deformed children may demonstrate human qualities in abundance. A deformity should be very major before an abortion is even considered and it should be demonstrated somehow that the deformity is so great that it will rob the fetus of any potentially personal qualities. After all, what is under discussion is the responsibility of one person to decide in advance for *another* person that this other person's future life will not be worth living. This is an onerous—perhaps an unreal—responsibility, and should never be lightly accepted.

We must now turn to the fetus and ask what degree of fetal abnormality may warrant an abortion. I do not believe hard-and-fast rules are appropriate, since our predisposition should always be against abortion. Hence, I am not suggesting that a fetus with condition *A* should *always* be aborted, nor that a fetus with condition *B* should *never* be aborted. The ideal would be not to abort either fetus. Nevertheless, if it appears that a family will be unable to cope with a severely handicapped child and if adequate alternatives are unavailable or unacceptable, and an abortion is contemplated, the extent of fetal abnormality needs to be taken into account.

The question now becomes whether it is possible to determine what conditions may rob a fetus of any potentially personal qualities. Two extreme examples may set the scene. On the one hand, potentially personal qualities will almost certainly be lacking in the case of a fetus with anencephaly, where major brain centres are lacking and where there is no prospect of anything remotely resembling human life. At the other extreme, a fetus of the 'wrong' sex quite obviously has all the qualities of personhood expected of a fetus at its stage of development. The anencephalic fetus could legitimately be aborted; the fetus of the opposite sex from that desired by the parents could never be legitimately aborted.

Between these broad extremes are the much more realistic situations regularly faced by expectant parents and clinicians, such as pregnancies affected by German measles or one of a whole range of viral infections that can occur during the first three months of gestation. Only a certain percentage of these pregnancies will result in the birth of deformed children, and the nature and severity of the deformities will vary considerably from one pregnancy to another. These infections are often sources of intense anxiety for the pregnant mother, and they should not be lightly dismissed. The element of uncertainty about the outcomes of *individual* pregnancies, however, is a source of considerable difficulty when generalizing. Nevertheless, my own predilection would be against abortion, since in most instances the fetuses (and consequent children) will display personal qualities in abundance.

My conclusion in the case of fetuses (and children) with Down's syndrome is the same; here again, I do not accept the legitimacy of aborting a fetus with Down's syndrome. These children display many qualities of personhood. This, however, should not lead us to underestimate the personal anguish suffered by some parents with a Down's syndrome child, especially if the parents are relatively old at the time of the birth. Support and care may be needed by some of these families for many years after the birth, and support of this order should be recognized as a major way in which Christians can uphold the dignity and value of all human life.

Very difficult decisions are presented by pregnancies in which the resulting children will have limited features of personhood and very severe behaviour disorders. An example is the rare Lesch-Nyhan syndrome, in which there is abnormal purine metabolism due to an X-linked genetic abnormality. All patients are males and are mentally retarded showing compulsive self-mutilation, biting and destroying fingers and lip tissue. They have difficulty in swallowing and frequently vomit. They may scream incessantly, and appear to be happy only when protected from themselves by being physically restrained. Sufferers with this syndrome cannot walk and cannot be toilet trained. Death generally occurs by the age of 10 years. Tay-Sachs disease also has serious clinical consequences, with a rapid deterioration of vision and motor skills after 6-9 months of age. Death ensues by 2-4 years. Its alternative name of amaurotic idiocy gives some idea of its behavioural consequences, and of the mental retardation implicit in the condition.

The good of all who might be directly involved in the birth of a severely deformed child needs to be considered. In making the decision, a balance needs to be attained between the pursuit of biological quality and the potential that a deformed child within a family holds out for that family to be humanized and to grow as a loving, human unit. Unfortunately some families cannot cope with such a challenge, and a compromise may be reluctantly adopted, namely, termination of the pregnancy.

God's love for the weak and fragile requires that we show comparable concern for the abnormal and for those likely to be rejected by society. Fetuses are not merely physicochemical mechanisms to be eliminated at will, even though the intentions may appear good. They are to be viewed with concern, because they are human and because all members of the human community are genetically imperfect. Genetic perfection is an unattainable ideal, and our actions in readily eliminating genetically defective fetuses are not to be guided by such an ideal.

Ours is a fallen world, and the genetically defective are one manifestation of that fallenness. Whatever way we cope with the genetically defective, therefore, is to reflect concern for the weak and defenceless, whether these be fetuses, distraught parents, or even a bewildered society. In general, helping the handicapped, not taking their life in advance, is the way to improve the quality of human life.

Christians should be careful that they do not lose sight of the tradition of mutual care, in favour of a concept of disposal. Mutual care is a constant obligation, no matter what the likely result of medical procedures. Disposal, by contrast, is a short-term technological solution to humanly insoluble problems. Of the two, mutual care is the human answer, based in the love shown by God for broken humanity.

My aim in this discussion has been to maintain the Christian ideal of life preservation in situations where abnormality and handicap seem likely to overwhelm individuals and families. In this context I have been prepared to allow that there may be extreme situations where abortion is undertaken in the face of what appear to be enormous difficulties. I realize that, for some, this will prove an unacceptable position, because fetal life must never be sacrificed and/or because the Christian path must always be one of protection of the handicapped.

I sympathize with both objections, since both point very clearly towards the ideal for Christians. Nevertheless a compromise is sometimes called for, whether this be a reluctant abortion, institutional care of the child, or adoption. Although the latter may signify the preference of many Christians, it may not be acceptable to the mother or family. Another way has then to be accepted.

The major objection to the position I have outlined is that abortion on genetic grounds violates the principle of justice. This is because defective individuals are being selected for destruction. To single out the handicapped for death goes against the whole spirit of the biblical ethos, according to which the godly have a special duty to protect the weak and disadvantaged. Gordon Wenham, in his treatment of this subject, also argues that to abort the handicapped is to deny the doctrines of our redemption, in that Christ identified with broken humanity and not with the physically perfect (Isaiah 42:19; 52:14).

These are principles with which I agree, and they are ones that have featured prominently in my treatment of genetic abortion. The major thrust of these principles is against the destruction of fetal life for eugenic purposes. To destroy a fetus because its quality of life is substandard is to violate God's care for the handicapped and down-trodden. When the fetus is viewed in isolation, therefore, these are critical guideposts for Christian thinking. However, when fetal considerations have to be weighed against the type of family considerations I have outlined previously, the course of action is not always as clear-cut. Appalling dilemmas do occur, and appalling dilemmas sometimes have to be faced. My argument has been that some of these appalling dilemmas may be resolvable only by therapeutic abortion.

## Living on a knife-edge

Abortion, especially for therapeutic reasons, confronts Christians with the agony of sometimes having to choose between what they recognize as the ideal—protection of fetal life—and what may seem inevitable in some circumstances—destruction of fetal life. For those Christians who find themselves in counselling and obstetric situations, this is an invidious choice to have to make. Some may argue that it should never be made—abortion is always wrong, and Christians in counselling roles should refuse ever to make a pro-abortion decision. It is better to refer the patient elsewhere than to make such a decision.

While respecting the integrity of those arguing in this way, I am unhappy with this course of action because it refuses to come to terms with all the relationships of which the woman seeking a therapeutic abortion is a part. Assuming that the abortion is being sought on serious therapeutic grounds, the woman is a human being in need not just of an abortion, but of advice, direction and perhaps comfort. And it is at all those points that Christians, as God's representatives, can contribute with comfort and wisdom alongside their counselling expertise.

Christians may well find that their inclination to preserve the life of a fetus is much greater than is that of many non-Christians. This is the source of considerable tension in this area. What then becomes crucial is the response to this tension—whether to increase it by stressing the gap between the opposing viewpoints or to decrease it by searching for common ground between the two positions.

If the viewpoints are seen as mutually exclusive, Christians will find themselves unable to function in therapeutic areas involving possible abortion. This, in turn, will isolate them from the needs of a major sector of health care. Such a stance, however, is required only of those for whom *abortion under all circumstances* is ethically unacceptable.

Alternatively, those who adopt a position on abortion similar to the one outlined in this chapter will seek to find points of contact with those holding more liberal positions on abortion. For myself, abortion is always a last resort, and is always an admission that a family (and society) will probably be unable to cope with the demands of a handicapped child. The factors which have to be weighed up when contemplating a therapeutic abortion are relative ones. Christians with a high view of human life will emphasize the preservation of life, and yet will also take into account the mental, spiritual and financial resources of the family and also the availability of social and welfare services for handicapped children in the community.

It is not sufficient for Christians to emphasize the inviolability of fetal life, and yet fail to provide support for those families having to look after mentally retarded and physically handicapped children and adults. Crusades in favour of life need to be matched by social services and appropriate schooling for the handicapped. Christian organizations and churches should be in the forefront of providing these services in communities where they are inadequately funded.

James, in his New Testament letter, writes on the quality of faith: 'What good is it, my brothers, if a man claims to have faith but has no deeds? Can such faith save him? Suppose a brother or sister is without clothes and daily food. If one of you says to him, "Go, I wish you well; keep warm and well fed," but does nothing about his physical needs, what good is it? In the same way, faith by itself, if it is not accompanied by action, is dead' (James 2:14–17). The application of these words to the preservation of fetal life with known deformities, and the subsequent care of those disabled individuals, is clear. The one must be accompanied by the other.

Christians are rightly alarmed at the little regard for human life shown by those who advocate abortion-on-demand. Such an attitude, however, should not be carried over into debates on therapeutic abortion without taking account of the many other factors relevant in the therapeutic situation. While this is not an argument in favour of a liberal position on abortion or of a low view of fetal life, it is a plea to Christians to respond to therapeutic abortion in ethical and not political terms. The condemnation of all abortion under all circumstances is an attractively simple solution to the evils connected with easy abortion. Nevertheless it may be a political rather than a theological solution, and it may have limited Christian content. Abortion for therapeutic reasons demands a serious response by those professing to follow Christ. All Christians will not recommend the same course of action in given situations, but they should all take serious account of the good of the fetus, the spiritual and human resources of the parents, and the help provided by society.

Throughout discussions on genetic abnormality care is required to maintain the distinction between the person and the disease. Otherwise the conclusion will soon be reached that the afflicted person or fetus *is,* rather than *has,* a disease. It is easy to slide from the language of possession to that of identity, so that 'he has haemophilia' becomes 'he is a haemophiliac'. When this transition occurs, the impression is given that the goal of abortion is the elimination of persons rather than the treatment of diseases. Christians need to cling to the value of the individual persons involved in any decision to abort a fetus.

They also need to cling to the context in which abortions are carried out. In this regard, a quotation ascribed to Mother Teresa is helpful:

> The biggest disease today is not leprosy or cancer. It's the feeling of being uncared for, unwanted—of being deserted and alone. The greatest evil is the lack of love and charity, and an indifference towards one's neighbour who may be a victim of poverty or disease, or exploited and at the end of his life, left by the roadside.

Genetic abnormality, with its resulting physical and mental deficiencies, should not be isolated from the neglect and abuse of a child, with their resulting physical and mental consequences. As far as possible the causes in both cases are to be prevented and the results are to be treated. However important the genetic and allied causes, it may well be that far more damage to children results from parental neglect, and from a lack of love and of a healthy physical and mental environment.

Whatever our practical response to genetic abnormality, handicapped fetuses, children and adults are constant reminders of the limitations of our present existence. Our flawed humanity is the context of life now. Decisions relating to the handicapped should always be difficult and will prove too onerous for some to bear. This is the knife-edge along which we walk. But as we do we should be encouraged by the prophecy of Isaiah that, ultimately, 'then will the eyes of the blind be opened and the ears of the deaf unstopped. Then will the lame leap like a deer, and the tongue of the dumb shout for joy' (Isaiah 35:5–6).

# 8
# Human technology and human values

## Towards an uncertain future

Our future inheritance can no longer be regarded as assured; whether we like it or not, it will undergo radical change. There is no escape from IVF, AID, amniocentesis, prenatal diagnosis of genetic disease, therapeutic abortion and many other consequences of technological medicine. It is just as certain that, in the near future, there will be no escape from surrogate motherhood, ovum transfer, cloning and ectogenesis. Whether or not we consider these to be the ingredients of the brave new world is largely irrelevant; they are the ingredients of *our* world, and we are the ones who have to contend with them.

They are also the ingredients of *God's* world. It is easy to overlook this when immersed in the myriad details of technological wizardry. This is God's world, just as much as the Middle Ages or the times of Christ were God's world. The principles of living enunciated by Christ are, therefore, just as relevant to the contemporary world as they were in AD 30. Although there are many areas where the teaching of Christ cannot be applied in a neat black-and-white manner, the principles laid down by him are still paramount in sorting out priorities and relationships, and in underlining the value of human life, the significance of individuals, and the place of mercy and compassion in dealing with people. Apart from such principles, technology will undoubtedly run wild and will transform human beings into robot-like mechanisms.

We are dealing with new issues, demanding creative and perhaps original answers. Control over many facets of human life is increasingly coming within the ambit of human responsibility and irresponsibility. Decisions are having to be made in areas where decisions were not previously required. From these decisions there is no escape; this is both a challenge to be welcomed and an area to be feared. Either way, there is no escaping dilemmas of untold and unexperienced proportions, which will tax our value-systems to the utmost.

Perhaps the supreme question confronting us is our own nature, because the dynamic of modern biology is rapidly bestowing upon the human race the ability to alter human beings in profound biological ways. The means to accomplish this are found in the realms of genetic engineering, reproductive biology, brain manipulation and psychological conditioning. Techniques in all these realms force us to examine our view of human nature in new and forbidding contexts.

While various issues have emerged in the course of the previous chapters, a number of general ones remain to be discussed. It is these which will be the focus of our attention in this final chapter.

## Quality control and foreknowledge

Quality control forces us to consider our expectations of what constitutes normal human experience. Technical advances in the realm of biological engineering have dramatically altered these expectations. Very easily the assumption is made that normal human life excludes, almost by definition, experiences involving stress, tension and deformity. Human well-being is readily equated with biological well-being.

Technological developments in biology and medicine are accompanied by changes in our expectations of normality; quality control takes this process even further. But should we equate fulfilment with biological excellence, and should we allow concepts of human biological normality to be transformed in this way?

For Christians, human beings are rooted in nature and, as such, share the finitude, creatureliness and death of all living things. Besides this, they are also made in the likeness of God and so can be addressed by God and can respond to the demands of righteousness and justice. Normality, therefore, while it can and does change, has limits and biological perfectibility, whatever that might mean, is outside those limits. This is a subtle factor we dare not overlook, however, because our expectations of what ordinary life will give us are undoubtedly very different from those of our grandparents. In this regard Christians are very much subject to the pressures of their society, and this means the pressures of modern biological and medical procedures. These procedures are drastically altering what we expect to get out of life and, if we are not very careful, they may also alter our view of what life means.

We are living in an age of enormous flux biologically, and this has dramatic implications for our Christianity. It touches us as individuals and as families, so that it has become impossible to ask what modern biology means without also asking what it means for each one of us as individuals. It is an immensely practical question, because it is now possible to think seriously about human fulfilment without taking God into account. And yet, in a Christian perspective, there cannot be true fulfilment apart from an active and meaningful relationship to God.

Quality control, therefore, brings us face to face with the relationship between human well-being and biological/physical well-being. Once we equate the two, we have made the profound statement that human existence can be reduced to a set of physical equations, and that human relationships, aspirations and endeavours are of no significance. Our desire for improving the quality of our physical lives, therefore, needs to be controlled by a human framework, and we should resist the temptation to make a fetish of quality. Important as quality control is, it is not an absolute, neither is it an end in itself. To make it a way of life is to deify it.

We are now being forced to make ethical decisions in situations which previously did not demand such decisions. For example, a hundred years and more ago, because of the high infant mortality rate, a couple was not faced with the decision of how many children to have. As infant mortality and human fertility have come under human control, so decision-making has come to the fore. How many children? How are they to be spaced? These may not appear major choices to have to make, and yet the process is taken much further with the advent of AID, safe and liberalized abortion, and IVF.

Foreknowledge, with all its attendant responsibilities, is not a light matter. It is associated with the ever-increasing likelihood of change in our lives and the ever-increasing freedom accompanying that change. Unfortunately there is a great deal we do not know and there are many decisions we are ill-equipped to take. Freedom, therefore, may pose as many problems as it solves. It is generally much easier to live in relative ignorance and cope with difficulties as they arise, than be faced with a conglomeration of decisions to which there are no ready solutions. It may even be argued that there is a certain level of ignorance of future events essential for mental health.

The repeated biblical injunctions against attempting to delve into the future may help at this point. Whether it was sorcery, as with Saul in the Old Testament, or simply the longing to know details of Christ's second coming, the principle is the same – it is the desire to view the present in terms of the future. For such desires the Bible, and Christ himself, have no sympathy, because they enshrine a lessening of present responsibilities and present realities.

The danger with too much foreknowledge in the scientific sense is that the complexities and conundrums coming with it become too great for us to cope with. Once this occurs, we become paralysed and are unable to deal effectively even with the simpler realities of the present. The realm of unlimited choice is not the realm of unhampered bliss; it is the harbinger of neuroticism and despair.

## Towards the ideal human

One of the more futuristic issues repeatedly raised by genetic engineering is that of transforming individuals, and even the human species, from what we are at present to something 'better'.

Although based in science, these are not scientific issues. What is 'better'? Is there an 'ideal' human? At a more prosaic level, is it possible to 'improve upon' the human condition? What would such improvement entail?

The very idea of the ideal human has roots in the belief that human beings are perfectible, a belief contrary to the fallenness of humans as depicted throughout the Bible. It is also opposed to the biblical insistence on the gulf between God, the Creator, and man, the created. To be perfect is to be god, to enter into the realm of the transcendent. This is the antithesis of the biblical emphasis on the transcendence of God and the finiteness of humans.

Even at the pragmatic level, however, it should be obvious that we are nothing like perfectible. So much that we touch suffers from the contact, rather than being enhanced by it. Our experience tells us that we are often ruled by self-interest and greed, and by national and racial prejudice, even when confronted by scientific possibilities that could benefit all.

Granted that the ideal human is not to be seriously considered, what about limited advance? Perhaps humans can be modified to bring about some measure of improvement. Even here, though, there is a difficulty. If humans are to modify humans, what models are available? In what directions would we like to see changes made, and why? Jacques Ellul has made the rather unflattering comment that those with the power of remodelling humans will make them in their own image. The new will not be new at all; simply a refurbishing of the old. However cynical we may think this response, it is a perceptive one. No matter how immense our technological prowess, the questions on which our studies are based are *our* questions, reflecting *our* attitudes and *our* expectations. The direction in which technology is pushed is the direction provided by us, a direction reflecting our presuppositions as well as our limitations. We are poor at answering long-term questions, and it is fatuous to suppose that we have any ability at all to provide an adequate basis for the most long-term of all biological goals – the production of an ideal human being.

No matter what our reaction to this issue, whether to regard it as a possibility or an absurdity, one thing is clear – it is not a scientific issue. It takes us into the area of values and aspirations which themselves depend upon our view of human existence.

I want to argue that our principal task in the biomedical area is to remedy defects rather than to attempt to construct the ideal person. I am suggesting that there is an important distinction between remedying defects and alleviating suffering on the one hand, and actually attempting to improve the human model on the other. The former course of action accepts humans as we know them as the norm; the latter strives to transform contemporary humans along biological lines. This is the contrast between remedial and manipulatory approaches.

We need to remember that, no matter how compelling some human achievements may appear, our capabilities remain very limited in very many areas. We cannot transcend our creatureliness to become something other than we are. Alongside this consideration should be placed another one, that of a fundamental dichotomy in our make-up between wholeness and destructiveness. In Christian terms this is inevitable, stemming as it does from our alienation from God and our consequent inability to find fulfilment and harmony in life. We strive for wholeness and yet find that failure and dissatisfaction mar our efforts. All too often, the things we can 'do' far outstrip our ability to control and direct those capabilities.

There is no 'ideal' in human efforts, but there are the realistic and all-important tasks of remedying defects and diminishing suffering. These are therapeutic goals that must not be submerged beneath a welter of implausible vistas. They are Christian ideals, because they seek to bring wholeness and purpose to real human beings contending with a real, if fallen, world. They enshrine the standards of Christ, with an emphasis on sacrifice and self-effacement. To achieve them, however, does not entail a biological revolution but a spiritual one; the transformation is one of attitudes, not of genes.

Talk of improvement, then, is useful, so long as it is removed from the biological context. Donald MacKay, for instance, suggests that improvement means an enhancement of people's capacities to relate better to God and to one another. This is a valuable principle which MacKay takes even further when he distinguishes between contentment with the unalterable and complacency with the alterable. This, too, is useful. In ordinary day-to-day existence, far away from the heady heights of genetic research, it is so easy to put up with mediocrity for no better reason than that we like apathy and sloth. So much could be improved, so many people's living conditions and standard of health could be ameliorated, but for these vices. Bad genes are not always to blame.

It may, of course, be difficult to decide what is alterable and what is unalterable. There is no doubt this is, to some extent, a relative matter. Nonetheless, from a Christian standpoint, the ultimate criterion must be: What will make the most acceptable possible offering to God? We must be prepared to work within the alterable/unalterable framework, recognizing the limitations bestowed upon us by human finiteness.

Bernard Häring, by contrast, in his book *Manipulation*, argues that, since man's biological nature is entrusted to his freedom and wisdom, he is the steward of his genetic heritage. This enables us to plan our genetic future, so that at some future time it may be possible to accelerate hominization by genetic means. For Häring, a Roman Catholic theologian, this position is based on the assumption that creation is an unfinished work calling for human co-operation in bringing it to 'greater perfection'. And so, according to Häring, human beings are called to become an even better image of God than at present.

The tenuousness of Häring's position is evident even from his own writings. He admits that acceptable criteria must be found to minimize the possibility of unrealistic and irresponsible interventions, while he ponders uneasily over the question of whether the intelligence that can be genetically influenced is the kind of intelligence most needed. This unease stems from the possibility, even likelihood, that improvement of biological quality and improvement of moral qualities, such as wisdom, moral responsibility and altruism, are unrelated. Biological quality control, therefore, is an issue on its own, to be debated on its own merits.

Häring is forced to draw a distinction between improvement of the genetic heritage of the human species and change of the species. By the latter, I take him to mean extreme forms of genetic manipulation that radically interfere with genuine human intercommunication. In practice, therefore, Häring would probably allow only limited self-modification. But if this is so, is it of any benefit to anyone? In the long run, the difficulties of his position outweigh any postulated advantages.

Another way of approaching this issue is via the incarnation. Not only are humans made in God's image, but the Son of God took to himself human identity, so revealing the image of God in human form. As a result Christ, who was one with God before the incarnation, became a real man at his incarnation without in any way ceasing to be God. More than this; when Christ ascended he maintained his manhood – albeit glorified and exalted. In remaining human, Christ has bestowed upon the human race, and human beings in their present form, an unequalled value. Consequently individuals as we now know them are of such value that we are to be satisfied with the type of body, brain and genetic inheritance we currently possess. There is room neither for the fashioning of a radically new type of human being, nor for the manipulation of individuals in the hope of producing improved and perhaps novel beings. On the other hand, recognized defects in individuals demand treatment in accordance with normal medical practice. We do our best to heal sickness and restore people to normal health, but we do not entertain grand visions of a science fiction type of human being who never suffers, is never ill and is invincible. Christ became like one of us, not like one of the heroes of a science fiction writer's imagination.

## Human responsibility

Our technological prowess has brought both the internal and external environments within the scope of our control. This means we have some control at least over our own potential as human beings. In this, I recognize an extension of the God-given mandate to subdue the earth and bring it within our control.

However, once we accept responsibility for nature, we cannot escape from continuing responsibility. We must treat nature in the same selfless fashion as we should treat our fellow humans. We are nature's keeper just as much as we are our brother's keeper. This should come as no surprise, because nature, like the human race, is the handiwork of God, who has lovingly brought it into being and continues lovingly to care for it. From this it follows that once we intervene in the processes of nature, continued intervention is imperative. Failure in this task is accompanied by a scarring of nature.

With respect to biomedical ethics, Thielicke draws out the principle in the following way. 'It is quite impossible', he writes, 'to intervene at only one point, and then at a second point to hold back and do nothing about the resulting disruption of the hereditary stream . . . It is rather a question of willingly assuming the further responsibility of intervening once again.'

Here we are confronted by the difficult relationship between the individual and the species. In alleviating the suffering of an individual, or allowing into existence an individual who would otherwise not have lived, we may be altering the genetic balance of the species. The dilemma is that we do not seem to possess acceptable criteria for making such a choice. So much of traditional bioethics is directed solely towards the good of the individual patient. Unfortunately the good of the individual has repercussions for the species and for nature, and these repercussions may not be overwhelmingly good.

There are two quite different levels of concern, namely, the individual level and the species level. The family doctor's concern must always be with the individual. The biomedical scientist, by contrast, is more concerned with the species, or at least with society. Technological possibilities are the realm in which the scientist works, whereas the application of these possibilities within a human framework and for real people is the sphere of the doctor.

Decisions regarding existence or non-existence belong ideally to the period prior to conception, when theoretical issues can be debated and when the pros and cons of bringing a person into existence can be dispassionately assessed. Once a fetus or an actual person exists, that individual is to be treated as of utmost importance, regardless of what deleterious genes he or she is carrying or what cost his or her upkeep is to society.

Technological progress needs to be viewed, therefore, with these different levels in mind, since they highlight different ways in which our technological abilities may be applied. What they emphasize is the short- and long-term uses of these abilities, the short-term revolving around the treatment of individual patients and the long-term their cumulative, and often unforeseen, effects on whole populations. Herein lies the ambiguity of technological progress, with progress and regress being intertwined. For instance, effective treatment of those suffering from diabetes or PKU may have consequences for those individuals later in life and, if they reproduce, will have further consequences for their offspring.

In these examples we catch a glimpse of the tension between the beneficial treatment of an individual and what may turn out to be the deleterious consequences of this treatment for that individual's offspring. A similar tension is seen in the beneficial effects of improved public health facilities for individuals, communities and whole societies, and the longer-term problems created by a subsequent explosion in birth rates. What emerges from these illustrations is that we are incapable of bringing about unambiguous progress. Human responsibility lies in balancing the advantages and disadvantages of our technological prowess. How do we do this?

An alluring point of view is that the long-term difficulties arising from technological advances are temporary ones, and that in the final analysis ambiguities reflect a lack of technological expertise. To an extent this is true. The replacement of a defective gene by a normal one, as envisaged by recombinant DNA technology, will in all probability revolutionize the treatment of diabetes and other comparable genetic diseases. And yet there remains a problem. Genetic diseases will not disappear overnight, just as infectious diseases have not disappeared overnight. The deficiency, even when treatable, remains. Our biological nature, even though modifiable, cannot be readily transformed.

Alongside this is the knowledge that humans in their sinful state will misuse the possibilities opened up by genetic or any other form of manipulation. This is not an all-or-nothing phenomenon; the good and evil uses to which it will be put are intermingled. More often than not any particular use will incorporate both aspects. This is a reflection not only of our sinful state, but also of the sinful world in which we live with its prominent manifestations of the fall. The ways in which genetic manipulation may mould us, therefore, will inevitably reflect what we are as sinners living in a world tainted by sin. While this is not an argument against the use of biomedical technology, it is a reminder of its limitations.

We have to live with the disadvantages, as well as the advantages, of biomedical technology. For Christians, it is important to ensure that the disadvantages do not fall unduly heavily on individuals. Technological procedures need to be assessed with the good of the individual patient in mind, so that the welfare of individuals is not sacrificed for the 'greater good' of the community, the state or the species. This is a difficult area, but we must beware of forcing others to make sacrifices they would not knowingly make for themselves.

Once an individual exists, human relationships are critical – relationships between that individual and others, between that individual and society, between that individual and the medical profession. Human concerns, rather than abstract principles, are paramount when an individual, or even a potential individual, is the object of attention. This is where Christian concerns, with their emphasis on compassion, forgiveness, the significance of human life, love for one's neighbour, and care for the weak and the frail, come into play.

Biomedical technology has the ability to decrease what is unknown in the biomedical domain. Nevertheless, it does not of necessity enable us to cope more adequately with the unknown in ordinary existence. However able we may become at increasing our control over the physical world, including our physical bodies, we must avoid the temptation to conclude that this enables us to live better controlled lives in the spiritual and social realms.

Biomedical technology, *per se*, does not lead to either environmental or inner peace. The words of Christ are just as applicable in a technological society as they were in an agrarian one: 'Peace I leave with you; my peace I give you. I do not give to you as the world gives' (John 14:27). To seek comfort, therefore, in a perfect body or in an exemplary level of physical health is to seek comfort in that which will disintegrate. And yet it is with the transient that technology deals. This is not to denigrate it, merely to place it in its appropriate context.

Technology neither leads towards, nor away from, God. Its level is that of the physical and material. In the biomedical sphere, it is concerned with our bodies and our physical welfare. The danger lies in our misunderstanding of it, because we misunderstand ourselves and the purposes of God. We expect biomedical technology to change us, as people, and to alter our goals and aspirations. Once we do this, we make technology a religion and it becomes an end in and of itself.

Technology is never a substitute for faith in the living God. Our technological expertise is a part of the riches bestowed upon us by God, and as such is to be employed wisely and responsibly. We are to be thankful for these riches, but we are also to realize the responsibility bestowed upon us to be faithful in our stewardship of such abundant resources. We are never to confuse these riches with faith. If we do, we confuse the creature with the Creator, and the difference between inordinate dependence upon man and worshipful dependence upon God.

## Suffering

The dynamic behind medical therapy, including genetic therapy, is the desire to relieve suffering. The distinction which needs to be made is between the relief of suffering within a wider human and ethical context and the relief of suffering *at all costs*. This is the distinction between regarding suffering as having positive as well as negative overtones, and viewing it as unmitigated evil. Our view of suffering will have repercussions, therefore, for our ethical system.

Suffering is a universal phenomenon. It is an integral part of the world we know and experience, with the result that we cannot conceive of a world devoid of suffering. Much of our experience is founded on either the direct sensation of pain or our response to some form of emotional trauma, so that the reality we know is woven around suffering and pain. Suffering is both a manifestation of a world in which sin is present and a means that God can use to direct and teach his people (*e.g.* Job 1:21; 2:10; 2 Corinthians 5:15; 1 Thessalonians 5:10; 1 Peter 4:1–2). Suffering, therefore, cannot be eradicated by changing either genes or the environment. This can never be the ultimate aim of genetic manipulation or any other medical therapy, although it may well diminish the degree of suffering experienced by individuals. Even here, however, suffering and its relief should not be isolated from the human condition.

In some senses, suffering is basic to human life. It can serve to place the limitations of human existence in perspective, reminding us that we are limited, temporal beings. On the other hand we cannot live with unbearable suffering.

Herein lies a conflict. Another expression of this conflict is provided by the importance of healing. Christ healed physical disabilities, but in so doing restored people to wholeness. For him, physical and spiritual problems were much of a piece. We too have a duty to restore people, as far as possible, to wholeness. This reminds us of the principle that the biological side of humans can never be separated from the whole person.

The goal of healing, including genetic counselling and genetic manipulation, is the benefit of the patient. This is the primary duty of medical care, with actual patients as 'ends' rather than 'means'. If this is the case, individuals and fetuses are more important than statistical risks, hypothetical individuals (ones as yet unconceived) or even the human species (a non-patient which cannot be treated). Herein lies further conflict. Neither future individuals nor the species are unimportant; nevertheless the object of medical treatment is always a real person.

It is imperative that the pursuit of physical perfection is not placed above the enhancement of specifically human characteristics. There is an inequality in biology, with which we must cope. This is epitomized by genetics. As Professor Charles Birch puts it: 'All men are different. Some are endowed with the capacity for developing many talents, others have a few. Still others are burdened with serious genetic defects that incapacitate them for life.' For Birch this realization highlights the unity of mankind, the cost of creation and the requirement of justice that we reduce and share the total genetic burden.

This sentiment brings us face to face with the essence of the human predicament, a predicament with roots in human sinfulness. To share the genetic burden of the human population is to become one with the afflicted, suffering with them and giving of ourselves in love and practical concern. To reduce the genetic burden may involve just this as well; however, it also ushers in the prospect of using genetic manipulatory techniques, some of which present few ethical problems while others are replete with hazardous ethical decisions. When compassion and ethical concerns appear to pull in opposing directions, we find ourselves at the heart of the human dilemma.

## Accountability

'Love of one's neighbour' emerges as a fundamental biblical principle in the area of social ethics. We are responsible for the welfare of our neighbour, whoever that might be. We are accountable to each other, in that we cannot go our own way totally regardless of the good of those around us. Individualism can be a self-centred excess, as well as a legitimate concern for the dignity of individual people.

To translate accountability at this general level into the accountability of a specific professional group requires a vast leap. Nevertheless, no profession can ignore its accountability to society. In terms of the issues discussed in this book, the profession we are concerned with is the medical profession.

It has become very clear that, in a world dominated by biomedical technology, it is easy for the medical profession to develop techniques that interest it regardless of their likely consequences for society. IVF became a viable procedure in both Britain and Australia against a background of few discussions on its social and ethical repercussions. Once viable, it raised the expectations of society and therefore generated pressures from society for the technique to be perfected and to be made available to all who might benefit from it. A vicious circle is soon set up, and from this circle neither the medical profession nor the community can readily escape.

These expectations and pressures within society should always be anticipated, and account should be taken of them before the biomedical procedures have advanced too far. Before this can happen, however, the medical profession has to recognize its accountability to society. Neither it, nor any other professional group, is a law unto itself. All within society are interdependent; all are neighbours. To neglect our interdependence is to ignore our neighbourliness, and to open the way to power struggles within society.

To argue that the medical profession is accountable to society is also to argue that the physical well-being of people cannot be isolated from their social and spiritual well-being. Quality of life encompasses all these forms of well-being; to have one at the expense of the others is to lack overall quality. An excellent genetic constitution is of little value to a severely malnourished person or to a child deprived of parental affection. The existence of a technique for alleviating a physical deformity or for correcting a malfunctioning organ is of little value if its cost is prohibitive to the individual or the community.

Biomedical advance needs to be seen within the perspective of a society's priorities. When one section of the medical profession is devoted to destroying potential human life, and other sections to heroic efforts at salvaging badly deformed life or bringing life into existence, it becomes evident that this technology is being directed by conflicting principles. The questions which arise are: what are these principles, and whose good are they serving?

If they are enhancing the total quality of life, they are to be welcomed. Alternatively, if they are serving greed and self and are life-denying, they amount to a negation of God's purposes for his creation. The ends to which new biomedical techniques are directed is a matter not only for the medical profession, but also for society as a whole, for ethicists and theologians, for lawyers and politicians, for social workers and nurses.

## Compassion and forgiveness

Our responses to the issues raised in the previous chapters have all been illuminated by biblical teaching. And yet with most of the issues there have also been areas of uncertainty, due to their inherent complexity, to our limited understanding of them or to our unwillingness to accept hard answers. For whatever reason, there are grey areas where exceptions to a general rule may have to be accepted.

Misunderstanding can very easily arise in situations such as these. Charges of compromise are made, a person's or a group's commitment to the Bible is called in question, and the issue itself is not tackled. The questions with which I have been dealing take us to the heart of human existence and the meaning of human life. Often there are no easy answers in this realm, and there is certainly no room for slick over-simplification.

A Christian, seeking to be guided by biblically-based ethical considerations, has to face quite realistically horrendously complex and frequently heart-rending dilemmas in the area of fetal life. Conflict situations all too often arise, and they have to be faced. Simple black-and-white absolute answers may not suffice in such instances. How do we respond to those torn in two by such conflicts? How do we respond to those whose decision is one which we ourselves would not have taken? How do we respond to Christian doctors and social workers who, in their dealings with patients having a quite different ethical stance from ours (and theirs), recommend courses of action of which we disapprove?

While the biomedical issues may be new ones, useful pointers to the attitudes we should adopt were provided by Jesus. When confronted by a woman caught in the act of adultery (John 8:1–11), Jesus did not simply deal with its sinfulness (Mark 10:19) but placed the incident in its human context. He was concerned not only with its illegality in terms of the law of Moses, but also with the motives of the teachers of the law and the Pharisees who had brought her to him, their own sinfulness, and the spiritual welfare of the woman. In allowing the woman to go, Jesus did not condone her adultery. He impressed upon her its wrongness, and the necessity that she change her way of life. However, he refused to condemn her, because the religious leaders who hoped to use her as a way of trapping Jesus were just as sinful in other areas of their lives.

This incident is a salutary reminder of the need for a balance between justice and mercy, ethical absolutes and compassion, ideals and practice. Forgiveness and understanding will feature large in our response to those who take what may to us be an unacceptable way out of a complex human dilemma. In these circumstances we should see as our priority the rebuilding of a life and the strengthening of a family unit, rather than astringent condemnation and judgmental rebuke.

This is no easy task in a society where scant regard is paid to ethical absolutes and respect for human life. Guide-lines, stemming at least in part from Christian thinking, are essential in the control of IVF, AID, therapeutic abortion and genetic engineering. Without guide-lines it is likely that all these techniques will be accepted in their entirety, or will be condemned outright. Constructive appraisal of techniques in general and their application in particular situations is what is required, not judgmentalism or sentimentalism.

Compassion and forgiveness also demand informed opinions on the part of all Christians. The ability to distinguish between abortion-on-demand and therapeutic abortion, and between AID and adultery, requires knowledge. With this, condemnation may not be as readily forthcoming on the part of some. Further, those who have taken the trouble to think these issues through will have been exposed to the human tragedies lying behind some of them.

When asked by his disciples: 'Who is the greatest in the kingdom of heaven?', Jesus called a little child (Matthew 18:1–9). He then proceeded to use the child as an illustration of the significance of children and also of childlike attitudes. This is an important emphasis for a discussion of biomedicine at the beginning of life, when the fetus and child are of paramount concern. Simplicity, trust, openness and honesty are central characteristics of children, and they are characteristics to be cultivated by adults. They are also seen as being foundational to Christian faith.

The child in all of us reminds us of the occasions when we do not understand the outcome of medical conditions or the implications of our decisions. It impresses upon us the magnitude of our ignorance alongside the dimensions of our understanding. There are many situations in which we should perhaps admit our lack of understanding and our inability to delve into the profound depths of a problem. In these realms we all are children.

To be prepared to admit this is the beginning of wisdom, because it recognizes our limitations. The openness and honesty of this admission are essential for those who would demonstrate compassion and forgiveness to those in need in the biomedical area.

They also give rise to adaptability – the willingness to

change one's attitudes and expectations in the face of rapidly changing technology. This is not the same as changing one's standards or ethical position; it is an openness to accept new solutions to biomedical problems, and to search for more adequate ways of expressing our humanity in the midst of highly impersonal technology. Christians, in particular, are called to be tuned in to change, realizing that the God of history is the same God who works today. The God who was relevant to the theologians of the Reformation is just as relevant to the technocrats of the biomedical revolution. Adaptability of this order is, however, made possible only by attitudes of openness, which expect God to meet us at our point of need, no matter what the context.

## Individual uniqueness

Regardless of which issues we may discuss in the area of biomedical technology, we are never far from the question of our uniqueness as individuals. Of the various ways of expressing this, the following are two striking ones:

I saw it in a book,
In a zoology book –
'Every individual is absolutely unique,
The first and last of its identical kind.'

Unique! The first and last!
Never anybody else just like me!
Never!
Never!
I am the only one just like me,
I am a race by myself;
When I die the world will have lost me
Forever.

Spermatogonia, spermatocytes, spermatozoa,
Oogonia, oocytes, ova –
Then oosperm!
And the three hundred thousand billionth chance
Produced me!
Think of it! The three hundred thousand billionth possibility –

Think if it hadn't happened.

But it did – and never can again. Never.
Chromosomes, chromomeres, chromogen, enzymes,
Protoplasm, germ plasm, cytoplasm, somato-plasm,
Permutation, maturation, segregation, differentiation,
Synapsis, mitosis, ontogeny, phylogeny –
All the combinations and changes and chances
That made me
Can never again come together
Exactly the same.

I am a person of distinction.
I am I.
I am that I am.

(John Barton, *Egomania*)

For you created my inmost being;
  you knit me together in my mother's womb.
I praise you because I am fearfully and wonderfully made;
  your works are wonderful,
  I know that full well.
My frame was not hidden from you
  when I was made in the secret place.
When I was woven together in the depths of the earth,
  your eyes saw my unformed body.
All the days ordained for me
  were written in your book
  before one of them came to be.

(Psalm 139:13–16)

It is appropriate that this topic is expressed poetically in both instances, because the scientific and religious merge at this point. While far more could be written about our uniqueness, this is as far as I wish to go in this book. Our uniqueness has been clarified by our technological skills in the biomedical realm, and this clarity serves to underline our dependence upon God and his purposes. Alongside this, our uniqueness emphasizes the care to be exercised in tampering with unique beings. Each one of us is a unique individual, biologically and in the sight of God, and we have the responsibility of caring for other unique individuals. This is the context in which our uniqueness has to be worked out, and it is the context in which the inevitable ethical dilemmas in biomedical technology have to be explored and resolved.

# Bibliography

In general, books are listed under the chapter in which they feature most prominently. In a few instances, however, some books appear in more than one place.

**Chapter 1**

Carey, G., *I Believe in Man*. Hodder and Stoughton, London, 1977.
Ellison, C. W. (ed.), *Modifying Man: Implications and Ethics*. University Press of America, Washington D.C., 1977.
Evans, C. S., *Preserving the Person*. Inter-Varsity Press, Downers Grove and Leicester, 1977.
Houston, J. M., *I Believe in the Creator*. Hodder and Stoughton, London, 1979.
Kidner, D., *Genesis*. Tyndale Press, London, 1967.
Lewis, C. S., *The Abolition of Man*. Collins/Fount Paperback, Glasgow, 1978 (first published 1943).
Macaulay, R. and Barrs, J., *Christianity with a Human Face*. Inter-Varsity Press, Leicester, 1978.
MacKay, D. M., *Human Science and Human Dignity*. Hodder and Stoughton, London, 1979.

Mascall, E. L., *The Importance of Being Human.* Oxford University Press, London, 1959.

Moss, R., *The Earth in Our Hands.* Inter-Varsity Press, Leicester, 1982.

**Chapter 2**

Allen, D. F., Bird, L. P. and Herrmann, R. L. (eds.), *Whole-Person Medicine.* Inter-Varsity Press, Downers Grove, 1980.

Henry, C. F. H. (ed.), *Horizons of Science.* Harper and Row, New York, 1978.

Hickman, L. and Al-Hibri, A. (eds.), *Technology and Human Affairs.* Mosby, St. Louis, 1981.

Illich, I., *Limits to Medicine.* Penguin, Harmondsworth, 1977.

Kennedy, I., *The Unmasking of Medicine.* Allen and Unwin, London, 1981.

Polanyi, M., *Knowing and Being.* Routledge and Kegan Paul, London, 1969.

Shinn, R. L. (ed.), *Faith and Science in an Unjust World,* Volume 1. World Council of Churches, Geneva, 1980.

Sugden, C., *Radical Discipleship.* Marshalls, London, 1981.

Taylor, R., *Medicine out of Control.* Sun Books, Melbourne, 1979.

Thomas, L., 'The future impact of science and technology on medicine', *BioScience 24*, 99–105 (1974).

Thorson, W. R., 'Reflections on the practice of outworn creeds'; 'Science as the natural philosophy of a Christian'; 'The biblical insights of Michael Polanyi', *Journal of the American Scientific Affiliation 33*, 3–11, 65–73, 129–138 (1981).

**Chapter 3**

Berry, R. J., 'Genetic engineering', *Christian Graduate 26*, 3–7 (1973).

Callahan, D., *The Tyranny of Survival.* Macmillan, New York, 1973.

Callahan, D., 'Health and society: some ethical imperatives', *Daedalus 106*, 23–33 (1977).

Darling, R. B., 'Parents, physicians, and spina bifida', *Hastings Center Report 7*, 10–14 (1977).

Fletcher, J., *The Ethics of Genetic Control: Ending Reproductive Roulette.* Anchor Books, New York, 1974.

Fletcher, J. C. and others, 'Prenatal diagnosis for sex choice', *Hastings Center Report 10*, 15–20 (1980).

Glass, B., 'Science: endless horizons or golden age?', *Science 171*, 23–29 (1971).

Jones, A. and Bodmer, W. F., *Our Future Inheritance: Choice or Chance?* Oxford University Press, London, 1974.

Kolata, G. B., 'Mass screening for neural tube defects', *Hastings Center Report 10*, 8–10 (1980).

Lappé, M., *Genetic Politics.* Simon and Schuster, New York, 1979.

Maynard Smith, J., 'Eugenics and utopia', *Daedalus 94*, 487–505 (1965).

McCormick, R. A., 'The quality of life, the sanctity of life', *Hastings Center Report 8*, 30–36 (1978).

Mertens, T. R. (ed.), *Human Genetics.* Wiley, New York, 1975.

Monteleone, P. L. and Moraczewski, A. S., 'Medical and ethical aspects of the prenatal diagnosis of genetic disease', in T. W. Hilgers, D. J. Horan and D. Mall (eds.), *New Perspectives on Human Abortion.* University Publications of America, Maryland, 1981, pp. 45–59.

Ramsey, P., *Ethics at the Edges of Life.* Yale University Press, New Haven, 1978.

Reid, R., 'Spina bifida: the fate of the untreated', *Hastings Center Report 7*, 16–19 (1977).

Restak, R. M., *Pre-Meditated Man.* Viking Press, New York, 1975.

Veatch, R. M., 'The technical criteria fallacy', *Hastings Center Report 7*, 15–16 (1977).

World Council of Churches, 'Genetics and the quality of life', *Study Encounter 10*, 1–26 (1974).

## Chapter 4–6

Anderson, N., *Issues of Life and Death.* Hodder and Stoughton, London, 1976.

Annas, G. J., 'Artificial insemination: beyond the best interests of the donor', *Hastings Center Report 9*, 14–15, 43 (1979).

Biggers, J. D., 'When does life begin?', *The Sciences 21*, 10–14 (1981).

Curran, C. E., *Politics, Medicine and Christian Ethics.* Fortress Press, Philadelphia, 1973.

Dunstan, G. R., *The Artifice of Ethics.* SCM Press, London, 1974.

Edwards, R. G. and Purdy, J. M. (eds.), *Human Conception In Vitro.* Academic Press, New York, 1982.

Fletcher, J., *Humanhood: Essays in Biomedical Ethics.* Prometheus Books, New York, 1979.

Geisler, N. L., *Ethics: Alternatives and Issues.* Zondervan, Grand Rapids, 1971.

Grobstein, C., 'External human fertilization', *Scientific American 240*, 33–43 (1979).

Grobstein, C., *From Chance to Purpose: An Appraisal of External Human Fertilization.* Addison-Wesley, New York, 1981.

Grobstein, C., 'The moral uses of "spare" embryos', *Hastings Center Report 12*, 5–6 (1982).

Hamilton, M. P. (ed.), *The New Genetics and the Future of Man.* Eerdmans, Grand Rapids, 1972 (including chapters by L. R. Kass, J. Fletcher and P. Ramsey).

Häring, B., *Medical Ethics.* St. Paul Publications, Slough, 1972.

Häring, B., *Manipulation.* St. Paul Publications, Slough, 1975.

Kass, L. R., 'The new biology: what price relieving man's estate', *Science 174*, 779–788 (1971).

Kass, L., 'Making babies – the new biology and the "old" morality', *Public Interest 26*, 18–56 (1972).

Kass, L., ' "Making babies" revisited', *Public Interest 54*, 32–60 (1979).

Lederberg, J., 'Experimental genetics and human evolution', *American Naturalist 100*, 519–531 (1966).

McCormick, R. A., *How Brave a New World?* SCM Press, London, 1981.

Moore, J. W., 'Human *in vitro* fertilization: can we support it?', *The Christian Century 98*, 442–446 (1981).

Muller, H. J., 'Should we weaken or strengthen our genetic heritage?', *Daedalus 90*, 432–450 (1961).

Nelkin, D. and Raymond, C. A., 'Tempest in a test tube', *The Sciences 20*, 6–9, 28 (1980).

Nelson, R. M., 'The ethics of *in vitro* fertilization and embryo transfer', *CMS Journal 14*, 19–25, 32 (1983).

Overduin, D. C. and Fleming, J. I., *Life in a Test-tube*. Lutheran Publishing House, Adelaide, 1982.

Ramsey, P., *Fabricated Man*. Yale University Press, New Haven, 1970.

Ramsey, P., 'Shall we reproduce? I. The medical ethics of *in vitro* fertilization', *J. Amer. Med. Assoc. 220*, 1348–1350 (1972).

Ramsey, P., 'Shall we reproduce? II. Rejoinders and future forecast', *J. Amer. Med. Assoc. 220*, 1480–1485 (1972).

Rorvick, D. M., *In His Image*. Nelson, Melbourne, 1978.

Scorer, C. G., *Life in our Hands*. Inter-Varsity Press, Leicester, 1978.

Shinn, R. L., 'Perilous progress in genetics', *Social Research 41*, 83–103 (1974).

Stirrat, G. M., 'Artificial insemination by donor – a Christian viewpoint', *In the Service of Medicine 29*, 13–16 (1983).

Thielicke, H., *The Ethics of Sex*. James Clarke, Cambridge, 1964.

Thielicke, H., *The Doctor as Judge of Who Shall Live and Who Shall Die*. Fortress Press, Philadelphia, 1976.

Thompson, C., 'IVF in the light of . . .the law', *On Being 9*, 46–47 (1982).

Walters, L., 'Human *in vitro* fertilization: a review of the ethical literature', *Hastings Center Report 9*, 23–43 (1979).

Walters, W. and Singer, P. (eds.), *Test-tube Babies*. Oxford University Press, Melbourne, 1982.

Wood, C. and Westmore, A., *Test-tube Conception*. Hill of Content, Melbourne, 1983.

## Chapter 7

Anderson, N., *Issues of Life and Death*. Hodder and Stoughton, London, 1976.

Camenisch, P. F., 'Abortion: for the fetus's own sake?', *Hastings Center Report* 6, 38–41 (1976).

Dunstan, G. R., *The Artifice of Ethics*. SCM Press, London, 1974.

Fletcher, J., *Humanhood: Essays in Biomedical Ethics*. Prometheus Books, Buffalo, 1979.

Gardner, R. F. R., *Abortion: The Personal Dilemma*. Paternoster Press, Exeter, 1972.

Geisler, N. L., *Ethics: Alternatives and Issues*. Zondervan, Grand Rapids, 1971.

Glover, J., *Causing Death and Saving Lives*. Penguin, Harmondsworth, 1977.

Gorman, M. J., *Abortion and the Early Church*. Inter-Varsity Press, Downers Grove, 1982.

Hilgers, T. W., Horan, D. J. and Mall, D. (eds.), *New Perspectives on Human Abortion*. University Publications of America, Maryland, 1981.

Humber, J. M. and Almeder, R. F. (eds.), *Biomedical Ethics and the Law*. Plenum Press, New York, 1976.

Langerak, E., 'Abortion: listening to the middle,' *Hastings Center Report* 9, 24–28 (1979).

Ramsey, P., *Three on Abortion, Child and Family*. Oak Park, Illinois, 1978.

Scorer, C. G., *Life in our Hands*. Inter-Varsity Press, Leicester, 1978.

Smith, H. L., *Ethics and the New Medicine*. Abingdon, Nashville, 1970.

Spitzer, W. O. and Saylor, C. L. (eds.), *Birth Control and the Christian*. Tyndale House Publishers, Wheaton, 1969.

Sumner, L. W., *Abortion and Moral Theory*. Princeton University Press, Princeton, 1981.

Tanner, J. M., *Foetus into Man: Physical Growth from Conception to Maturity*. Open Books, London, 1978.

Thielicke, H., *The Ethics of Sex*. James Clarke, Cambridge, 1964.

Wenham, G., 'Abortion: what about deformity before birth?', *Third Way 4* (18), 9–11 (1981).

**Chapter 8**

Birch, C. and Abrecht, P. (eds.), *Genetics and the Quality of Life*. Pergamon Press, Sydney, 1975.
Dunstan, G. R., *The Artifice of Ethics*. SCM Press, London, 1974.
Ellul, J., *The Technological Society*. Alfred A. Knopf, New York, 1964.
Häring, B., *Manipulation*. St. Paul Publications, Slough, 1975.
Jones, D. G., *Genetic Engineering*. Grove Books, Nottingham, 1978.
MacKay, D. M., *Human Science and Human Dignity*. Hodder and Stoughton, London, 1979.
Mascall, E. L., *The Importance of Being Human*. Oxford University Press, London, 1959.
Thielicke, H., *The Doctor as Judge of Who Shall Live and Who Shall Die*. Fortress Press, Philadelphia, 1976.

# Index of names

This index does not include biblical names nor those found only in the bibliography.

American College of Obstetricians and Gynaecologists, 80
American Medical Association, 56
Annas, George J., 90
Apocalypse of Peter, 173

Barrs, Jerram, 21
Barton, John, 206
Berry, R. J., 57
Biogen, S. A., 96
Birch, Charles, 200
British Medical Association (BMA), 112
Brown, Louise, 83f.

Callahan, Daniel, 73
Calvin, John, 172
Carey, George, 16, 18
Carr, Elizabeth, 83
Cetus Corporation, 96
Curie-Cohen, M., 90

Department of Health, Education and Welfare, 116
Didache, 173

Edwards, Robert, 82ff., 86, 109f.
Einstein, Albert, 133
Eli Lilly, 96
Ellul, Jacques, 30, 191
Epistle of Barnabas, 173

Fletcher, Joseph, 48f., 56f., 164f.

Galton, Francis, 57
Geisler, Norman, 126, 177f.
Genentech Inc., 96
Genex Corporation, 96
Glass, Bentley, 55
Grobstein, Clifford, 108, 113, 118
Gurdon, John, 93

Häring, Bernard, 113, 193f.
Hastings Center, 73
Haydn, Joseph, 138
Hertwig, Oskar, 93
Hitler, Adolf, 133
Hoffman-La Roche, 96
Houston, James, 17
Huxley, Aldous, 4, 132

*Index of names*


Illich, Ivan, 36, 44
Institute of Child Health and Development at the National Institutes of Health (NICHD), 59

Josephus, 173

Kass, Leon, 23f., 76, 102, 106, 113ff., 118
Kennedy, Ian, 44
Kidner, Derek, 12, 19

Lappé, Marc, 70
Leonardo da Vinci, 138
Lorber, John, 67f.

Macaulay, Ranald, 21
MacKay, Donald, 193
Mao Tse-Tung, 133
McCormick, Richard, 75
Medical Research Council (MRC), 111
Mozart, Wolfgang Amadeus, 133, 138
Müller, Hermann J., 92

National Health and Medical Research Council (NH and MRC), 112
*Nature,* 112f.

Oppenheimer, Robert, 25

*Parthenos,* 93
Philo, 173
Polanyi, Michael, 26

Ramsay, Paul, 101, 104f., 161, 168ff.
Reid, Candice, 83
Repository for Germinal Choice, 91, 130
Rorvick, David M., 94, 134
Royal College of Obstetricians and Gynaecologists (RCOG), 111
Royal Society, 111f.

Scorer, Gordon, 176
Singer, Peter, 110
Sinsheimer, Robert L., 94
Stanford University, 97
Steptoe, Patrick, 84, 86
Stirrat, Gordon, 125
Sugden, Chris, 38

Taylor, Richard, 44
Teresa, Mother, 186
Thielicke, Helmut, 10, 124f., 142, 170f., 195
Thomas, Lewis, 41
Thomson, Colin, 120

United States Supreme Court, 63, 97

Veatch, Robert, 67

Wenham, Gordon, 183
World Council of Churches, 55
World Health Organization, 35

Zachary, R. B., 66, 68

# Index of Scripture references


**Genesis**
1:26 8, 11–13, 15, 17
1:27 8, 13
1:28 12, 13, 17
2:7 8, 11
2:16–17 15
2:19 12
3:6 18
3:7 19
3:8–13 13, 19
3:22 20
4:1 158
5:1 13
9:6 13
16:2 158
25:23 159
29:31–32 158
30:22–23 158

**Exodus**
21:12 172
21:22–25 171f.

**Deuteronomy**
25:5 126

**Judges**
13:7 159

**Ruth**
4:13 158

**Job**
1:21 199
2:10 199
10:8–12 159

**Psalms**
8:5 12
8:6–8 12, 17
139:13–16 158, 173, 206

**Ecclesiastes**
11:5 159

**Isaiah**
35:5–6 186
42:19 183
49:1 158
52:14 183

**Jeremiah**
1:4–5 162
1:5 158

**Matthew**
5:27–28 125
18:1–9 204
19:5 125

**Mark**
10:19 203

**Luke**
1:34 125
1:41–44 158

**John**
8:1–11 203
14:27 198

**1 Corinthians**
6:15–17 125
11:7 13
15:45 21

**2 Corinthians**
5:15 199

**Ephesians**
1:4 158

**Colossians**
1:22 15
3:10 13

**1 Thessalonians**
5:10 199

**James**
2:14–17 185
3:9 13

**1 Peter**
4:1–2 199

**2 Peter**
3:11–12 15

# Subject Index


Abortion (on demand), 20, 119–122, 147, 150, 164f., 175f., 178, 185, 190, 204
Adoption, 119, 121f., 128f., 179, 182
Adultery, 90, 203f.
  and AID, 90, 125f.
Alpha-fetoproteins, 59
  in neural tube defects, 62, 65
Amniocentesis, 4, 23, 51, 53, 58, 60–62, 64, 107, 187
  and sex choice, 63
  and therapeutic abortion, 63
  description of, 58
  ethical status of, 62
  in IVF, 86
  in neural tube defects, 65
  risks of, 59
Amniotic fluid, 58, 60, 62, 65
Anencephaly, 61, 180
Artificial insemination, 4, 89–92, 103, 122–131
  AID, 89–91, 116, 123–130, 133, 136, 147, 187, 190, 204
  AIH, 89, 103, 123f., 129
Askenazi Jews, 54

Beta endorphin, 96
Biological foreknowledge, 72
Biological normality, 33, 154f., 189
Biological perfection, 130
Biomedical ethics, 73, 195
Biomedical model, 30f., 34, 36
Biomedical revolution, 6f., 205
Biomedical technology, 3–6, 10, 13f., 16f., 20–22, 31f., 37, 44–47, 155, 197f., 201f., 205, 207
  and over-medicalization, 46
  and simplicity of life-style, 39
  benefits and hazards of, 20
  ethical decisions in, 17
  levels of, 41
  misuse of, 20
  risks and side-effects of, 44
  successes of, 32
Birth, 79, 155–158, 162f.
Blastocyst, 79–81, 84, 113, 118, 169f.
Brain damage, 74f.

Caesarean section, 103, 107
Cancer, 42–44, 109, 168
Chance ethics, 49
Choice ethics, 49
Christ Jesus, 22, 30, 32, 35, 38,

40, 136, 140f., 158, 190, 194, 200, 203f.
as human being, 22
as last Adam, 21
fully human and fully God, 14, 21
Critical stage approach, 156, 164
Chromosomes, 89, 92, 111, 155, 206
abnormalities of, 50, 56, 58–61, 88, 150f.
number of, 50
sex, 51
XYY, 70
Cloning (asexual reproduction), 82, 88, 92–95, 116, 127, 132–149, 168, 187
reasons for, 94f., 138f.
Clowns, 143–145
Conception, 78, 80, 104, 106, 111, 119, 123, 129, 156, 164, 167, 170, 172, 176f., 196
definition of, 80
moment of, 82
natural/artificial, 104
Contraception, 41, 80, 111, 129f., 176
Copernican revolution, 7
Coronary heart disease, 42, 44
Cystic fibrosis, 50, 52

Darwinian revolution, 7
Dehumanization, 19, 30, 34f., 102, 117, 146f.
Dementia, 52
Diabetes, 41, 148, 196f.
Down's syndrome, 49–51, 59, 74, 147, 151f., 181
incidence of, 50, 60f.

Ectogenesis, 88, 103, 187
Embryo(s), 78–86, 99f., 106–115, 118, 120, 156f., 159f.
banks, 82, 88
destruction of, 120
experiments using, 111, 118
frozen, 83, 86, 108, 112, 117
genetic manipulation of, 112
post-implantation, 110
potential of, 113
pre-implantation, 88, 109–113
rights of, 108f., 119
sex determination of, 88
spare (superfluous), 83–87, 108f., 112, 114f., 117f.
status of, 112, 118f.
transfer (ET), 80, 82, 85f., 88, 104, 108, 112, 115–117, 137
use in research, 88
Encephalocoele, 61
Environment, 57, 72, 76, 136, 138, 143, 162, 168, 186, 195, 198f.
*Escherichia coli,* 97f.
Eugenics, 57, 76, 90–92, 123, 130, 136, 183
negative, 55f., 58
positive, 56–58, 77

Faith, 185, 198
Fallopian (uterine) tubes, damage to, 86, 117
Family (life, unit), 7, 103, 112, 116, 127, 129f., 138, 141, 146f., 153f., 166, 178f., 181f., 184, 203
Fertilization, 78–84, 89, 106, 108, 111f., 114, 116f., 119
artificial, 105
in cloning, 93
in parthenogenesis, 93
internal, 105f., 109, 117
interspecies, 111
mechanisms of, 89
Fetoscopy, 4, 58, 60
Fetus, 58, 64, 78f., 81, 88, 104, 114, 120f., 129, 147, 151–186, 196, 200, 203f.
as potential person, 15, 156f., 162, 164f.
consent of, 105–107
defective/healthy, 63, 151
destruction of, 172, 179, 183
harm (damage) to, 105–107, 115
previable, 114
risks to, 105f.

Roman Catholic position on, 164, 166–168
status of, 14, 153, 155–164
Freedom, 18, 29, 140, 144, 146, 165f., 171, 190
individual, 7, 33, 57, 155
misuse of, 18
of choice, 33, 155
unrestricted, 16

Galactosemia, 65
Garden of Eden, 15, 19
Genes, 52, 57, 76, 79, 89, 96–98, 129–131, 135, 138, 154f., 193, 199
abnormal, 53, 150f., 185f.
defective, 55, 70, 76f., 88, 95, 98, 181, 197, 200
deleterious, 50, 196
detrimental, 56, 152
dominant, 52
recessive lethal, 24, 54, 57
surgery, 57
Genetic control, 7, 82
Genetic counselling, 32, 51, 108, 139, 150, 168, 200
in spina bifida, 68
Genetic diseases, 7, 23, 50, 57, 71, 108, 115, 139, 187, 197
and cloning, 95
carriers of, 52–56, 61
cost-benefit analyses in, 154f.
dominant, 51f.
prenatal diagnosis of, 49, 58, 62
recessive (X-linked), 51–53, 60f., 181
sex-linked, 51
Genetic engineering, 4f., 32, 56–58, 76, 88, 94, 96f., 133, 145, 168, 188, 191, 204
definition of, 56
Genetic information, 70f.
Genetic manipulation, 7, 9, 41, 76, 96, 148, 194, 197, 199f.
Genetic research, 148, 193
Genetic screening, 4, 50, 53f., 64, 66, 70–72, 88
and familial polyposis, 71
and hypercholesterolaemia, 71
mass programs of, 65, 69
Genetic therapy (treatment), 76, 82, 98, 147, 149, 199
Genetic uniqueness, 70
German measles, 151, 180
Glucose-6-phosphate dehydrogenase deficiency, 50
God, 15–24, 27, 32, 39, 47, 72, 129, 131, 135, 140f., 158–160, 162, 165f., 168, 171, 173–174, 177, 191, 193, 195, 198f., 205f.
co-workers with, 18
Creator, 8–11, 14, 18, 102, 130, 141f., 145, 175, 187, 191, 199
dependence upon, 9
love of, 182f.
moral qualities of, 16, 31
purposes of, 171–175, 202
relationship to, 15
response to, 75
separation from, 19
sovereign will of, 11, 168, 171
Growth hormone, 96

Haemophilia, 51, 61, 98, 148, 151, 186
Healing, 200
Health, 35–41, 46, 72, 154, 194
and just social relationships, 39
as a social phenomenon, 36
expectations of, 32, 73
in spina bifida, 68
lack of, 30, 34
standards of, 155, 193
Human-animal hybrids, 20, 88, 116
Human beings (existence), 17, 128, 130, 133–135, 139–146, 155f., 162f., 179, 188–195
Adam/Eve, 13–16, 18f., 21
as ends in themselves, 17
as image/likeness of God, 8, 11, 13–18, 20–22, 69, 74, 141, 165, 174, 189, 193f.
as created beings, 8–10, 14, 102, 191
as physical machines, 31, 37

creativity of, 12, 19, 76, 135f.
creatureliness of, 9–11, 21, 127, 175, 189, 192
dominion over creation, 17f., 195
exercise of control, 10, 12, 31, 33, 137, 145f., 168, 195
fallen, 18, 21, 131, 170f., 174f., 182, 193
finiteness of, 10f., 13f., 150, 191
humanness of, 21, 33, 74f., 81, 114, 118, 142
ideal, 76, 148, 191f.
improvement of, 94
individuality of, 144, 146f., 155, 162, 188f., 195–197, 205
laboratory production of, 98, 102
limitations of, 12f., 20f., 143, 153, 192, 199, 204
part of natural world, 11f.
personhood of, 14f., 18, 35, 38, 69, 74f., 102f., 109, 120, 126, 138–142, 146f., 154–158, 161–175, 177–183, 185, 196, 200
potential of, 109, 113–115, 118f., 156f., 161, 202
relationship with God, 13f.
responsibility of, 10–19, 24f., 29, 32, 42, 72, 107, 137, 141, 144, 148, 153, 162, 168, 175f., 188, 190, 194–199, 207
significance of, 35
sinfulness of, 20f., 200, 203
uniqueness of, 205–207
value of, 144
Human dignity, 16f., 32, 38f., 45, 69, 75, 131, 141f., 144, 155, 160, 165, 169, 174
'alien' dignity, 32, 142
Human life, 79f., 144, 147, 155, 162, 168, 172f., 184f., 188, 198f., 202, 204
beginning of, 78f., 81f.
potential, 81, 175
sanctity of, 174
value of, 81
Human nature, 136
base elements of, 19
Humour, 143f.
Huntington's chorea, 52, 70
Hydrocephalus, 60, 66f.

Illness, concept of, 37
Implantation, 80, 84, 86, 88, 108, 111, 118f., 156
Inborn errors of metabolism, 54, 58, 60f.
Incarnation, 22, 141, 194
Infanticide, 165
Infertility, 50, 83, 86, 89, 95, 99, 101, 105, 109, 111, 115f., 119, 122f., 127
alleviation of, 87, 100
bypassing, 20, 99
idiopathic, 87
social significance of, 88
types of, 87
Insulin, 96, 98, 101, 148
Interferon, 96
*In vitro* fertilization (IVF), 4, 7, 42f., 49, 80–83, 88f., 94, 99–123, 127, 133, 137, 147, 168, 187, 190, 201, 204
applications of, 87, 114f.
as impersonal process, 102
assessment of, 115–119
clinical, 87, 103, 114, 118f.
compared with microtuboplasty, 86, 101
costs of, 99f.
description of, 84–86
donors in, 108–112, 116, 120
human control in, 102
laboratory, 87f., 113f.
legal issues in, 119–121
Melbourne program, 100
Monash program, 87
research uses of, 109–115, 117, 119f.
success rate of, 85
use of clomiphene in, 84
use of human pituitary gonadotrophin in, 84

IQ, 58, 90
  and humanness, 81

Lesch-Nyhan syndrome, 181
Life expectancy, 44

Maple syrup urine disease, 65
Marriage, 125–130, 146f.
  (married) couples, 116, 121, 123, 126f.
  status of, 7
Mental retardation (deficiency), 50f., 53, 58, 69, 142, 178f., 181, 185
Murder, 120, 167, 172, 175
Muscular dystrophy, 51, 61

Natural law, 168
Neural tube defects, 4, 60–62
  genetic screening for, 65

Organ transplantation, 41, 139
Ovum (egg), 78–84, 88, 92, 118, 121, 134, 205
  banks, 88
  in cloning, 93f.
  in IVF, 108, 111f., 116
  transfer, 82, 88, 120, 187

Parthenogenesis, 93
Phenylketonuria (PKU), 50, 53f., 65, 196
Plasmids, 97
Potentiality principle, 156f., 161f.
Preconceptive control, 56
Prenatal control, 55
Procreation, 102–105, 125, 162

Quality control, 7, 32f., 49f., 57, 72f., 112, 146, 150, 188–190, 194
  and foreknowledge, 189f.
Quality of life, 4f., 7, 44f., 48, 74f., 142, 152, 165, 181–183, 194, 201f.
  decisions, 48f.
  in spina bifida, 67f.
Quickening, 156, 166

Rape, 177f.
Recombinant DNA technology, 41, 96–98, 139, 148f., 197
Redemption, 21, 141, 183
Reductionism, 4, 34, 49, 131, 147
Restriction enzymes, 96f.
*Roe v. Wade,* 63

Science, and values, 26
  ethical guide-lines and, 27
  fear of, 27
  fiction, 144, 195
  foundations of modern, 25
  hypotheses in, 26
Scientific enterprise, 24–28
Sexual intercourse, 123, 125f., 128, 146
Sexual reproduction, 92, 134–136, 140
Sickle-cell anaemia, 4, 50, 53, 60, 65, 98
Situation ethics, 57
Sperm, 78–84, 88, 92f., 112, 116, 121–125, 129, 205
  banks, 89f.
Spina bifida, 61f., 65, 68
  acetylcholinesterase levels in, 62
  closed, 62, 65
  non-treatment of, 68f.
  open, 62, 65–67
  treatment of, 66–68
Spontaneous abortion, 50
  in amniocentesis, 59
  in fetoscopy, 60
  with anencephaly, 61
Suffering, 12, 107, 128, 140, 152–154, 192, 195, 199f.
Surrogate motherhood, 20, 82, 88, 109, 112, 116, 120f., 134, 187

Tay-Sachs disease, 50, 54, 61, 65, 151f., 181
Technology, 20–24, 34, 36, 39, 47, 83, 125, 137, 143, 155, 188–192, 196–198, 205

advances of, 33f.
and AID, 127–130
and biomedical ethics, 30
and freedom, 29
and human life, 28, 145, 187
and IVF, 99–101, 104, 109, 117, 119, 122
as end in itself, 30
control of, 12f., 33f., 40, 45, 48f., 72
expensive, 31
fusion of science and, 28f.
half-way, 41–44, 99
high, 7, 31, 39, 41, 44, 148
material benefits of, 24
materialistic attitudes of, 30
modern medicine as, 37, 75
non-technology, 43f.
religious overtones of, 28
reproductive, 103, 108
risks of, 45
Thalassemia, 60
Therapeutic abortion, 4, 24, 54–56, 62, 81f., 150–186, 204
and amniocentesis, 63
and genetic screening, 69
criteria for, 55
ethical acceptability of, 64
direct/indirect, 167f.
for fetus, 152–154
for maternal illness, 151, 168–171, 177
for parents, 154, 179f.
for society, 154f.
genetic, 150–158, 170f., 181–183
grounds for, 178–183
in Down's syndrome, 51, 181
in IVF, 86, 119
in Tay-Sachs disease, 54
in X-linked recessive disorders, 61

Ultrasound sonography, 4, 58, 60, 65

Viability, 156f.

Zygote, 78–81, 174